A SONG FOR EVERYONE

ALSO BY JOHN LINGAN

Homeplace: A Southern Town, a Country Legend,
and the Last Days of a Mountaintop Honky-Tonk

A SONG FOR EVERYONE

THE STORY OF
CREEDENCE CLEARWATER REVIVAL

John Lingan

 hachette
BOOKS

NEW YORK

Hachette Books
Hachette Book Group
1290 Avenue of the Americas
New York, NY 10104
HachetteBooks.com
Twitter.com/HachetteBooks
Instagram.com/HachetteBooks

First Edition: August 2022

Published by Hachette Books, an imprint of Perseus Books, LLC, a subsidiary
of Hachette Book Group, Inc. The Hachette Books name and logo is a trademark
of the Hachette Book Group.

The Hachette Speakers Bureau provides a wide range of authors for speaking events.

To find out more, go to www.hachettespeakersbureau.com or call (866) 376-6591.

The publisher is not responsible for websites (or their content) that are not owned
by the publisher.

Print book interior design by Linda Mark

Library of Congress Control Number: 2022937046

ISBNs: 9780306846717 (hardcover); 9780306846700 (ebook)

Printed in the United States of America

LSC-C

Printing 1, 2022

For Justyna

and for Nina, Albert, and Roch, the youth of today

We do not feel like a cool, swinging generation. We are eaten up inside by an intensity we cannot name.

RADCLIFFE COLLEGE
COMMENCEMENT SPEAKER, 1968

Contents

They left San Francisco with a crowd waving good-bye in the gray damp evening, then disembarked to even more shouting young people standing welcome in the English mist. The band was famous everywhere by this point, including at home. But this was London, the global rock and roll capital, and they were being greeted as conquerors. The door of the jet opened and four humble and denim-covered young men were set upon by writers, photographers, label brass, and hangers-on. Behind a barrier, the prime of Young Britain were ecstatic.

It was April 1970 and for all but Stu, it was their first time outside the United States. John, Doug, and Tom had barely left California two years earlier. But now they stood on the Heathrow tarmac as mainstays of the Top 40 for nearly eighteen months. A half-dozen singles and three LPs had stuck in the UK charts like tune-up grease, a barrage like nothing since the Beatles five years earlier.

The original funny-haired quartet had also been together since the late '50s, playing old Black music in unglamorous circuits, but now they were moving relatively slowly. The rumors from the last few years involved heroin and threats of quitting. These Californians, by comparison, were up-and-comers only now getting their due, and not taking anything for granted. In 1969, they did what no other group had managed for half a decade: they outsold the Beatles.

In the days leading up to their arrival, a press release announced Paul McCartney's first solo album through a "self-interview." The article referred to his "split with the Beatles," and he gave an unusually terse answer to the question of whether he'd ever write songs with John Lennon again: "No." Suddenly there was no one left to outsell.

Given the circumstances, the English press and those screaming fans might have expected more excitement. Instead they only got four young suburban men. Hairy, bashful, a tiny entourage. A little stoned? Which one was even John, the front man? From the airport they floated through London in black cabs toward their hotel. That evening the label took them to a lavish dinner, then to the Thames dockside where a big party embarked on a cruise aboard the H.M.S. *Proud Mary*, which the record company had chartered for the evening and christened for the song that started it all only a year ago. A group of cute girls greeted the band, all with big smiles to match their baggy mock-naval costumes. A treat even if the band members were all married. They weren't accustomed to food, girls, and nighttime boat rides with the bosses. They weren't used to celebrations.

London was the beginning of the trip but not the beginning of the tour. They started with two shows in Rotterdam, then another in Essen, equally manically received, before returning to the English capital for their debut at the Royal Albert Hall. Television cameras awaited them. They were going to be seen across the nation, preserved for posterity in the city's best-known venue. Doug could never lose sight of the pure blinding unlikelihood of it all. He had a long thick beard, and behind the drums he was the rangiest, most eye-catching character onstage. The only one who challenged John for control of the band when they were fully engaged and in formation, flying through their filler-free setlist.

On his stool, with his veiny arms waving, his cymbals swirling in the lights like fireworks, Doug bashed the songs that had been ringing through London's shops and clubs: "Green River," "Fortunate Son," "Bad Moon Rising," "Travelin' Band." Songs that he and his bandmates had eternalized for every kid in America, and they never sounded better than in the Albert Hall's grand palace of ancient curtains and looming rococo boxes.

The set ended with "Keep On Chooglin'," like always. John wailing on guitar, then harmonica, then guitar again, Doug thumping and crashing, building everything continuously upward for nine minutes. The Albert crowd likes to roar, they'd been told. And roar they did. Standing off to the side of the stage as the house lights rose, the band watched six thousand Brits rise and scream as if they were prepared to continue it all night. Five minutes passed and they were still on their feet.

Surely tonight, Doug thought, looking to John. Doug had his towel over his shoulders and was trying to read those hidden eyes, the ones that were always locked beneath heavy pageboy bangs. Surely tonight we'll go back out for an encore. What else have we been working for but this?

Then John turned away just like every night, making for backstage. Doug watched him go, and watched Tom and Stu, who he knew agreed but would never speak up and tell John just how stupid the no-encores policy was. Stupid at home in Oakland, stupid in New York, Miami, everyfuckingwhere.

Now it had been ten minutes. The fans were still rapturous, the band was still in their claustrophobic greenroom just behind the stage. They could hear the applause, feel their fans vibrating the hall with excitement. The promoters came back to explain: The crowds at Albert Hall don't leave without encores. They're waiting everywhere, in the corridors, outside. It would be impossible for the band to leave until the audience was satisfied and finally dispersed. Supposedly McCartney was in the venue along with George Harrison and Eric Clapton. Those three wanted to come say hello but they couldn't leave their box because the crowd was still there, cacophonous.

Twenty minutes. John was still silent. The band's US label boss, Saul Zaentz, who was following his golden goose around Europe, explained the policy yet again: The band doesn't do encores. They do their show, play the songs they planned, and that's the gig. The Englishmen were vexed.

A half hour went by like that, with some of the country's biggest musicians, guys they idolized, waiting to pay tribute. They could only wait for the audience to leave the venue out of their own tired, confused volition so the band could leave unswarmed. Doug stewed. Just on the other side of a curtain, his drums sat unattended on one of the world's eternal stages while thousands of his admiring peers beat their seatbacks, cheering. He and his bandmates sat in growing silence while the last of a thinning crowd chanted "CREE-DENCE, CREE-DENCE, CREE-DENCE . . ."

ONE

CLASSMATES

Homerooms in Portola Junior High were arranged alphabetically, so Doug Clifford and Stu Cook first saw each other on day one of seventh grade. James Dean was dead three years but his ghost still hovered over all would-be greasers. The boys looked at each other and saw only competition: another tough guy in jeans and a T-shirt and a leather jacket. They both took their seats near the front, nearly snarling. They were thirteen. It was 1958. The US flag hanging above them had forty-eight stars.

By lunchtime, all ill will had vaporized. Both boys lost the massive chips on their shoulders when they learned of their mutual love of KWBR, AM 1310, the station that broadcast just down the road out of Oakland. They heard a lot of KYA too, but that was parents' stuff—Henry Mancini, Patsy Cline, Rosemary Clooney, Percy Faith. KWBR was where R&B happened. That was where Black music lived. In that first conversation in the halls of Portola Junior High, Stu and Doug didn't talk about the awkwardness they both felt among new peers. They didn't reveal that they were each expecting to get their asses kicked by bigger guys like always. They just talked about the radio.

That KWBR music sounded like a different solar system than El Cerrito, the staid, mostly white suburb where they lived. They heard Fats Domino, James Brown, and Chuck Berry, then at night, the cool San Francisco air carried KRAK, a country station, all the way from Sacramento, and they got Johnny Cash, Porter Wagoner, and Hank Williams if they toggled the dial just right and listened close.

Once they established the overlap in taste, the next question was obvious: What records do you have? They both collected 78s like other boys had baseball cards. It was the height of doo-wop airplay, but Stu and Doug liked the darker, rougher stuff, which is to say, southern Black music rather than its urban street-corner variety. From KWBR deejays like Jumpin' George Oxford and "Big Daddy" Don Barksdale, they heard Jimmy Reed and John Lee Hooker, whose songs were direct transmissions from a South that still shuddered with racial violence. The Black men and women of 1950s Macon, Augusta, or Memphis had seen the extent of white cruelty in the twentieth century, and their music opened a new range of human expression. Some of it made Stu's and Doug's parents nervous, like Etta James's raunchy "The Wallflower (Work with Me, Henry)." Others only made Doug's father roll his eyes. He used the worst word imaginable to diminish this music and these people. But Doug and his friend could not dismiss something like Bo Diddley's "Bo Diddley," which sounded like the past and future all at once: a beat that a baby could bang on a countertop, with an attitude that could drain the blood from a suburban mother's face. They couldn't ignore Chuck Berry, who took the rhythms of Black music and wrote narratives that appealed to everyone.

Berry's stories and his sharp guitar would have fit perfectly on the whispering country station, if only anyone had the sense to ignore more obvious boundaries.

This friendship felt cosmic. Not just the names. Not simply that they both loved "race music" at a time when even East Bay residents burned a cross in the front yard of a Black judge who purchased a house in a white neighborhood. It turned out that Doug was only twelve hours older than Stu. He was born April 24, 1945, while his new buddy was born April 25. Both had only one sibling, a brother. And both were routinely dismissed as "cut-ups." Soon their greaser sneers were replaced by inside jokes and plays for classmates' attention.

It was a friendship too big for school walls, even the sprawling campus of Portola Junior High. Stu invited Doug over on a weekend and told him to bring his records. Doug was not poor, not exactly, but he knew he was going to see a different kind of lifestyle when Stu said they could play "the big piano."

In the 1950s, El Cerrito was the quiet pocket of the northeast region of San Francisco Bay—less industrial than Richmond to its north, less intellectual and moneyed than Berkeley to the south, and less diverse and urban than Oakland to the south of that. Above it all loomed the Berkeley Hills, a mountain range that trapped the wind and clouds as they rolled off the Bay and the Pacific. The Hills did something else, too: They gave El Cerrito an easy way to distinguish rich from poor. The higher a house's elevation, the more expensive it was, and the highlanders, as they were called, could literally and figuratively look down on the flatlanders, who were squeezed inside gridded streets and I-80. Flatlanders got the region's overcast weather and its sprawl, but none of its life-affirming vistas, at least not at home.

Doug lived in between. Neither high enough in the Hills to watch the sun set beyond San Francisco, nor down amid the shops and the two interstates—I-80 and its spur, I-580—that were perpetually under construction. He was also new to the neighborhood. His father was a blue-collar worker with a temper that kept him from staying too long at any one job. The family had lived throughout California, most recently in Manhattan Beach and Palo Alto, where Doug's father worked on a refinery floor for Standard Oil. At least, he did before his foreman hassled him one time too many and he got the man up against a wall. Then it was time to move the family once again.

His brother, Doug's uncle, owned a machine shop in Richmond, so the Cliffords went to the East Bay. They arrived in the middle of an enormous regional migration that had started during the war. The Richmond shipyards employed a hundred thousand people then, and the Bay Area's population grew by half a million. The age of prosperity continued after Allied victory. Many of the new arrivals were Black families, and two major companies, Sears and Safeway, hired their first Black employees during this time. When Doug's family arrived, that new middle class had joined the area's final World War and Korea G.I. Bill graduates and pushed into the sleepier suburbs, including El Cerrito. The *San Francisco Chronicle* described this Cold War period as a "second Gold Rush." El Cerrito's population was only six thousand in 1945; within five years it tripled.

The change in demographics changed the civic character. Since its founding in 1917, El Cerrito had been the Bay Area's haven of sin. Racketeering, gambling, and bootlegging proliferated during prohibition. The downtown strip of San Pablo Avenue was lined with lurid spots: Club Rio, Club Compiano, the Cave, the Acme, the Miami. The dog races at the southern end of San Pablo started in 1932. Stu grew up hearing about this era from his grandfather, who said you could always tell the lawbreakers because their car trunks sagged from the weight of illegal liquor. But when the post-war arrivals swept in to make their middle-class fate, it all went away. A newly formed Good Government League banished the hooch and slots. The dog track became a drive-in movie theater in 1948, then a shopping mall, El Cerrito Plaza, ten years after that. Forty years of iniquity gave way to quiet wholesomeness. A bored, aimless teen in the late 1950s would hardly believe that they did the family shopping on the ruins of a West Coast capital of vice.

Doug arrived in town right as the transition became complete. His mother did her best to bring color to the home. She had been a singer on Bay Area radio as a young woman. Doug and his brother, Chuck, grew up with Perry Como and "Mr. Sandman" bouncing through their many houses alongside big-band jazz. Mrs. Clifford was doting and boundlessly kind to her boys, but her artistic dreams were long past. Once the family settled, she became a makeup clerk at Capwell's, the anchor store in El Cerrito Plaza. But she found ways of expressing her bohemian open-mindedness to the boys. Doug attended a local Bahá'í congregation for childcare and spiritual education, where he heard about the elemental oneness of all things. This was not a mainstream statement for white boys to hear in the 1950s, but neither was "Mojo come to my house, ya black cat bone / Take my baby away from home." There was something to take from both.

And Doug needed survival strategies. There was his lisp, which a speech therapist had helped him overcome in grammar school. There was Chuck, his loving but straight-and-narrow brother whose grades, they both knew, would always be higher than Doug's, his promise a bit greater. And there was his father, the man who was dumb or daring enough to beat up his own foreman and wanted his sons, above all, to be *serious*. Doug found this impossible. He coped with everything by imitating Jerry Lewis, who the family watched on TV while Mr. and Mrs. Clifford enjoyed their nightly Manhattans. Enlisting Chuck as his straight man, Doug would wait for commercial breaks and emerge into the living room in a clown outfit stitched by his mother. The Clifford family watched three or four hours of television a night, as much as the networks offered, and the boys performed for their parents' pennies during commercials. Doug "sold" Mom and Dad bowls of cereal for a nickel. Clowning, Doug learned, was the key. If he kept his father laughing, the belt wouldn't come off. When the family moved, often in the middle of the school year, clowning was his way of fending off ass-kickings. He memorized Milton Berle's jokes and perfected his Rocky and Bullwinkle impressions, and when the new school's reigning bully inevitably sought him out for a showdown, Doug knew how to disarm him. At Portola Junior High, as in so many similar concrete buildings throughout California, Doug knew exactly how to style his clothes and exactly what routines to perform in order to get the roughneck benediction: "If anybody fucks with you, you tell 'em I've got your back." This was how he learned that performance could change his life.

Stu needed no such saving, at least not at home. His mother, Dolores, named for San Francisco's Dolores Mission, had an artistic bent as well. She was a trained dancer who also studied classical piano and practiced as a painter, potter, and silk-screener, and she had the luxury of still occasionally working in all of them thanks to her husband's successful legal career. Herman Cook was a senior partner and contract law specialist at Hardin, Fletcher, Cook & Hayes, an Oakland law firm whose clients included Lloyd's of London and the Oakland Raiders. Herman had his own creative past: he put himself through college playing jazz trumpet before busting his lip during a rugby game. Other than late nights when sufficiently drunk, he no longer played.

Unlike Doug, Stu was born in the East Bay and spent his whole childhood there. He got the occasional beating from high schoolers in the neighborhood, but Stu's early life was otherwise completely free of struggle or drama. Weekends meant family trips in their enormous car—often to the Playland amusement park on the San Francisco shore, maybe stopping at the nearby Cliff House restaurant or the nineteenth-century public baths. Some days they'd head north, over the mist-trapping hills and into the perpetually sunny Central Valley farmlands. Often the destination was Mrs. Cook's family in Sacramento, where Stu's extended relatives owned a music store and his uncle led a big band. On the way to and from, his parents would stop off and buy Stu and Gordon, his younger brother, glasses of fresh-squeezed orange juice from a farm stand, or they'd get a meal at a family-run, agricultural-kitsch restaurant like the Nut Tree in Vacaville or the Milk Farm in Davis.

Through it all, less out of fear than good business sense, Herman never let on that he was Jewish. His own father had been named Chernovsky and served as an architect in Belarus in the early twentieth century. When he fled, he landed in Hayward, California, where, under his new all-American name, he became a sign painter and chicken farmer. Herman's success—reviewing banking paperwork and getting the occasional football player out of jail—was the reward for such immigrant hardship, and in the casually antisemitic atmosphere of the postwar United States, it was too risky to reveal his background. It might have cost him a client or a country club membership. Stu's mother was Roman Catholic but religion played no role in their family life except as a means of assimilation. On Sundays, Mr. and Mrs. Cook would bundle the boys and send them to the nearby United Church of Christ. There was a boulder in the church parking lot and Stu and his brother would climb on it and enjoy the view of San Francisco until the congregation let out, then head home to show their parents what good, unassuming Christians they were.

Stu learned trumpet in grammar school, then took classical piano lessons for a few years. But there was never any question, even in his young life, that he would one day become a partner at his father's firm. For all their trips and luxuries, Stu grew up with a sense that his family was a duty, not a launching pad. Especially as the oldest boy, he could feel the years ticking by in his adolescence. He was marking time, embodying his mother's sense of artistic accomplishment until he could fulfill a paternal destiny. In the evenings the family would gather around the hulking television set and watch black-and-white programs on the plate-sized screen. There were no hijinks as in the Clifford home, just midcentury calm and ease. But then came Elvis.

The new teen idol secured his monumental fame with three performances on *The Ed Sullivan Show* in 1956 and 1957 that were watched by nearly the entire possible US viewing audience. Elvis was a pied piper for white children, like Doug and Stu, who had a love for Black music but hadn't yet felt it up close. Elvis had. His television dispatches were made from Los Angeles and New York, but his hips were from Memphis. He'd been inside that famous city's blues and gospel palaces. Elvis knew that music intimately, but he found the perfect accompaniment for his specific talent. Just guitars, drums, bass, and a voice, and this guy from nowhere became the most important person on earth for millions of people.

When Doug first arrived at Stu's house, the Cooks were still living only halfway or so up the Hills. They kept a car on blocks in the driveway and the boys swapped back and forth between the passenger and driver's seats, shifting gears and dreaming up a getaway. Then they went inside to listen to records and dink around on the piano, which, to Doug's shock, was perfectly in tune.

They spent alternating weekends at the Clifford house, which had its own luxuries. Doug's parents, unsurprisingly, were the first on their block to own a television. But within a year of that initial hangout, Mr. Cook's law firm was a runaway success. The family moved higher into the Hills above Richmond, ascending to a final gentile-worthy castle next to Wildcat Canyon on the boundary of Tilden Park. On clear days you could see seventy miles, all the way to San Jose. But the boys were more taken with its subterranean treasure: a huge rumpus room, big enough for the piano and more.

Doug had grown to love drums, but you can't buy a drum set with love. Instead, as always, he made the most of his limitations. While "doing homework" in his bedroom, he'd keep the radio low enough to hide it from Mom and Dad, then play along by tapping his foot and hitting the bell of his conical desk lamp with a pencil. But as he and Stu began learning songs rather than just listening to them, his ingenuity grew. At the Portola woodshop, a friend helped him sand down two dowels into makeshift drumsticks. In the metal shop, he welded rods so they functioned as a hi-hat stand. From neighbors he gathered a beat-up snare and an old marching bass drum. With the snare balanced on a flowerpot stand, he had something to work with.

By spring, the boys were now fourteen and had the makings of something that the newly cleaned-up El Cerrito had never seen. Whatever the look of Doug's Frankenstein'd drum set, it held a beat behind Stu's piano. Stu couldn't play much, only a little stride and boogie-woogie, but with Doug's drums he sounded somewhere in the vicinity of the radio broadcasts they knew well. They made a racket, and they didn't know anyone else who was capable of making one. As far as they knew, no one else in the neighborhood was even interested in it.

Doug was lean and energetic, so he naturally played sports and spent time around the Portola gymnasium. The school was still new, one of the first big structures to be physically built into the mountains, and the gym was one of a few satellite structures down the hill from the main building on the other side of a wide, sunny courtyard. Walking back one day, Doug heard piano. It wasn't classical or even Pat Boone. It was Little Richard. Doug followed the sound in disbelief. Soon he found himself in the doorway to the music room, which shared a covered outdoor walkway with the gym. There he saw a white boy at the upright piano, stiff-backed and hunched at the shoulders, facing the room's rear wall. He played Little Richard, start to finish. Then he started Fats Domino. This was not a racket. This kid was a musician.

When the boy finished, Doug jumped. "I have those records," he said. The kid was shy, but he clearly had his own capacious record collection. They started listing songs they loved. "Rumble." "Honky-Tonk." "Deep Feeling."

"Do you want to be in a band?" Doug finally asked. The kid was short and shy, with the same tight crew cut that everyone wore. He seemed up for the invitation. It was hard to tell.

TWO

THE COMBO

He should have known John Fogerty. How many of his classmates liked Bill Doggett? All year, Stu and Doug had been fantasizing about hearing themselves on the radio, dreaming in each other's basements, in class, at the furniture store in downtown El Cerrito where they bought their records. It was impossible that Doug had somehow missed the other gangly white soul brother in the same grade, learning piano solely by ear and KWBR—and learning it faster than them.

John was the middle of five brothers, a flatlander all his life. His father, Galen, had worked in the printshop of the *Berkeley Gazette*, but he was a troublesome drinker. When John was eight, after the birth of his youngest brother, Bob, his parents divorced and Galen moved to Santa Rosa, north of San Francisco. John and his brothers stayed with their mother, Lucile, and visited Galen only occasionally.

John had been walloped by Elvis just like Stu and Doug, but he'd heard him from his brothers Tom and Jim, who were four and eight years older, respectively, and on their way out of the nest by the time John could even hit an octave with one hand on the piano. When Doug met him in the music room, John was living in his family's wet basement while his mother made do on a schoolteacher's salary and Galen's inconsistent child support payments. His thoughts were consumed with shame and self-consciousness about his parents' divorce and the shabby house. John felt poor and lonely. He didn't love music because it was rebellious; he loved it because it might allow him to escape.

Lucile and Galen had their own history of fleeing to freedom. They had moved to the Bay Area in 1941 after enduring the Depression in their hometown of Great Falls, Montana. Lucile was a drinker as well, but she brought a love of folk music and old-time Americana into her boys' lives. When the annual Berkeley Folk Music Festival began in 1958, she brought John and his little brothers. When he showed a growing interest in guitar, she sought out the festival's founder, Barry Olivier, to teach him in the style. But perhaps her most important gift was an earlier one, a record that she gave him when he was just a small boy, not yet even in school. "Camptown Races" was on one side, "O! Susanna" on the other. There was music in their house all the time, as there was in Doug's and Stu's thanks to their own mothers. But Lucile told John that both these songs were written by the same man, Stephen Foster. That piece of information struck him, even then: songs are *written*. Those pieces of spinning plastic that made people dance and sing and cry—someone had to make them up.

The plastic objects themselves also interested John. He liked records, the energy of them, the perfection of them. Listening to

KWBR or his own growing collection of 78s and 45s, he could tell that some were made more carefully than others. He didn't know what "separation" meant, but he could appreciate that the melody instrument needed to be heard more clearly than the drums, and that the bass and snare needed to be in balance. He could hear that certain recordings, especially Carl Perkins's, felt like they had "air" in them—room vibrations, echo, space. When he heard something he liked, he wanted to own that sound, study it. On a visit to Santa Rosa he heard a song on a grocery store jukebox, Elvis's "I Want You, I Need You, I Love You," and John knew he needed that guitar part in his life. He needed to know who the guitar player was. He felt the same about "Rock Around the Clock," Bill Haley's immortal dance-blues. Somehow, he would conjure those guitarists' sense of drama and control. He was certain.

When his hands were big enough to command the keys, John taught himself music using records. The family had a woefully out-of-tune piano, and he set the record player next to it and put on Jack Fina's "Bumble Boogie," a bopping novelty remake of "Flight of the Bumblebee." The record was a 78, but he played it back at 33 rpm so he could keep up. There was a cheap acoustic guitar in the house as well, made by the Stella company. Who needed friends?

John already had a library of music in his head when he reached Portola Junior High. He entered eighth grade as his older brother Tom was nearing the end of high school. Tom studied singers with the same devotion that John had for instrumentalists, and he had been singing with East Bay groups for years. The Stella was quaint, but the brothers weren't looking to pluck and fingerpick. They wanted the fullness that only electricity could bring, so they agreed to split the cost of a Silvertone amp and guitar. They were $39.95 each; contributing $5 per man per month, they could pay it off in less than a year. Plugged in, the first thing John taught himself was Jody Reynolds's atmospheric ballad of teen near-death, "Endless Sleep." It barely required more than an open E chord. On an electric guitar, that was plenty.

Doug may have first seen John on the piano, but guitar was where John wanted to go. He knew the names of those great guitarists for Elvis and Bill Haley—now he could say he wanted to play like Scotty Moore and Danny Cedrone. He knew other guitarists too: Duane Eddy, Chet Atkins, Ricky Nelson's sideman James Burton, and of course the great, swinging Carl Perkins. Stu and Doug knew how the music sounded and felt. John knew how to put it all together. And though he was bashful, he didn't lack ambition. He fantasized too, elaborately: In his mind he saw himself as a Black singer-bandleader, Johnny Corvette, named for the new car that had turned every preteen boy's head since its debut in 1953. He saw himself standing onstage in a blue rhinestone suit that sparkled in the lights. There was an audience in that dream, somewhere, but they were secondary to all that dazzling blue and the band that followed his every cue.

When Doug heard him in the music room, he invited John over to his house and bragged about his drums. Then John arrived at the Clifford home and saw the flowerpot stand, which put him at ease. Here was someone with the same unwarranted faith in himself that he had. From that day forward they started meeting up after school to indulge their mutual delusions of radio stardom. In Stu, Doug had a friend that shared his love of music, but they both had other interests and other friends. They were quintessentially well-rounded boys. John was single-minded. After a few months banging on the snare and Silvertone, Doug asked if they should include a piano player. He knew a guy, and the kid even had a good place to practice.

He hadn't even bothered asking Stu if he wanted a third member of their amateur rock and roll club, let alone if his parents would abide a full trio in the basement. By this point Mr. and Mrs. Cook were beloved to him. He spent enough time on the Hilltop that he chided Stu for not being nice enough to his dad. He watched Stu back-talk his father and expected the man to summon his son with the belt. But punishment never came. Stu put off easy chores and ignored his dad's requests with impunity. He even cussed at the guy. Doug was a good influence by comparison. If there was somehow an issue with the third boy, he would joke his way back into the Cooks' good graces.

No need to worry. Of course his part-time parents were fine with it. John came over with the Silvertone guitar and amp, Doug brought his patchwork drum kit, and they had plenty of room around the piano. Mr. and Mrs. Cook, with their backgrounds in music, particularly jazz, smiled admiringly at the boys' ambition. "The boys have a combo" is how they described it.

Immediately Stu recognized that Doug was right. The two of them knew how to make noise, but John knew honest-to-god *parts*. He could play Jerry Lee Lewis flourishes on the piano and could re-create bass lines with his left hand. He even sang a little—the combo tried Johnny Horton's new single, "The Battle of New Orleans"—but mostly they stuck to instrumentals, a practical choice for a group with no microphone and also a creatively sound one: mainstream rock and roll stars had become regular attractions on television, but the charts were still flush with wordless hits, from "Rumble" to "Red River Rock," "Tequila," "Sleep Walk," and Duane Eddy's "Rebel-'Rouser." John recognized the potential that they had, but he also knew he was the only one who could push them to the next level—gigs, records, radio. In his mind, within the first few practices, they were already his band.

John didn't let on how the Cook house made him feel. He didn't tell his new friends that he'd never spent so much time so high in the Hills before, or that the Cooks' two new big-finned Buicks were the wildest cars he'd seen in a peer's driveway. The Fogerty home didn't have a fireplace; the Cooks' had two, including one in the rumpus room. Lucile had supplied her boys with an old violin and that little acoustic Stella guitar, and they had the family upright that John could plink on (Doug joked that the instrument was in the "key of X"), but he'd had to scrape together paper route money just to split an electric guitar on layaway. He lived with a sense of multi-layered self-recrimination—as a middle child, as a poor young man, as a Catholic, and as a white guy who wanted only to play Black music. His life was defined by self-consciousness. Meanwhile here was Stu, a well-meaning goofball who didn't even appreciate what a gift it was to have an in-tune piano, let alone a father in the house.

When the three of them started meeting up at the Fogertys, Stu understood the source of John's drive. He saw the bedroom in the basement, with concrete floors that were cold even in good weather. In the winter the room flooded. Lucile had admirably met the challenges of raising five boys with ages ranging across sixteen years, but those challenges were real and plentiful. John's oldest brother, Jim, was a married CPA in his twenties, while Tom was already eyeing family life with his high school sweetheart, Gail. They were not expecting any financial help from their mother as they set out on their own, and in fact they welcomed the challenge and freedom despite that. Lucile's interest in the Berkeley Folk Music Festival was no surprise given her wider love of music, and the concerts had the added benefit of introducing her boys to a sense of class consciousness. They heard songs from Appalachia and the Blue Ridge there, songs that predated record-making and commercial concerns at all. Barry Olivier brought artists like Jean Ritchie and Frank Warner to the Bay for the first time to share songs that they had collected and curated, not written. The blues and R&B singles on KWBR were astonishing dispatches from the Jim Crow South, but at Olivier's studio and in the audience for the local Pete Seeger performances that his teacher also produced, John received a different kind of cultural inheritance, one that came closer to the isolation he saw on the family's sole trip back to Montana to visit Lucile's people.

These were faraway concerns on those first weekend afternoons in the Cook home. The boys tumbled their way through a handful of popular instrumentals and Stu's parents shrugged their shoulders, preferring that din to the thought of their boy running pell-mell in the streets. Whatever subconscious forces were pushing John to take this stuff so seriously, at the expense of sports or cars or more earthly adolescent interests, Doug and Stu could see the benefits of it. On a break from music-making they went outside to shoot baskets. They started asking each other: What are we doing this for? They all agreed: the goal, the only goal, was to be on the radio. From there, anything might transpire.

Doug held the ball. "Someday," he told his new bandmates, "we're going to make a hundred dollars a night." John and Stu paused to consider the unimaginable, then Doug brought the dream to new heights.

"Each!"

They had heard of "beatniks." They knew that the city across the Bay was supposedly awash in them, and some of their teachers wore the telltale beads or groomed themselves groovily. But they did not know what beatniks did, what they stood for or stood against. They did not know of the bookstore on the border of Chinatown and North Beach, the one where Italian immigrants bought anarchist newspapers and the organizers of the Chinese New Year parade kept their dragon in the basement. They didn't know of the owner, Lawrence Ferlinghetti, who landed a US Navy boat on Normandy Beach and came to the city in 1951 as part of the same migration that attracted the Cliffords and a half-million others. The boys were not aware that Ferlinghetti was a publisher of ostensibly obscene poetry, or that he was a poet in his own right, whose debut, released in 1958, was on its way to selling a million copies. There was a poem in that book, "Autobiography," where the reformed seaman recalled his early life. "I was an American boy," he wrote. He recalled the thud of newspapers as he threw them on porches on his own predawn route.

> I thought I was Tom Sawyer
> catching crayfish in the Bronx River
> and imagining the Mississippi.

He wrote about potato salad picnics and the wholesome creeds and cults of his youth. Then the poet recalled his lifelong hunt for new experiences, which started with his interest in Black music. In Ferlinghetti's case, he fell for Kid Ory, the early New Orleans jazz pioneer, the first from that city to record. "I am looking for my Old Man," the poet wrote, "whom I never knew."

THREE

A GROWN MAN

A band needs a name and John had one that worked as well as any: the Blue Velvets. It had class, with its echo of Tony Bennett. A name with mystery and sophistication. If someone saw that name on a record sleeve or marquee, they'd never guess that the group didn't have driver's licenses, or even a real cymbal stand.

Doug was working on that one. He became his parents' housekeeper and gardener for extra allowance money. They paid him to do the dishes, make the beds, and vacuum. Then he picked up lawn-mowing jobs in the neighborhood to supplement that, and whenever a gift-giving occasion arose, he asked for cash. That allowed him to replace the flowerpot pedestal with a real snare stand, then he got real cymbals. The most affordable kit he could find in El Cerrito was a relic from the 1930s with bottom heads that were literally tacked on, impossible to tune. He paid $200 for it. The drums had been spray-painted bright red, not exactly a match for the group's new name, so he brought it to his garage, stripped all the paint off, and glued on mother-of-pearl contact paper. There were wrinkles in the paper when he finished, and he had no money to his name, but by god he had real drums now.

With that and John's Silvertone rig, the Blue Velvets were a certifiable novelty at Portola. Once they started eighth grade in the fall of 1959, they played five songs at a sock hop dance and were suddenly the town band—literally the only one. They started playing gigs at the El Cerrito Boys Club, an after-school hangout for junior high students who weren't old enough to drive around and get into gang brawls at Mel's Drive-In in Berkeley like the high schoolers. The Boys Club had a boxing ring for the region's punks and farm boys to bash each other, and a social hall for Friday night dances. When the Blue Velvets plugged in for one of those occasions, the response was immediate. At long last, rock and roll had come to El Cerrito. Stu, Doug, and John had seen their heroes on TV, driving girls to screaming madness and boys to howling excitement. With their five-watt amp, an upright piano, and a hand-finished drum set that was nearly as old as Elvis, they found a version of that heaven themselves.

Soon they were Friday night regulars, and word spread. After playing a Portola sock hop, they had the admiration and gratitude of every adult who was trying to keep El Cerrito's *Blackboard Jungle*–era youth from waywardness. The Portola administration invited the Blue Velvets to perform at assemblies, then farmed them out to high schools around the region for the same purpose. John had been a regular truant for years. During the 1958 World Series, a rematch between the Yankees and the Milwaukee Braves, Lucile let him stay home and watch a game. That small indulgence evolved, unbeknownst to her, into a monthlong festival of unexcused absence and

Silvertone practice. Now the school was pushing him out the door to represent Portola wherever other administrators were starved for student entertainment. Just because he knew a few cover songs.

At the Boys Club, they made five dollars per show—each. Then they became the regular band for dances at El Cerrito High School, too. Doug was making more money as a drummer than he did as the family help, which earned his father's grudging respect.

There was no precedent for the Blue Velvets regionally, certainly not among anyone the boys knew. San Francisco had produced one Black pop act of some renown, Bobby Freeman, whose 1958 single "Do You Want to Dance" was a favorite of John and his older brother Tom. It was an exquisitely simple song, just a few chords played mostly on piano and hand percussion, given life by Freeman's energetic, soaring vocal. For their duets, John grabbed a pair of bongos that Lucile had somehow procured for the house, and he focused on re-creating the part from the record while Tom played the pounding piano. The older brother's true talent, however, was in his voice. John sat by the piano and marveled as Tom hit the smooth high-tenor lines that made Freeman a teen idol. He wasn't only a mimic—he had a natural singer's confidence and a real sound, a pleading croon in the ballpark of Ritchie Valens or Phil Everly.

Tom was only four years older than John, but that is a monumental difference to a fourteen-year-old. It was also enough of a gap that Tom's early musical education had begun well before Elvis. His earliest loves were West Coast vocal groups like the Five Satins, the Penguins, and the Medallions. That's where he learned that high, mellow tone that entranced John, and his younger brother was not the only one who recognized its beauty.

When he was still a teenager, a group of older local musicians with a Crickets-inspired name, Spider Webb and the Insects, wanted

Tom to join them as a singer, and even came to the Fogerty home to audition him. He sang Valens's "Donna" as his little brother watched, awestruck. In March 1959, before John had gotten his own group going, Tom went with the Insects to Los Angeles to audition for Del-Fi Records, the label that released "Donna" and was now reeling from Valens's recent death. They recorded two songs but nothing came of them, and the tapes did not survive.

The Blue Velvets' domination of East Bay sock hops and social dances rolled on through their eighth-grade year, which was Tom's final year of high school. Undeterred by the rejection in L.A., he proposed another recording session, this one local, at an Insects practice. Tom offered to pay for it all as well. Whatever it took to get them a real product, something to sell at dances and bring to radio stations. The band was confused. Would they get paid? Would there be chicks there? When Tom explained no, this was a down payment on future success, a stepping-stone, the band said they'd rather work on their cars. Tom had heard enough. He knew time was ticking by. It was foreordained that he would marry Gail after graduation and take a laboring job. It was a given that they'd start a family. He saw from his own mother that a mere interest in music didn't guarantee a career, even an amateur one. If he wanted to make a future with that voice, he needed partners who took this as seriously as he did. Maybe they were four years younger, but it looked like John's group was doing something that people responded to.

John told his bandmates that his brother wanted to sit in. He and Tom had even written a few songs together. Stu and Doug could hardly believe their luck, and when Tom showed up for rehearsal they could've fallen over. Here was a grown man. Eighteen years old, soon to be married, muscular, handsome, with experience behind a microphone and in a recording studio. A million miles from their own gawky midteen awkwardness; they were still being driven around by their parents. Jesus Christ, he'd been to Los Angeles.

And then he sang. John had not lied. Tom's voice was powerful and exciting, like gleaming clean chrome. He was a front man, the piece they lacked. And when they started talking about records, he knew everything. Obscure, mainstream, white, Black, harmonized, instrumental, the entire theology of contemporary R&B — if a record had been played or sold in the East Bay, Tom had it in his head.

When he asked if the Blue Velvets wanted to back him up, Stu and Doug felt that a door to the adult world was opening. All they had to do was grab hold of this guy and let him carry them to stardom. John had made them musicians, now Tom would make them a band.

And shockingly, he was kind. Tom started coming to Blue Velvets gigs and sitting in for a few songs each set. There was rarely any setup to speak of. Most of the time he would sing without a microphone. Stu and Doug knew they were no savants as players, but Tom was never less than encouraging. He had his own small-time piano skills, but he knew music as well as anyone they'd ever met. His enthusiasm meant as much as any squealing girl, though they noticed that whenever Tom sang, the squealing grew.

Tom's hope still rested on records, so he scrounged for local studios that would take a quartet with three barely pubescent members. Deliverance arrived in the form of Dick Vance, an Oakland man in the HVAC business who owned a studio on Grand Street, near downtown. Tommy Fogerty and the Blue Velvets arrived and brought their gear to the second floor, where they entered a studio that was barely big enough to hold them. Doug set up his papered drums only to find that he had no room to sit. No worries, Vance said, and cracked the window so Doug could sit on the sill. They recorded two songs with Doug's ass hanging out over Grand.

They had seen that their music worked at this point. They were a dance band; the point was to drive their peers to a frenzy. Now, in Dick Vance's closet-sized dream factory, they gathered around the console and heard, for the first time, the details of their sound. As the speakers played the Fogerty brothers' compositions "Baby Doll" and "Sandy Lou," the young guys went out-of-body. It was surreal to hear themselves. It was also humbling: they were connoisseurs enough to recognize that their well-intentioned thumping lacked the spark and subtlety of their favorite records. But they were on tape now. Right in the studio, Vance pressed the songs to acetates — impermanent lacquered discs meant to serve as master copies for vinyl duplication. They took the records and drove home to El Cerrito, having made it halfway to eternity.

Tom shopped the demos around while the trio kept to their steady live schedule. Since there weren't many places to play in their hometown, the Boys Club owner launched them out to foreign worlds like the orbiting satellites and so-called astronauts that were always in the news those days, to other sleepy East Bay towns with euphonious names like Pleasanton and San Leandro. He got them additional gigs at the summer 1960 Alameda and Sacramento County Fairs. During these shows they met a Black singer from North Richmond, James Powell, who wrote songs and sang. Powell needed a backing group to cut a record. He couldn't afford professionals, and the boys weren't picky about opportunities. A brief marriage of convenience was born.

Powell's songs were all named for women. He wanted the Blue Velvets to help him cut "Beverly Angel" and "Lidia," which were cookie-cutter doo-wop, not the boys' preferred style. Nevertheless, they threw themselves into the project, and John even borrowed an upright bass from a neighbor so they could enhance the bottom end. Doug had recently upgraded his drum set, too. He now played a modern Slingerland kit that he got at a discount because the sun had damaged its finish while it sat in a shop window. He didn't know if it had started as aqua or gold sparkle, but now it was an unholy swirl of both. Powell arrived in El Cerrito, and they loaded it all into his car and set off for North Richmond for their first practice.

Their knowledge of Black life and culture was still mostly limited to records. Now the boys drove up through the industrial sector in Powell's wide car and arrived in a blighted urban neighborhood that felt nothing like the dusty fairgrounds and low-ceilinged teen venues they were used to. Powell was older, though how much older was difficult to tell. His mother accompanied them and never left his side, even at the microphone. He carried a handkerchief to catch the saliva that perpetually dribbled from his chin. When practice finished, Doug began loading his drums back into the car before his friends shouted worriedly from the doorway. They pointed down the street to a man with a shotgun who was screaming at two girls who appeared to be prostitutes. Doug ran back inside, and they waited for the scene to disperse before leaving for good.

Powell had a contract to cut his two songs for Christy Records, an independent label in Vallejo. It was not a long session. In 1960, few were. When playback revealed that Doug hit a microphone with his brushes at the end of "Beverly Angel," the Christy engineer simply assumed no one would notice. "Lidia" utilized the same four-chord progression, and they were both less than two minutes long. The former was a waltzing slow dance, a flagrant copy of "In the Still of the Night," while the latter had a snappier Latin style, a familiar A-side/B-side template. The band went uncredited and the boys weren't paid. And while no deejay or record collector would confuse them for virtuosos, the playing was soulful beyond any reasonable expectation for suburbanites of their age and experience. Stu kept the rhythm on "Beverly Angel" with thudding block-chord triplets. Doug painted between those with swinging fills. At the bridge, John crept in on the Silvertone, bending his strings high on the neck in a way that added a bluesy flair to Powell and his harmonists' falsetto harmonies. The song also featured a real ending: the band dropped out and the harmonists brought everything back down to earth before one final resolution, no fade-out. There was echo all over the track. It sounded like real music.

The Black tastemakers of Oakland agreed: "Beverly Angel" was played on KWBR. Not often, and not enough to move many copies of the 7-inch single. The boys didn't even love the song. It didn't rock. But how could they care? They were fifteen years old, nearly all their heroes were Black musicians, and now, for a brief glorious moment, they were in rotation among the saints. When they heard themselves on the radio, on KWBR, out-of-body didn't describe it. This was beyond dreams.

"Beverly Angel" arrived around the election of John F. Kennedy, the first Catholic president and the first born in the twentieth century. His victory was the final act of a transformative year. Back in May, down the road in Berkeley, the police had fire-hosed a thousand students just slightly older than Tom for participating in a multiday demonstration against Bay Area hearings by the House Un-American Activities Committee. In February, Black students in North Carolina organized the Greensboro Sit-in, the first of its kind. That one action inspired similar sit-ins in fifty-five other cities, which in turn spurred the formation of the Student Nonviolent Coordinating Committee by summer. 1960 was a period of fear and bravery for young people, and the Blue Velvets had experienced their own modest, sheltered share of each. They had a record to show for it, too. But the nightly news was increasingly full of police crackdowns and racial uprisings, and it wasn't at all clear that the students leading the way would look for sustenance or inspiration in something like "Beverly Angel." For many of them, that was the music of their childhood, and they were learning that their childhood had not prepared them for the world.

FOUR

BLUE AND GREEN

Tom drove a truck, he worked in an Oakland steel mill, then in spring 1961 he got a position with Pacific Gas & Electric, the regional utility. It was fine, dull work, even if he occasionally served his ex-classmates from his Catholic alma mater, St. Mary's College High School, many of whom were now in college or working toward real careers. His three bandmates were entering high school and took inspiration from their leader. They pushed into music like laborers. It was their job to start parties, and they treated it as such.

It wasn't their only responsibility, though. Lucile tried to straighten John out by enrolling him at St. Mary's. John struggled immediately. He had no patience for authority as it was. He was singled out as a Fogerty by priests, the third to enroll. John made friends at St. Mary's, though, more musicians. He formed a group with boys he met in his freshman class, Ronnie White, John Tinonga, and Baynard Cheshire. John taught Cheshire how to play rhythm, and the classmate let him borrow his National guitar, a much more solid instrument than the Silvertone, as thanks. They wanted to call their band the Untouchables but another band in Richmond had already claimed that name and they had a record out locally. So instead they went with the Centennials, because they were in the class of '63, a hundred years since the school's founding. They practiced occasionally and performed before a couple school events in the gym. They even got a gig at a dance at Oakland's Sacred Heart Church Teen Club. These were meaningful experiences, but John couldn't tolerate being the school's sole "long-hair." He lasted barely a year, and it marked him. He saw the hypocrisy of authority figures, including priests who railed against rock and roll but couldn't be trusted alone with any of the boys.

After winter break in their sophomore year, he rejoined Doug and Stu at El Cerrito High, forgetting the Centennials instantly. He respected those guys, but there were just so many reasons why he couldn't stay at St. Mary's, from his disdain for the priestly hypocrisy to the weight of his two older brothers' reputations on his back. But on some level he was simply drawn back to Stu and Doug. They had already started their work, they were already the Blue Velvets. They were already his band.

When the trio played their first El Cerrito High student assembly, they were still awkwardly in thrall to Black culture: John brought a bicycle pump onstage and pretended to shoot up with it, like the heroin-addicted jazzbos that many white Bay Area parents still associated with Black music. He wasn't usually so rebellious or lighthearted. He took on night shifts at a gas station near his house, which kept him in guitar strings. He bought a small tape deck with a tweed cover, too, and started recording his own multipart demos. He taught himself rudimentary mixing in the cement basement by turning the volume down on the rhythm parts and cranking up the leads.

Doug, meanwhile, was splitting his time with the El Cerrito High football team. He came home sweaty every night and immediately headed to the drums. This interrupted the Cliffords' evening ritual of Manhattans and Milton Berle, so they gave him an ultimatum: sports or music. To their shock, he chose music, no hesitation. The football coach grumbled disappointedly when he learned he'd be losing his lanky, sprinting sophomore. Mr. Clifford couldn't understand it either. Nevertheless, Mr. Clifford helped get the boys to and from their sessions and gigs, even helped load the aqua-gold drums in the car. One night, after waiting outside yet another Blue Velvets gig and hauling his son's burdensome, bulky equipment out of one more foul-smelling teenage social hall in the dark, he chided the boy.

"Goddamn it, Doug," he said, "why couldn't you have played the piccolo?" Doug had another five-dollar bill in his jeans pocket from the night.

"Well, I don't know a single piccolo player that's working," he said.

Mr. Clifford couldn't argue with that. It wasn't only the money. The boys practiced. They worked. He might not have liked the music, but he respected their ethic.

So did Tom. Even Stu, who didn't need pocket money and didn't need to upgrade his equipment, put the time in. He got better at his instrument, and on the rare occasion when they secured a gig that didn't have a piano at the venue, he was out with his bandmates, loading one into a pickup truck just to make sure they didn't miss the chance for fifteen dollars. He was having fun, he was trying his best to get with the girls who danced and stared while the group played, but that wasn't the point. This was not a goof. Like Stu and John, he took his cues from their older leader—mentor, really—who was no longer a student but a nine-to-five working man with a family. The least they could do was treat it like a job.

Their ambition wasn't delusional. Tom's hustle got the attention of Orchestra Records, a nascent local label that offered him studio time for some of the songs that he and John had worked up together. The first they cut was "Come On Baby," a song so simple that they scarcely deserved their songwriting credits. A rollicking rock and roll blues, it better suited the boys' taste, and the performances reflected that. It kicked off with a quick New Orleans–style piano turnaround by Stu, then the group launched in together. John played the "bass" on his guitar's lower strings, then overdubbed a brief, sharp solo. Doug's drums were low in the mix, just enough of them to keep things propulsive. And Tom's vocals were strong enough to lead a band. It broke no ground musically, it simply hit hard and fast. Casey Kasem, a deejay at KEWB in Oakland, was impressed. Tom brought the record to the station, and though it never made a dent in terms of airplay, Kasem's three encouraging words—"Hang in there"—were enough to strengthen his resolve.

Better still, and a minor hit on KEWB, was the A-side they recorded a few months later, "Have You Ever Been Lonely." Another Fogerty brothers composition with an overly familiar chord progression, this one could have been more doo-wop by numbers. Instead, Doug played it fast and busy, with a Latin pattern that used every drum in his kit. It was John on piano for this one, and his solo on that instrument was even more expressive and technically accomplished than his earlier guitar breaks. He added blues feeling that contrasted with Tom's plaintive vocal. The singing on this track was the kind that made his little brother marvel in the living room. "Sweet" was the only word, and not faint praise. It took talent to sound this open, this guileless. Tommy Fogerty and the Blue Velvets were proof of that.

Now that they were in high school, they found a new place of business. Rather than the sock hops and adolescent dances of the East Bay, the band soundtracked fraternity parties at UC Berkeley. Their audiences were not the students who had stood up to HUAC, and they were not destined to participate in the Peace Corps, which was established by President Kennedy in March 1961 as a way to put the United States' growing youthful vigor to world-changing use. They were certainly not the white kids who spent 1961 pushing their way into the segregated South to fight alongside their Black peers for racial equality in the interstate bus system. In May of that year, the same month that Tom joined PG&E, white opposition to the Freedom Riders was so intense that a bus was firebombed in Anniston, Alabama, and the young people who escaped the flames were beaten with pipes by a Klan-led mob. It was Mother's Day.

The party scene on Berkeley's frat row was no moral crusade. It was cascades of beer, rivers of it, even for the Blue Velvets. It was bopping and howling. It was the Blue Velvets—surely familiar to some of the attendees from El Cerrito High School dances—running through their repertoire with growing confidence and musical ability. And it was twenty dollars for the band. Tom would join them when his schedule allowed. Sometimes the frat brothers would cut the young road dogs a deal, giving them sixteen bucks and four dollars' worth of lager, which was plenty. On nights like that, Stu and Doug would head down to Berkeley, make money by driving these future bankers and their girlfriends to sickness and oblivion, then head back to their own high school parties with cash and alcohol in hand. Applause greeted them everywhere.

John was not the kind to enjoy himself so much. His parents' struggles scared him off drinking, as did an incident at one of the Berkeley bacchanals where he hesitantly borrowed a sip from Doug's beer right as a cop entered the room. The straightest of them all, John got caught can in hand. This only underlined his belief that gigs were jobs, not excuses to party. He was there to perform a task: make people move. When that task ended, it was back to the other job, which he loved even more: make good-sounding records.

He quickly learned all he could from messing with the tweed tape recorder, so he went to the phone book. Rock and roll was new to the Bay but recording studios weren't. He found one, Sierra Sound Laboratories, on Alcatraz Avenue in Berkeley. It had just opened in 1961, and the owner, Bob DeSousa, was taken with the young man, newly of driving age, who wanted nothing more than to come by in his off-hours to play guitar and twiddle knobs. DeSousa knew an effect that John loved, the slapback, a bedrock for Elvis and his contemporaries at Sun Records in Memphis. Just a little onetime, instantaneous echo on the guitar, like the sound was bouncing off a nearby wall, made it seem like its own spectral double. It added space—air.

DeSousa recognized that John was a talent, not merely a tech-minded invalid. He used the kid on a few sessions as a pianist, particularly on country songs, where John could do a reasonable Floyd Cramer impression. Cramer was one of a handful of instrumentalists reimagining the template of country and western down in Nashville in the early 1960s, using the same methods that John was teaching himself under DeSousa's supportive watch: separation, subtle studio effects, and dramatic arrangements. Motown and Tamla, founded by the young descendants of displaced Black southerners in Detroit, were updating the doo-wop sound with similarly sophisticated songwriting and rhythms.

But none hit John so hard as Stax and its subsidiary label, Volt, out of Memphis. The first shot from this new independent label arrived in May 1962, when John was deep into his extracurricular studies at Sierra. The A-side of Volt 102, "Behave Yourself," didn't move radio listeners, but its B-side, "Green Onions," was an event to rival John Glenn's orbit of the Earth just a few months earlier. John Fogerty heard the song as a summation of his every interest. The instrumental was a twelve-bar blues led by a churchy Hammond organ and embellished with stabs of gnarled guitar, a walking bass line, and straight, deep-pocketed drums. In the famous formulation, it was Saturday night and Sunday morning simultaneously— roadhouse gospel, or, as it would soon be known, Memphis soul. "Green Onions" was a radio phenomenon: no. 1 *Billboard* R&B, no. 3 overall. By the end of the summer, when the Blue Velvets were preparing to enter their senior year, the single was rereleased with the sides reversed.

Most importantly to John, every instrument had its place and the band sounded relaxed, like they were rolling slowly down Beale Street, top down. The song's power came from its rhythm, style, and mixing, and he became an acolyte for the group who wrote and recorded it, Booker T. & the MGs. As far as he was concerned, this new quartet from Sun Records' backyard was now the greatest band in the world, and Stax, where they served as house band, became the primary label he looked for in the record stores. The Blue Velvets lacked a Hammond, but that was a small obstacle. "Green Onions" entered the repertoire and became their North Star.

Booker T. & the MGs released a full debut LP by year's end, inevitably titled *Green Onions* as well. But the record was not a filler-padded cash-grab by an overnight sensation. Instead, the group stretched across genres, performing instrumental soul versions of songs by Ray Charles, Philadelphia vocal group the Dovells, and a contemporary English easy-listening ballad, "Stranger on the Shore." They pulled out two by Motown's homegrown songwriting genius Smokey Robinson, and even a jazz tune, "Comin' Home Baby."

It was the perfect record for an in-between time, when popular music in the United States straddled old and new. The biggest mainstream record of the year wasn't even music, it was comedy—Vaughn Meader's send-up of the Kennedys, *The First Family*, which debuted on the charts sitting between the Crystals' "He's a Rebel" and Ray Charles's "You Are My Sunshine."

The Charles song sounded familiar to the Blue Velvets, particularly John, who revered the pianist's *In Person* live album above all others. The Crystals, however, were yet another group of young people on an independent label, Philles Records, founded at the dawn of the decade by another wunderkind producer, Phil Spector. "He's a Rebel" was Philles' first no. 1, and something of a mission statement for Spector's entire worldview. He aimed his orchestral four-chord pop directly at teenagers who had a nostalgic affinity for vocal-group harmonies and bad-boy chic, but who now yearned for epic and otherworldly sounds to match the news. Something like "Telstar," the Tornados' spiraling instrumental hit of 1962, named for the first orbiting communications satellite that launched during the summer. Vaughn Meader turned the president's beautiful family into hi-fi entertainment—a television variety show without the pictures. "He's a Rebel" and "Telstar," meanwhile, caught the teenage feeling of the time: one foot in the 1950s, with eyes watching heaven and outer space.

The Blue Velvets were approaching their own crossroads. Senior year was just another step in Stu Cook's forward march in his father's footsteps. He kept his grades high enough to guarantee college admission, enjoyed the rollicking weekend nights that music afforded him, but a dark shadow had been cast over the family: Dolores had developed lung cancer. Stu wasn't one to discuss his emotions, even with his friends. Instead, the pressures mounted and he remained testy with Herman. Doug arrived for a customary weekend at one point and heard the old man ask Stu to trim the hedges and take the clippings to the dump. Instead, Stu told him off and kept on with his friend. By the second day, even Doug began to ask, why not just get it over with? Doug was a semi-professional mower at this point, and offered to help. They could even drive the bags in Stu's own 1957 Chevy, purchased by his parents for his sixteenth birthday. Stu refused. Finally, by Sunday evening, the dump was closed. Three days of arguing, for nothing; Doug couldn't grasp it. Why would his friend make such a fuss about basic work? And why wouldn't Mr. Cook simply smack the kid until he did as he was told? Instead, Stu hastily clipped the bushes and tossed the green branches into a cement oven on the property, dousing it all in gasoline before tossing in a lighted match. Within seconds, Stu and Doug were blown back by the force of the explosion. Stu was alight, and the yard was dotted with gas fires. Mr. Cook simply drove them to the hospital, and his son missed a week of school with second-degree burns.

Doug had his own explosions and fallouts to worry about. Back in his Portola days, he'd learned of ongoing problems between his parents. He was too young to know any specifics but old enough to recognize that they were not making each other happy. Things came to a violent head when his mother started spending more time outside the house and his father grew even more distant, then despairing. Mr. Clifford was finished with El Cerrito and all the baggage he'd brought there. The family sold the house, moved into a smaller apartment, then Doug's father announced that he was moving to San Jose to invest everything he had in a new manufacturing company. He made it clear to Doug that the boy was on his own now.

While the band was his passion, Doug still had a social group outside music, most of it centered around the Delmar Club, a sort of high school fraternity. One of their benefactors was a Standard Oil executive, Jack Fleming, who had four daughters but no sons, and who was taken with Doug's flamboyance and hard work. Hearing the boy had nowhere else to go, Fleming offered Doug a place to stay for his senior year. He moved in during the summer.

As 1962 passed into 1963, nothing was certain for the Blue Velvets. Stu would be heading to college, but his life had been bruised. Doug's family had seemingly dissolved, and he was drinking more as the pain of that realization set in. John only knew that he would follow Tom's lead—into blue-collar work, semiprofessional music-making, and married life with his high school girlfriend Martha. The weight of adulthood bore down on all of them in different forms. Pop music was evolving, but their individual worlds were shrinking. Orchestra Records, where Tom had found them a home for occasional singles, had lost interest in Tommy Fogerty and the Blue Velvets, a group that for all their excitement had yet to sell many 45s.

Around this time they received a clue as to why. After finishing "Green Onions" at one of their gigs, the Blue Velvets were approached by a Black attendee. He was moved by the white boys' efforts. He could tell they really got this music, understood it. That's why he felt comfortable telling them that something was missing. *Swing,* you might call it, or *grease*—the ineffable feel that sets real musicians apart from the amateurs, at least in Black styles. If the band was going to play Booker T. & the MGs, he told them, they needed to find that in themselves.

The Blue Velvets graduated high school in spring of 1963, and Stu and Doug prepared to enroll at San Jose State. Martin Luther King Jr.'s March on Washington for Jobs and Freedom, held in late August, was yet another watershed moment in the media depiction of Black America. The event played in millions of homes and was covered by more television cameras than the Kennedy inauguration. The Blue Velvets were ahead of most white people in their knowledge and interest in Black culture, yet they were simultaneously a galaxy apart from any kind of East Coast mass movement. They spent the summer playing out their usual round of Elks Lodge and teen-club shows, thinking of the unknown man who had taken interest in their sound. Importantly, he had not laughed or made them feel they should give up. He said they were on their way. But deeper secrets would need to be unlocked.

FIVE

FANTASIES

I n 1963, the San Francisco city government began Phase A-2 of an ongoing "urban renewal" project centered on the Fillmore district, the so-called Harlem of the West. A new eight-lane expressway along the former Geary Street had already led to a mass relocation of nearly thirty thousand residents, mostly Black, across hundreds of city blocks in the previous decade. Stores and churches followed. Phase A-2 called for the relocation of an additional thirteen thousand people across sixty square blocks, which would rob the storied neighborhood of its lifeblood and further deplete the audience for some of its most revered buildings, including the Fillmore Auditorium.

In the spring, as the Blue Velvets graduated high school, the Associated Press reported on a massacre of South Vietnamese leadership by an insurgent group, the Viet Cong. Journalist Malcolm Browne described US troops laying out the bodies for transport. It was the first glimpse on the home front of young American men taking part

in this tropical fight, one that few US citizens even knew was taking place. Since the scene featured young Americans, it of course
included music. Browne reported that the loudspeakers overhead
blared Pat Boone.

The Fogertys were still in El Cerrito, pumping gas and working
the electrical lines. John remained a regular at Sierra Sound and at
Ray Dobard's Music City, another Berkeley studio where he served
as a gofer and apprentice. The latter had gained some renown for
producing one bouncy R&B hit, "W-P-L-J," which stood for "White
Port and Lemon Juice." When John worked there and occasionally
brought in his bandmates to try out new songs, it still retained its modest charm. The only soundproofing was literal egg cartons on the wall.

Doug and Stu were pursuing more formal education at San
Jose State an hour away at the Bay's southern end. For Stu, it was a
mere requisite for law school. For Doug, it was a chance to remain
near Stu. Very little kept him in El Cerrito now that his father had
forced him into independence. The friends moved in together and
started their newest dual adventure. In his previous moves, Doug
had charm and humor to fall back on. In San Jose, he took only a
partial class load because it was all he could afford, and he worked
as a night-shift janitor to keep up on rent and tuition. The band was
the only continuity that Doug had, as it was for Stu. They made
weekend trips back to town and kept their fraternity gigs going.
The Blue Velvets played three to four of those per month, making
twenty dollars a man. When they didn't have gigs, they practiced or
recorded. For most of 1963, they were a devoted commuter cover
band with nothing to rely on but a shared need to keep each other's
musical hopes alive. They couldn't even settle for being good-for-
high-school. They were men now, the same age as Tom when he
seemed like their blond, crooning savior.

To make things more confusing, it wasn't clear what a pop act was supposed to look or sound like in early 1963. A quartet of boys in suits? A trio of gyrating girls in spangled minidresses? An interracial instrumental group from Memphis led by a black organist? Twirl the dial in the car and you might hear Roger Miller, Ray Charles, Bing Crosby, Jackie Wilson, or the Singing Nun. After rock and roll hit its commercial peak in the boys' early practice days, the tallest figures of that genre were since toppled, captive, or dead. Elvis had gone to Germany in the Army and returned as a teen-movie heart-throb. Little Richard became a religious artist. Chuck Berry had been arrested for licentiousness and Jerry Lee Lewis was spurned for statutory incest. Buddy Holly was lost in a blazing plane crash alongside two compatriots, the Big Bopper and Ritchie Valens. And then in 1963, another young upstart in her own genre, Patsy Cline, died in the exact same manner, on the cusp of claiming a new realm of country-crossover fame. There was no single type of pop star, and thus no obvious reigning pop royalty.

The biggest halfway recent hit to come out of San Francisco was "Cast Your Fate to the Wind," released in 1962 by an all-white jazz group, the Vince Guaraldi Trio. If that could work, three white boys banging out blues and R&B standards on guitar, drums, and piano seemed viable. The Blue Velvets weren't missing any crucial element for popularity that they could see.

That changed on December 10, when *CBS Evening News* re-broadcast a five-minute feature on the "epidemic" overtaking British youth at the time: Beatlemania. It was the same mob imagery in every similar feature in the UK. Kids getting shaggy bowl cuts. Girls screaming at previously unimagined decibel levels. The Beatles' impact was so immediate that the media started watching the audience the minute they started covering the band. The audience *was* the story for many people. Whether you focused on the hair or the crowds or the total domination of national pop charts, it was clear that a new type of attention was being paid, and a new type of emotional response was possible. Those mobs of girls were shaking in their souls, crying and shouting, feeling the spirit. The cameras feasted on them.

The program initially aired on the morning of Friday, November 22, and CBS intended to rerun it that evening before all other news—and the wider national consciousness—was overwhelmed by the assassination of President Kennedy. The average US household watched ten hours of commercial-free television the next day. It took until early December for the media to deem the country ready for distraction again. The Beatles segment rose from oblivion, introduced once more by Walter Cronkite.

The Beatles differed from other youth entertainers mostly because they were self-contained. They played their own instruments and had a signature unkempt hairdo that no other boys dared until John, Paul, George, and Ringo made it required. They even wrote their songs, and lord, what songs. "I Want to Hold Your Hand" was the one that broke the dam, a tough and fast amalgam of American styles: street-corner harmonies and distorted guitars performed with the breakneck teenage enthusiasm of Motown or, one could argue, a frat-party house band. But there was no confusing them with the Blue Velvets. The Beatles' music was sophisticated and vibrant, not just dance fodder.

Within weeks, the plans were made for them to bring their live show to American television. John, Stu, Tom, and Doug watched *The Ed Sullivan Show* on Sunday, February 9, 1964, along with seemingly every other young person in the country. The band performed three songs to kick off the episode, then gave way to three more acts that seemed instantly passé, including a scene from the musical *Oliver!* featuring child actor Davy Jones as the Artful Dodger. Then they returned for their finale, closing with "I Want to Hold Your Hand." The Blue Velvets loved the band's sound, but the Beatles were a visual revelation as much as a musical one. Not just the hair or their smiles, but the sight of three upright guitarists flanked by amplifiers with a drummer behind them on a riser. Every element of their sound was visible and balanced. They smiled while they played, owning the wide stage from their designated positions, then huddled at their microphones to harmonize with beaming grins. When they bowed, they did so in formation.

A purported seventy-three million people watched the Beatles on television that night. But the group stirred teenage minds more than adult ones. *Newsweek* would scoff at their "tight, dandified Edwardian beatnik suits and great pudding-bowls of hair" and their purported lack of talent: their "merciless beat that does away with secondary rhythms, harmony and melody. Their lyrics (punctuated by nutty shouts of 'yeah, yeah, yeah!') are a catastrophe, a preposterous farrago of Valentine-card romantic sentiments." But a rumor grew that no major youth crimes were reported anywhere in the country during *Ed Sullivan* on February 9. A new four-headed fount of youth identity and fascination had arrived overnight.

For Tommy Fogerty and the Blue Velvets, the Beatles had an immediate impact during a driftless period. They dropped the two-part name, for one, resolving to record only as a cohesive unit. And after a year of uncertainty, they finally saw the shape that their band needed to take. One guitar and a thunking piano would do no longer. It had to be two guitars and a bass, all positioned toward the audience, on their feet, in front of the drums. They needed to face forward, literally and otherwise.

Well-meaning resolutions aside, they still had no label or immediate prospects. And San Francisco was not London, where the English group was signed to EMI. In terms of rock and roll, it more closely resembled Liverpool, the city that the Beatles left to find fame. Los Angeles, hours south, was the capital of West Coast show business, and the closest place for a young, tested band to capitalize on the newly raging market for white boys with a Black sound.

Barely a month later, they learned otherwise. On March 18, John and Tom watched the second episode of a new series, *Anatomy of a Hit*, on the San Francisco educational station KQED. The show was focused on the Vince Guaraldi Trio's "Cast Your Fate to the Wind," one of 1962's many unlikely pop sensations. The song appeared on the trio's *Jazz Impressions of Black Orpheus*, a consummate example of the frictionless, easy-listening style already known as "West Coast jazz." The interviews and group performances took place at the studio belonging to one of that genre's leading independent lights—Fantasy Records, right across the Bay.

The *Anatomy of a Hit* episode featured Fantasy's co-managers and co-owners, brothers Soul and Max Weiss. Their dynamic was clear: Soul kept the books and managed the business side, while Max, the creative spirit, spent his interview in a philosophical reverie while fondling a revolver, wearing some kind of fur hat. He mentioned at one point that the label was looking to move into the pop side; their limited non-jazz roster at the time included a singer, Roy Chauncey Huff, and a teen group, Tommy and the Hustlers. They'd just had a major success with an instrumental song, and the Fogerty brothers had a handful to play for this little on-the-make label. Tom and his little brother made quick plans to bring their demos to the other set of brothers on Treat Avenue.

This was no small thing for John, who by this point had only been to "the city" a handful of times. He was eighteen now, an adult, and a seasoned performer at that, but his life remained curiously small. He didn't visit his friends at college in San Jose—didn't do much, in fact, besides make music and take occasional breaks to work at the gas station. Even as political turmoil grew on the Berkeley campus, a place he'd come to know well, his world remained limited to records and guitar. Standing on Treat Avenue, steeling himself to enter the warehouse where the Weisses ran their small operation, he was about to take the most ambitious step of his life, and even then, he had his older brother there to help.

Soul and Max were not really record men. They had come to the industry through a back door: plastics. In the late 1940s, Jack Sheedy, owner of the Dixieland label Coronet Records, recorded an unknown local pianist named Dave Brubeck, then fell behind on his bills. The Weisses were one of his creditors. They ran the pressing company that supplied Coronet and other labels, and they were given Coronet's master tapes when Sheedy couldn't pay. After taking control of the operation, Soul and Max named their new label for a popular pulp science fiction magazine, and, like true plastic magnates, gained a reputation for producing records in unusual colors, including green, red, and blue translucent vinyl. The brothers built on Brubeck's commercial momentum by recording other rising local jazz names, but their early moneymakers had little to do with piano. They released spoken-word records from Lawrence Ferlinghetti and Lenny Bruce, and numerous albums of Chinese opera, which were mainstays in San Francisco's many Asian households.

By the time the Fogertys came in the door, the Fantasy roster had grown to include West Coast jazz luminaries like Gerry Mulligan and Cal Tjader, as well as music by Miles Davis, Thelonius

Monk, and Charles Mingus, whose sister was married to Fantasy's sales manager, Saul Zaentz. The yin-yang scene captured on television was obviously not a put-on. Soul Weiss was barely to be seen, and instead kept to his office in the warehouse's second floor while his avuncular brother Max sat behind a first-floor desk enjoying his role as chief executive hipster. He had a mustache and goatee and wore his Russian-style hat along with Day-Glo socks under his sandals. He spoke of music as "groovy."

The Fogertys brought their records into a different room and played some of their band's instrumentals for Max, who responded positively. But it was the Beatles' world now. He asked if they had any songs with words. If they did, Max would have them in the studio.

John had written a few, and Tom was of course the author of forgotten classics like "Have You Ever Been Lonely," but the invitation to record for Fantasy compelled them to approach songwriting with greater sincerity and ambition. Seeing that the Beatles' songs were mostly Lennon-McCartney cowrites, they began working together, even giving themselves evocative aliases for the purpose: Tom became Rann Wild and John, Toby Green. The new Green-Wild team brought some of their new material to their bandmates at the next practice, eventually settling on two songs for their Fantasy debut, "Don't Tell Me No Lies" and "Little Girl (Does Your Mama Know)." The quartet, with Stu now playing a bass that they'd borrowed from their go-to music store and Tom on rhythm guitar, arrived at Fantasy to record their demo in late March.

The studio was a step up from their usual—Fantasy even owned two four-track recorders, though one only had three working tracks. The facilities were still not fancy. The studio was an empty room, essentially a lean-to built on to the main building with the lumber still exposed. When sessions went longer than Fantasy's neighbor liked, the man banged noisily on the wall. Max was excited but felt "The Blue Velvets" needed updating. After a quick discussion, the band decided to rename themselves the Visions, which sounded forward-thinking and mysterious. Demo completed, the group left the studio to await the Weisses' verdict on their prospects.

Fantasy's openness to an unknown teenage group was one of a million small, hopeful corporate revolutions playing out in the wake of that fateful *Ed Sullivan* episode. In Los Angeles, record companies were scrambling for guitar quartets, and even the movie and television industries were looking for ambassadors to this strange, unkempt new world. The same month that the Visions recorded their demo, Screen Gems, the TV arm of Columbia Pictures, hired a young new executive, Bob Rafelson.

Rafelson was only in his early thirties but had already done a lifetime's worth of traveling, seeking, and rebelling. The son of a Manhattan ribbon manufacturer, he was simultaneously macho and privileged: he attended multiple prep schools, then Dartmouth, courting expulsion wherever he went due to a hair-trigger temper. But he had an artistic bent as well, and made pilgrimages to meet literary heroes like J. D. Salinger and Wallace Stevens. After his own attempt as a New York salesman (selling ties, not ribbons), he enlisted in the Army, serving on a base in Japan where he subtitled movies.

Back in the city, he took a job writing for *The Play of the Week*, a Screen Gems production, where he worked for an executive named Bert Schneider. Buoyed by these small tastes of filmmaking, Rafelson moved to Los Angeles in 1962 and brought his temper with him. In a meeting with Lew Wasserman, a famously cranky but legendary Hollywood producer, Rafelson threw an award across the office in a fit of pique about what constituted "reality" in movies. He was reunited with Schneider at Screen Gems after holding a few similar middling studio jobs. The most recent one ended when Rafelson overturned an executive's desk during a screaming matching about recuts. He felt the movies could be better if the suits just got out of the way and followed the new youthful energy that was taking hold all around them. Schneider, who just happened to be the son of the head of Columbia Pictures, grew convinced—and sympathetic.

The Visions were hardly exemplars of this rising energy. They still played their bread-and-butter 1950s covers, and Fantasy wasn't an obvious place to carve out a niche in the teen market. But it was the one chance they had. They had a real record man's interest and couldn't afford to say no. John took the same attitude he took toward any opportunity, large or small: he resolved to grasp it with a fury, to not even run the risk of losing it. He knew he had talent, but lots of guys had talent. Not all of them grew up in a leaky basement, however. John would never be outworked. And now he had the platform to make that clear.

SIX

FREEDOM SUMMER

In April 1964, Ford introduced the first car explicitly aimed at the young, the Mustang. It was coming-of-age time for all those children born in the years after the war, including John, Stu, and Doug. A million more Americans turned seventeen that year than in 1963. Demographic trends showed that the number of teenagers would double by 1970. Introducing the new hot rod, Lee Iacocca, Ford's president, called these boys and girls "the buyingest age group in history," and music was central to their practice.

Even the tame and sleepy East Bay caught the fever. A thirty-mile stretch from Albany down to Fremont, both even smaller than El Cerrito, embodied the teen-beat boom. Bands like Tom Thumb and the Hitchikers, Harbinger Complex, Lucky 14, and Peter Wheat and the Breadmen played to packed rooms with names like Rat Fink a Go Go, Frenchy's, the Penthouse, and Soul City. At the southern end of the route were venues like Carlo's Pizza in Fremont, a GM factory town. To the north was Oakland, a port city with its own boom of newly minted teenagers. In the middle were the Newark Pavilion, the Sound Factory, and Little Richard's.

This ecosystem of young entertainment was blooming by the summer of *A Hard Day's Night*, and its epicenter was a heavenly club-strewn stretch of San Leandro's Fourteenth Street known as "the strip." Sylvester Stewart, better known as Sly Stone, was a studio prodigy not unlike John and had a band that played Frenchy's regularly, as did another locally revered soul-rock band, the Spyders. It was a multiracial party music coalition, something that the British bands, for all their blues and James Brown affectations, couldn't boast.

The Visions were made for this scene, yet they remained literally peripheral to it. San Jose, where Doug and Stu lived, was just south of Fremont, while El Cerrito, still John and Tom's home, was just north of Albany. John spent his few off-hours on the Berkeley campus, where he frequented La Val's, a little eatery near the College of Architecture. He even entertained diners in the restaurant's courtyard in the fall of 1963, where his guitar playing was impressive enough that one student, Mike Byrne, approached him to ask about joining his group.

Byrne was a keyboardist who had one close musician friend in the College of Architecture, Tom Fanning, but otherwise struggled to get a working band together. The need to play wasn't just extracurricular. Like John, he had grown up among multiple siblings and even served as a caretaker for his younger ones before heading to college. Music, he felt, could be a way to make money and help pay for his education. He had the same tastes as John, and he shared the younger guy's commitment to playing seriously, not just to get laid or drunk. But music was a means to an end. He was on a path to design buildings and wasn't reliant on music to secure a life outside of the gas station graveyard shift.

Mike and Tom Fanning's group was called the Apostles, and they played a similar mix of the Blue Velvets' early rock and soul. Like John's band, they performed at fraternity parties as well as country clubs as far away as Palo Alto, but they hadn't yet secured a permanent lead guitar player. With his friends in college, John joined the Apostles when he could.

In spring 1964, Mike and Tom got the Apostles a recurring Thursday night gig at a small jazz bar just across the Oakland line, the Monkey Inn. The group built a reputable sound thanks to John's Freddie King–inspired playing and Mike's blaring piano, achieved with a stage mic dropped under the lid, right near the strings. But with summer coming, they knew campus would empty and their party nights would evaporate. Tom and Mike's fraternity had a chapter in Portland, Oregon, a perfect destination for a good summer field trip. The Portland scene had produced harder-edged bands like the Sonics, the Kingsmen, and Paul Revere & the Raiders, which gave it a reputation as the West Coast's party-punk outpost. The Northwest bands were thunderous and pounding, largely thanks to their big horn sections and blaring, tonally unwavering organs like the Farfisa. These were all genuine justifications for the trip, though Tom didn't reveal another reason that Portland appealed: his girlfriend was living there at the time, training for the Peace Corps.

John had to get up there himself after Mike and Tom scouted out a place for them to stay. He brought his tape recorder and guitar—by this point he'd gotten a sunburst Supro at three-quarter scale to accommodate his small hands—and went up through the Northern California mountains to join his fellow Apostles. For someone who had barely gone across the Bay just a few months previously, this nine-hour trip must have felt like a voyage to foreign lands. Except for one family vacation to Montana, almost his whole life had been spent near San Francisco. He was nineteen now, and other than the Monkey Inn adventures of the previous few months, his entire musical evolution had taken place alongside the same three guys. But he had prepared for this in small ways—by finding the courage to play that piano at Portola Junior High, learning and writing songs with his older brother, or impressing a handful of small-time studio operators in Berkeley and environs. Portland wasn't a bigger step than those. He wasn't expecting to find greater glory than the Fantasy opportunity, the details and future of which remained unclear. Instead, this was a chance to try something new, perhaps even something untethered to the pressure of making a living in this work. If he was actually playing in a band away from home, he wouldn't have to obsess over escaping.

Tom and Mike found a rural house to rent by the time John arrived. It was a bucolic place outside the city with chickens and friendly neighbors who supplied them with fresh vegetables and eggs. After placing an ad for a drummer and signing up for the local musicians union, they had a full band and took a nightly gig playing from eight to midnight at a bar that catered mostly to older couples.

Their setlists were familiar. "Hully Gully" and the Northwest's biggest hit, "Louie Louie," were standard. John brought his tape machine and recorded everything they played, then the band would come back to the house and stay up until the late hours listening back and drinking beers. Mike could yelp a bit, but John became more ambitious with his role in the band. He wanted to sing. He started studying his own vocal work in the way he'd studied his favorite records at slow speeds, trying to identify his limitations and overcome them. He also started playing harmonica, bringing the same devotion to that instrument that had made him a guitar prodigy.

John's goal with both was simple. He wanted a gritty singing voice like the men he most revered: James Brown, Wilson Pickett, and Little Richard, who he considered the best singer in rock and roll. On the harp, he wanted to sound like the unquestioned king, Little Walter. He wanted the grainy growl and howl that Black vocalists and bluesmen brought to US pop music, the same soul element that last year's supportive listener had called out the Blue Velvets for lacking. On guitar, John's heroes included white boys like James Burton and Carl Perkins, and even if he imitated Black players like Lightnin' Hopkins or Albert King, that was finger work and technique. Singing, as evidenced by John's reluctance to try it, was more personal, especially the singing that grew out of Black slave and church traditions.

He was attempting to learn his way into southern Blackness. And though John was humble and well-intentioned toward his influences, even reverential, he fit a prototype of the era. He was drawn to the earthier realm of Black music because he felt, in his blinding self-consciousness, that it would make him seem manlier. There was no shortage of white-boy would-be soul and bluesmen at the time, some of whom were inspired, including John Hammond Jr. in New York and Charlie Musselwhite in Chicago. And by 1964, every white kid in the country felt part Black anyway. If their favorite artists weren't Black, they likely approximated Black songs and dance styles so fully that the influence was even more striking. Civil rights leaders recognized this disparity in white America's engagement with Black culture. Speaking to a Birmingham crowd in 1963, Ralph Abernathy noted, "The white man can learn to do the Twist and Slop in two weeks, but it has taken us two hundred years to learn to live with each other."

Even outside the pop world, more white people than usual were getting formative educations in Blackness in the mid-1960s. The March on Washington had shown a broader sampling of these traditions to more US homes than any event to that point. Not only Martin Luther King, who was now the best-known Baptist preacher in US history, but also Mahalia Jackson, the queenly gospel singer who compelled him to his "I Have a Dream" reverie, and John Lewis, a young man about Mike Byrne and Tom Fanning's age who had co-organized the event after a childhood spent among Deep South sharecroppers.

That same spring, the Student Nonviolent Coordinating Committee also began plotting the Mississippi Freedom Summer, a voter registration effort focused on the state with the lowest level of Black participation in the franchise. Starting on June 13—almost simultaneous with John's trip to Portland—about a thousand out-of-state volunteers descended on Mississippi to help its beleaguered Black populace exercise their rights. Nearly all were college-aged, and some were Black. But 90 percent were white, drawn from prestigious colleges including Berkeley and the Ivies, bearing what the *New York Times* referred to as "a distinct middle-class stamp." These well-intentioned young people were fans of Motown and Bob Dylan. Some had been inspired by images of Black suffering that now peppered the nightly news. Yet many, like John Fogerty—like most people in other regions of the country—knew the South only from media, especially TV programs like *The Beverly Hillbillies* and *The Andy Griffith Show*, and it was through media coverage that their unsuccessful yet inspirational campaign became famous, especially after three white volunteers were killed by oppositional racists.

John needed no convincing that Black people were equal; in fact he worshipped their traditions and sought their approval. His Portland trip was a rumspringa by a true believer to practice his art, not a rich boy's fight for others' dignity. John yearned in his chest to make music worthy of James Brown despite their obvious differences. And Portland was where he first grew convinced that he could do it fully. The bucolic setting, the nightly shows, the supportive older bandmates, and the total, if temporary, lack of worry about career-making presented him with something new: a monthlong period where music was merely a defining aspect of his everyday life rather than a desperate attempt to escape self-doubt. The Visions were still his band. He had no intention of remaining in Portland. But thanks to Mike Byrne and Tom Fanning, he was granted a chance to simply have fun and build his skills as a working artist, and he jumped on that with the same enthusiasm that he brought to his writing and recording.

Eventually the three musicians had to return to the Bay, but the Apostles were fun enough that they continued their regular Thursday night standing gig at the Monkey Inn. They still lacked a drummer, so John suggested they bring in Doug, who made the trip up from San Jose every week while balancing his janitorial night shifts, his own fraternity life, and as many university classes as money and time allowed.

On the weekends, Visions rehearsals continued as well, and John had brought his newfound confidence down from the Northwest. He now wanted to sing his songs, a final step of the transformation that began with Stu's move to bass and Tom's adoption of rhythm guitar. You couldn't have a crooner playing in front of two guitars; even Lennon and McCartney could wail when their songs required.

Incredibly, Tom agreed. Only months earlier he had been the undisputed front man and namesake of the group, but he could recognize the change that Portland had wrought in John. He had watched his little brother grow from a kid who liked 45s to a man who made them well. He'd seen John pick up guitar and piano and blaze past the neophyte stage on both. The guy had regular gigs before he could drive. Why wouldn't he sing and play harmonica now? Give him a few hours and he'd probably get a good sound out of a tuba. John's voice was the right one to lead the Blue Velvets into their new stage as the Visions. John, after all, had the vision.

Fall 1964 saw the largest-ever college enrollment in the United States, and since half of the band was already playing Thursday nights at the Monkey Inn, the Visions also took a night to entertain the Berkeley arrivals who were now fully in thrall to the British sound. This wasn't exactly a fraternity house, but it was close enough. John plugged a microphone into his guitar amp and developed a habit of facing the wall instead of his audience while singing. The drunken, sweaty crowd got only his profile as he brought his first howls and original songs to his hometown.

Finally, in November, word came from Fantasy. The records were ready. The group's first reaction was surprise—they thought their session back in spring was a tryout, a demo at best. But Max and Soul had gone ahead and pressed the songs as a 45. Aflame with anticipation, the Visions went over the Bay Bridge to see their debut record, "Don't Tell Me No Lies" b/w "Little Girl (Does Your Mama Know)," on the same label as "Cast Your Fate to the Wind."

Max handed them a box with twenty-five singles and the quartet opened the cardboard to see their new identity in full flower. Instead, they thought a horrible mistake had been made. Rather than the Visions, the records were credited to the Golliwogs. They looked to Max, expecting him to share their confusion. Instead, he took credit. This was 1964, after all. English bands were the rage, and "Golliwogs," named for a UK children's doll that resembled the stateside Sambo caricature, sounded almost parodically British. Panic set in, tempered by joy, anger, gratitude, nervousness. They couldn't possibly keep this name, yet they had no other options. It was more than five years since this group of friends had made their first noise together. Now their choice was embarrassment or oblivion.

SEVEN

HUMILIATION

I t wasn't only the Golliwogs who felt untethered and ambivalent at the end of 1964. The whole country shuddered with
uncertainty, the Bay Area most of all. On December 2, students at
Berkeley occupied the campus's Sproul Hall in defiance of growing administrative restrictions on political expression at the university. The Free Speech Movement had been building since October,
and the December occupation catalyzed a resistance of thousands.
Hundreds were arrested, Joan Baez performed folk songs in solidarity, and student activist Mario Savio, a recent arrival to California,
gave an impromptu, instantly famous speech exhorting his peers:
"There's a time when the operation of the machine becomes so
odious, makes you so sick at heart, that you can't take part. You
can't even passively take part. And you've got to put your bodies
upon the gears and upon the wheels, upon the levers, upon all
the apparatus, and you've got to make it stop. And you've got to
indicate to the people who run it, to the people who own it, that

unless you're free, the machine will be prevented from working at all." The Berkeley rebellion embodied the defiant spirit that impressed historian Howard Zinn, who observed earlier in the year that "young people are the nation's most vivid reminder that there is an unquenchable spirit alive in the world today, beyond race, beyond nationality, beyond class. It is a spirit that seeks to embrace all people everywhere."

There was no youth monopoly on anger, however. Lyndon Johnson's unsuccessful opponent for the presidency, Barry Goldwater, had mobilized a widespread group of dissenters to the government's mounting liberalism. Some were rock-ribbed anticommunists with doomsday fears after the recent Cuban Missile Crisis. Others opposed Kennedy-era business regulations, and plenty were simply that era's share of perpetually terrified white folks, disgusted by the seemingly ceaseless demands of civil rights leaders and their race-traitor enablers. The sight of a state university under siege by its own student body only deepened this faction's conviction that the new youthful idealism was a challenge to decency and order.

The Bay Area had become a lodestar for those who felt equally apocalyptic and idealistic — Savio's people. Steve Reich, like Savio, was another native New Yorker drawn to the region for education. He entered Mills College in the late '50s for graduate studies in music composition. In late 1964 he stood in Union Square in San Francisco's Tenderloin District, less than a mile from the Fantasy Records studio on Natoma Street, and listened to a Black Pentecostal preacher named Brother Walter. Reich was struck by the musical quality of Walter's sermon about Noah and the flood. The man's voice seemed to hover between speech and song. Reich had a tape machine on him and recorded clips of the performance and the ambient noise surrounding it. At home he played with small bits of Brother Walter's voice that struck him as particularly musical. One was a snippet of just three words: "It's gonna rain." Shortening the clip to just that ominous phrase made the words' meaning simultaneously deeper and more elusive. When Reich tried to synchronize two tapes of the recording, he became entranced as they grew slowly out of phase with each other, until Brother Walter's already musical voice had become an overlapping, rippling babble of microtonalities outside any time signature or traditional notation. Then the two recordings naturally began to "catch up" to each other, finding synchronicity again, a process that registered to Reich as a physical sensation. He felt more like an audience member than a composer.

Reich began to perform the resulting piece, "It's Gonna Rain," in early 1965. It was a breakthrough in the use of supposedly nonmusical source material in the classical world, as well as in the technical development of electronic music. And though it wasn't as straightforward an example as John Fogerty willing himself to sound like Wilson Pickett, "It's Gonna Rain" was also a watershed in the interaction between Black and white culture, in this case a Jewish composer's use of a southern preacher's literal voice to achieve a sort of music-beyond-music, a pure soundscape where established rules of tonality and composition didn't apply. The piece made Reich's reputation as an artist with his body against the gears of Western music, forcing it to embrace everybody everywhere.

The Golliwogs, however, were still banging on the outside of an industry that had yet to accept them. San Francisco was no L.A., and the East Bay was no San Francisco, and they took this double-outsider status to mean that they would simply have to work harder to realize their goals, which were still unchanged from 1958: radio and records. Fantasy hired a new booker, Paul Rose, and opened a new subsidiary label, Scorpio, both of which were intended to help the Golliwogs break into a younger audience.

But god, that name. They could barely say it out loud. At best, it sounded silly. At worst, for a band that was consciously channeling Black music, it was obscene. Golliwogs were a type of nineteenth-century rag doll with coal-black faces and bright toothy smiles. The group ran the risk of offending the very people whose music they were trying to elevate and master.

Max's awkward attempt at Anglicization had another component, this one arguably even more awful. The British groups tended to dress alike—and sharply. The Hollies had gray suits with black trim, the Zombies wore vests, everyone seemed to wear skinny ties. So Max concocted a Golliwogs uniform fit for California and his Day-Glo temperament.

From the bottom up, the uniform started with Beatle boots, pointy and high-heeled and ankle-high. Then came plaid golf pants, slightly bell-bottomed and patterned with a mishmash of every color imaginable, like a cartoon Scottish clan. The band's shirts were long-sleeve with purple paisley trim, worn under dark-green suede vests. The group could tolerate all that. But the true insult was the hats. Max chose a tall Cossack-style tower covered in white fur of unknown origin, an inch or two long. It looked like a towering cake and felt like a heat lamp when they wore it onstage.

The band was mortified, afraid to say their name or even be seen. But what recourse did they have? They were paying Max to be their manager. He was the only person who was offering them a chance at fame. It only made sense to take his advice. And his advice, always—at recording sessions and in the booths at Original

Joe's, San Francisco's famous Italian restaurant where he took clients for lunch—was "You gotta have a gimmick." After the meal, he'd write "Vince Guaraldi" on the check for his accountant, who would never believe that he'd taken on a group called the Golliwogs.

Paul Rose got to work as well, sending the band over the Hills and into the San Joaquin Valley, where parched small towns sat on Route 99 like resting crows on power lines. Up and down that long, flat highway, young people were growing restless with the energy they absorbed from the radio and television. For years, the teens of Yuba City, Fresno, Marysville, Modesto, and all their farmland neighbors had been hearing the new music and seeing its white stars on-screen. A real band in town was something more than *Where the Boys Are*, however. The Golliwogs, even with their inane costumes, were something to stand up and move to—a rare local *Hullabaloo*, the nation's first rock and roll TV show, which premiered in January 1965. The band did their sweaty job, then sped off into the night. Every day after a show, Doug's neck hurt from hiding his face underneath his humiliating hat.

They drove in a '58 Volkswagen bus that was still decorated with the name of its previous owners, the Du-All Floor Company. Doug bought it, so he did most of the driving. It had no gas gauge. When they ran out of fuel, they pulled a lever to switch to a reserve tank that gave them enough time to find a filling station. The engine was in the rear and it piped heat to the front, but in the back, where the only insulation was the single sheet of frame metal, two band members, often the Fogertys, had to lie down amid the equipment, shivering until home.

Paul Rose found them more than just faraway youth-club gigs. The Golliwogs also played roller rinks and bowling alleys like the

Lucky Lanes in Richmond. In between bowling or skate rounds, the owners would dim the lights and move chairs to make a space for the band, who would set up in their four-man formation and pound out the new rhythms that got the audience, most now younger than them, to dance. That summer, the summer of "I Got You, Babe," the Golliwogs even opened for Sonny and Cher at the San Diego Civic Theatre. In front of their largest audience yet, they played well past their brief allotment as the famous couple's handlers stood on the side of the stage making throat-slitting gestures. When they finished, the Golliwogs took their customary Beatle bow, for once unashamed of their getups, and Doug took his rock-star moment to hurl the Cossack hat into the crowd.

The summer of 1965 was a good time to spend endless hours in the car with your friends. The radio was a cavalcade of rhythmic and attitudinal shocks: "Satisfaction," "Papa's Got a Brand New Bag," "We Gotta Get Out of This Place," "Do You Believe in Magic?," "Tracks of My Tears." The Golliwogs heard them all as they traveled everywhere the VW bus could manage. They drove through moss-strewn towns and farmland in the Sacramento–San Joaquin Delta, a sort of California bayou. At one point they arrived for gig night in a bar that was empty except for nine brawny fruit pickers, none of whom looked like Motown fans. The Golliwogs had been hired to play four sets over the course of the night, and each went the same way: they played in their getups, none of the men moved, and at the break the bar owner approached the band and asked them to turn down. When their final, barely perceptible note ended, they'd received not a smidgen of applause all evening. Now the owner explained he wasn't paying them. They had played too loud. In their goofy clothes the band tried to stick up for themselves before all nine customers stood up at once.

"I think you should get out while you still can," the owner said. The band packed quickly.

Rose, an ex-military man, saw opportunity in the many bases near San Francisco. For its wealth of universities and proximity to Asia, the region had long been fundamental to the US war industry. During World War II and Korea, hundreds of thousands of men shipped out of the city's nearby installations, and Berkeley had been more closely connected to the development of nuclear power than any university in the country, so much so that one campus room had to be permanently sealed after the war to contain radioactive contamination. The work continued into the Cold War, when a new element was synthesized on campus and given the name berkelium in tribute.

In 1965 the area was once again a hub of military activity. There were only 23,000 deployments to Vietnam during the previous year but the number ballooned as all those instant classics filled the radio. Operation Rolling Thunder, an aerial bombardment without precedent in US military history, began in February, followed by the arrival of ground troops in Danang. In the summer, 10,000 young men were being inducted monthly, and most of them left for Vietnam from the Bay Area. In total, 185,000 boys were shipped off to fight in 1965, and the Golliwogs played dozens of shows for these terrified peers as the nightly news slowly revealed the horrors that awaited.

Though President Johnson still had majority support for the war, these escalations precipitated the first widespread protests. On March 16, Alice Herz, an eighty-two-year-old professor and devotee of Martin Luther King Jr., parked her car in front of the federal building in Detroit. She filled her mouth with cotton, doused herself with dry-cleaning fluid, and lit a match. Herz survived ten days in the hospital, and when she died her handbag contained leaf-lets proclaiming, "To make myself heard I have chosen the flaming death of the Buddhists . . . May America's youth take the lead toward LIFE!" She was the first antiwar casualty of the Vietnam era.

While Herz still lay in the hospital, three thousand people, mostly students, debated the war for twelve hours at the University of Michigan. This model of youth-led discussion and information-sharing set the terms for future "teach-ins," including the opposi-tion it attracted. Counterprotesters made multiple bomb threats and marched on campus with flags reading "Drop the Bomb" and "Peace Through Strength."

The dichotomy grew. In April, the Student Nonviolent Coordi-nating Committee organized a 25,000-person march in Washington against the war. The *New York Times* reported that "students clogged the sidewalk" as they walked through the city to hear speeches at the foot of the Washington Monument. "Many marchers appeared to be newcomers to the 'peace movement,'" the *Times* wrote. By late July, that movement had grown popular enough that President Johnson began to fear and punish it. His announcement that an additional fifty thousand troops would be sent to Vietnam revealed only half the actual number deployed. He also increased the draft numbers among eligible young men, those born between 1945 and 1950. The next hammer fell in August, when an amendment to the Selective Service Act made it a crime to destroy draft cards, with punishments up to five years in jail and a $10,000 fine.

This was the audience for the Golliwogs' military gigs: boys be-tween eighteen and twenty from all over the country who were be-ing sent across the world at gunpoint despite crumbling support for their purpose or mission there. These shows weren't dances, they were distractions. Instead of pretty girls eyeing them on the stage, the band played in front of guys their own age in crew cuts and a veneer of macho bravery. They were aware that their songs might be the last live music that some members of their audience would ever hear. The Golliwogs knew this fear. All except Tom were born during the draft window, and early in it too, at a time when draftees were chosen largely by age. Sometime soon, especially the way this war was building, they might play their final notes too.

EIGHT

A MAN OF NATURE

John picked up a job at Fantasy working in the loading dock. It supplemented his gas station paycheck and put him in closer touch with the people who worked at the label, including sales manager Saul Zaentz, who struck him as smarter and less aloof than Max Weiss. At least Zaentz started in entertainment, not plastics. His background was in jazz, and he buzzed with ideas for how to build Fantasy's catalog. While getting to know his business associates better, John married his girlfriend, Martha Pais, who he had dated since high school. These were stabilizing forces, but they didn't spare him from the threat of military service. He wasn't in college and didn't yet have kids.

Stu had a struggle of his own to contend with. His mother Dolores died of cancer in 1965. As usual, he wasn't talkative about his problems, not even to Doug, but inside he felt the loss bring him closer to his band. They were his longest-running friends and his greatest hope for a life outside his father's shadow. Herman, now a widower, still operated under the assumption that there would eventually be another Cook at the firm. Halfway through college, the deadline to break free of that life was closing in on Stu. But the bass was a new frontier. He had a new role in the band, one that brought him into closer alignment with Doug as well. The drums and bass are what give a guitar quartet its downbeat and heavy power. The old class clowns were now driving a train that could make the Monkey Inn rumble or impress an arena of Sonny and Cher fans.

They hadn't lost their boyish sides. They lived together in a San Jose State fraternity house that was constantly littered with trash and heaps of uncleaned dishes. When their half-dozen housemates finished a chicken wing or grew tired of a pizza crust, they just threw it in the corner of the living room. Roaches and ants swarmed everywhere. It was too high a price to pay for the occasional offered joint or toga party. Doug gathered the housemates for a meeting and explained, truthfully, that he was an amateur entomologist since childhood with a particular interest in ants and butterflies. He knew how to kill an infestation, but they had to play their part by cleaning up. Everyone agreed, so Doug bought poison at the hardware store and set about laying traps and toxic food throughout the entryways. It took two weeks but eventually the bugs were gone, and Doug was now respected for his command over the natural world.

This came up at a party, where Doug was drunkenly referred to by his frat name, "Clifford C. Clifford," prompting someone to ask what the middle initial stood for.

"Cosmo," one of his brothers announced to the silenced crowd. "He's cosmic, a man of nature." And so it was.

Tom drove their studio work. He now had two kids and knew that records, not bar gigs, were the path to money. The Golliwogs wouldn't find their place among the glut of new bands unless they made a hit. Despite Max's urging and costuming, they had no gimmick, no unique draw. PG&E was still Tom's life, and not the life he longed for. The band released two singles on Fantasy in early 1965, and Tom sang on the A-side, "Where You Been," with John on harmonies for the B, "You Came Walking." But on the next 45, John sang both songs, "You Can't Be True" and "You Got Nothin' on Me." As their titles declared, they were a bit meaner than the material Tom had grown up on and made his name singing. John hadn't achieved his sought-after growl, but Tom's rhythm guitar brought bite and high end to the group's increasingly blues-based approach. They weren't playing pop. The Golliwogs weren't jangly like the Byrds, Los Angeles's kings of sunny radio harmonies (Stu adored their transformation of Dylan's "My Back Pages"). They were dry and blown-out like the Brit bands who had grown up playing in literal rubble: the Animals, the Who, Them, and the Stones. That year, Mick Jagger explained the mark that such an upbringing left on this music. "If you listen to all popular songs ten years ago, very few of them actually mean anything, or have any relation to what people are doing," he told an interviewer. "The songs didn't have any relation to what people actually spend their lives doing, like getting up, washing, going to work, coming back and feeling very screwed up about certain things."

John Fogerty knew more about those subjects than anything else, though he wasn't writing songs about them. In October, however, the Golliwogs recorded a track that could stand with anything by those groups. "Brown-Eyed Girl" didn't really even have a riff. Its hook was a three-chord progression that came close to Link Wray's "Rumble," which the group had been covering since they were the Blue Velvets. On top of this endless vamp, John layered organ, harmonies, and a vocal performance unlike any he'd recorded to that point, including an early falsetto howl that proved his voice now fit his imagination. Doug lurched and tumbled underneath, moving the beat from a shuffle to double time. Paul Rose, who oversaw the session, considered this the first "John" record, something that he made nearly by himself. There wasn't even guitar by Tom. Off it went to Max and Soul, to see what magic they might find this time.

The routine—gig, record, gig, gig, record—was so established, so taken for granted, that the Golliwogs completely missed the growing emotional tenor of their own audience, especially in Berkeley. When Pope Paul VI spoke to the United Nations in October, he specifically said that he came on behalf of "the young who legitimately dream of a better human race." A capstone to that effort arrived only ten days later, on the International Days of Protest against the Vietnam War. The global weekend-long days of action corresponded with the first major battle of the war, at Drang Valley. In Berkeley, ten thousand people including Allen Ginsberg, Dick Gregory, Ken Kesey, and Lawrence Ferlinghetti marched from Berkeley to Oakland Army Base for a "Peace Invasion." For the Golliwogs, it was gig night at the Monkey Inn, and the bar was suddenly surrounded by protesters' chants. Outside, the crowd flowed by like an undammed river, and like always, the Monkey Inn's front door was open to entice passersby. Once again, Doug played with his ass hanging out a window, this time for the Bay Area's mobilized peaceniks to see.

The bar emptied that night. The band lost their crowd to the heady mass rush against the war. And the Golliwogs understood. They weren't marchers by temperament, and they figured the fighting itself would be over before too long anyway. But it obviously meant something that this many people were standing up against the Vietnam conflict. That night, John, Tom, Stu, and Doug went safely home. When the peace marchers reentered Berkeley hours later, they were attacked and beaten by Hells Angels, who shouted, "Go back to Russia, you fucking Communists!"

In L.A., it was the early days of Raybert Productions, the media company founded in frustration and defiance by Bob Rafelson and Bert Schneider. They were determined to prove themselves right: they had better sight for movies than the studios. Now Raybert was advertising opportunities for "Folk & Roll Musicians-Singers for acting roles in a new TV series" in the *Hollywood Reporter* and *Daily Variety*. Specifically, "4 insane boys, age 17-21," which could have described any number of young men showing up to Oakland Army Base at this exact time. The cattle call attracted four hundred musicians, including Stephen Stills, who auditioned for an unknown company with noticeably younger executives than the average.

The pilot script and the mass auditions were in service of a Rafelson project, *The Monkees*, a youth-oriented scripted sitcom based around a studio-conceived insta-band. They sold the concept to CBS and now they were building the group, which would naturally have four young men and would take advantage of all the studio luxury and splendor available to them. This was Rafelson's big triumph after years of hectoring executives and complaining about his bosses' idiocy. He had creative control of a well-funded project aimed right at the heart of a youth consumer boom that journalists were comparing to pandemics and typhoons. *The Monkees* could make him.

John Fogerty wasn't even that close to the cusp. He ended 1965 with every reason for optimism and very little to show for it. Yet his vision was focusing. He was married. His voice was nearly where he wanted it. That year he looked longingly at the charts and saw a lot of Marvin Gaye, who became a force in 1965. Gaye was now making hit songs like chip shots. He was also handsome as hell, radiant enough to stand high on the bill of *The T.A.M.I. Show* with James Brown, the Stones, and the Beach Boys. That year his two big solo dance tunes, "I'll Be Doggone" and "Ain't That Peculiar," sat on the charts alongside duets with Mary Wells and Kim Weston. He had the Motown finger-snap beat, but the church in his voice made it unique, like Memphis soul that never touched the ground. Nobody on the radio moved like Marvin Gaye. His songs tickled you.

Gaye had earned those hits after years of work for Motown as a writer and a performer. He tried on a half-dozen styles and personae before finding success in this clean-cut, smooth R&B mode. Now he had the clout for a personal project, and released *A Tribute to Nat King Cole*, his most recent attempt to prove himself as a dinner club balladeer, in November. Gaye was six years older than John but shared many of the Californian's experiences, including an unloving father and a fraternal but competitive relationship with his brother Frankie. Gaye's musical tastes were formed in the 1950s, too. In a fundamental way, he still lived there, among a DC street-corner group-harmony scene where he first sang secular music. That capital doo-wop community no longer existed, but it was where he began, in a group that got their start working with Bo Diddley. John didn't literally live early rock and roll in the same way, but he did the best that a poor kid with a few local radio stations and record racks could manage. He had his own compulsion to return to those earlier days as if he had lived them—as if they still lived in him. He had his own *Tribute to Nat King Cole* to share.

Gaye's LP didn't chart. But that wasn't the point anyway.

NINE

NITTY-GRITTY

In December 1965, Charles Sullivan wasn't sure he could continue operating the Fillmore Auditorium, formerly the Majestic Hall. The Black former sharecropper had moved west from Alabama long ago and made his living by entertaining the Fillmore District. Now the city was killing him by killing the neighborhood around him. And then came Bill Graham, looking for a place to hold a party. He was calling it "Appeal II." Its organizers knew it as the second acid test, hosted by the Grateful Dead, but Graham promised he knew all the other San Francisco bands too: Jefferson Airplane, Quicksilver Messenger Service, Moby Grape. He could bring the hall back to life. After learning that Graham was a Holocaust survivor, Sullivan let him have the permit for six months to see how he could do. "You just go back downtown," Sullivan told him, "and you beat those white motherfuckers."

Graham was born Wolfgang Grajonca in Berlin and knew something of Sullivan's displacement by state violence. Raised Jewish, his mother and sister were killed by Nazis and another sister survived Auschwitz. He was sent to a Paris orphanage but fled on foot with his sister and sixty-two other children. He was nine, she was thirteen. She grew sick in Lyon, where he left her in a hospital and never saw her again. He boarded an ocean liner in Lisbon and went to New York by way of Casablanca and Dakar. Adopted by American parents, he was drafted at eighteen and sent to Korea, where he was awarded a Bronze Star and Purple Heart. After gaining citizenship, he brought two of his remaining sisters to the United States from Israel.

One sister, Rita, moved to San Francisco, where Graham visited her. He loved it immediately and felt he was finally living in a place that "wasn't always life and death." He was introduced to the city's musical subculture through the San Francisco Mime Troupe, an anarchist art collective who hired him as a business manager in 1964. He didn't even like rock music. But the Fillmore Auditorium became the lab where this death-defying refugee experimented with ultimate freedom.

Attendees at Appeal II were invited to take acid around five or six in the evening to achieve maximum flight by the time the Dead played. Tom Wolfe was there, in "the big ballroom in one of San Francisco's big negro slums," as he put it, tracking the movements of the Dead and their comrades in psychedelia, Ken Kesey's Merry Pranksters. He saw "hundreds of heads and bohos from all over the Bay Area turned out, zonked to the eyeballs," while satirist Paul Krassner thought he saw thousands, though he agreed they were "stoned out of their everlovin' bruces in crazy costumes and obscene makeup." A machine played the roar of thunder, balloons flew everywhere, and strobe lights flashed and flickered as the Dead set began around nine. By the time the police arrived to shut it all down at 2 a.m., the place was filled with dancers who were lost in themselves and oblivious to the multiple microphone-wielding ringmasters imploring them to keep moving, keep living, keep feeling the night's holy glow.

On Christmas Day two weeks later, the *New York Times* reported on a different kind of pandemonium. Only a few years earlier, Nam Dinh, Vietnam's third-largest city, had a population of ninety thousand. Now, the *Times* reported, US bombing campaigns had reduced it to twenty thousand. The paper reported 12,464 homes destroyed, eighty-nine people killed, and 405 wounded. "No American communique has asserted that Namdimh [*sic*] contains some facility that the United States regards as a military objective," they went on. "It is apparent, on personal inspection, that block after block of ordinary housing, particularly surrounding the textile plant, has been smashed to rubble by Seventh Fleet planes."

A strange background for boom times. At the dawn of 1966, a teenage boy in the United States lived in a world that was devoted to meeting his every sensory whim and desire until his eighteenth birthday, at which point he became cannon fodder in the fight against communism. One day and you went from rock and roll, color television, and Mustangs to Selective Service mailings and a designation at the local draft board. And the danger of such a fate was not ebbing. More US soldiers died in Vietnam during the first ninety days of the year than had died there in the previous five years combined.

The growing East Bay social scene provided a perfect escape for the many terrified young men awaiting draft age, or those celebrating their last night before deployment. The chief attraction was the Rollarena in San Leandro, a skating rink that another enterprising promoter named Bill converted into a club on weekend evenings. Bill Quarry was in semiretirement after an Army career and recognized a business opportunity on the strip in Fremont. He held the first dance party on New Year's Eve 1965. Before long he hosted Them's first US show and additional gigs by the Byrds and Neil Diamond. By September 1966, Quarry's purview had expanded to public relations, and he founded Teens 'n Twenties Promotions, announcing it with a grand press release: "In this era of the go-go set, many people have set out to make good on the business of capitalizing on the enthusiasm of the young, and young at heart. Here in the Bay Area, teenagers and people in their early twenties flock to where they can get some of this energy loose. They want to listen to the wild and pulsating sound of ROCK 'N ROLL."

Quarry's venues hosted Bo Diddley, Etta James, the Coasters, and more. Teens 'n Twenties operated a network of venues including the Carpenter Hall in Hayward, the American Legion Hall in Redwood City, the Rollarena, Highlands a Go-Go in Clearlake, Scout Hall in Antioch, and the 1966 Alameda County Fair. Their posters documented the panoply of bands arising in the region: U.S. Male, the Misanthropes, Plasmatic Conception, the Baythovens.

The Golliwogs had once been the only band in the region, and now a whole East Bay ecosystem was rising in their wake and they had nothing to do with it. Their sights had shifted west to the city. Their label was there, and the new Bill Graham shows were bigger and more exciting than any roller rink in the suburbs. And finally, in 1966, the Golliwogs had real success to back up their ambitions.

"Brown-Eyed Girl" was released in November 1965 and a handful of regional radio stations leapt at it. Best of all, it went to no. 1 in San Jose. Doug woke up one day and walked to history class when the sound of a portable stereo stopped him. A guy was sitting alone on the building entryway steps with a radio. Doug heard his drums driving it, twisting, John's howl, that ominous guitar.

"That's my band," Doug dazedly told this stranger, who gave him a look up and down.

"Fuck you," said the guy.

Others were more impressed. The record sold ten thousand copies. The band's gig fees quadrupled, enough to get Stu a real bass amp and Doug a set of tortoise-shell Ludwig drums, just like Ringo's. Everything still went back to the band; they'd have a new van before any of them bought a car with music money. But without a doubt this was a breakthrough. Their schedule was now packed with every highway exit in the Valley: Sacramento, Stockton, Turlock, Modesto, Clear Lake, Santa Rosa, Marysville, as far as Yuba City, down to Hanford, out to Merced to the east.

John of course still managed to worry. An opportunity granted was a possible opportunity lost. Now that he had a hit song, he needed to write another one. Who wants to peak with one regional single? He worried that the band wasn't up to the sound he'd made in the studio. He worried that live, onstage, they sounded soft, like the Monkees.

The television show about the made-for-television band was announced in the spring of 1966. The *Washington Post* saw it as "concocted to woo the younger generation away" from the current age-group hit, *Batman*. The first Monkees recording sessions began around the time that "Brown-Eyed Girl" found regional chart success, and despite John's feelings on the result, they featured musicians like James Burton, one of his original guitar heroes.

For John and for all of them, Max included, the next step was obvious. They went back to the Fantasy studio to capitalize on the huge boost in recognition that "Brown-Eyed Girl" had given them. "Fight Fire," their next A-side, arrived on Scorpio in early 1966. It had an even quicker tempo, an even catchier riff, and an even more compulsive groove than "Brown-Eyed Girl." The song was simply unstoppable. John's vocals weren't would-be Howlin' Wolf either. He gave his song a big swooping melody on top of its central, buzzing guitar theme, double-tracked in the manner of John Lennon's material at the time. It was clear he knew the Portland bands and their furious R&B as well. The band and the label braced for liftoff. "Fight Fire" didn't sell.

Their resulting frustration was understandable. The song couldn't have been better suited to the cultural mood. Even the very young had confrontation on their minds, and their elders knew it. The biggest mainstream hit of the past year was SSgt. Barry Sadler's "Ballad of the Green Berets," which the singer said he wrote to push back against "draft card burning and dissent by American youth." Meanwhile, in a private internal memo at the FBI, J. Edgar Hoover warned about countercultural indoctrination at US colleges, with risks including "a turbulence built on unrestrained individualism, repulsive dress and speech, outright obscenity, disdain for moral and spiritual values, and disrespect for law and order." The top levels of corporate entertainment and government were determined to find and exploit evidence of degradation and degeneracy among America's young, just as they were determined to use as many of them as necessary to secure the Vietnamese jungles.

Vietnam hung like a guillotine over the Golliwogs. Stu had asthma and was a full-time student, good enough for a deferral. Tom was a parent and outside the age range of the draft anyway. But John and Doug lived in fear of envelopes from the draft board, and if either of them got the notice, particularly John, they all knew that the band might be done forever. In the meantime, they drove all over central California in their freezing Du-All van, half the group packed like steerage, in service of an idea of musical fame they had formed eight years ago. They played like fate was following them through all those highways, over and back again across the Berkeley Hills, from the teen halls of the Valley to the military bases on the Bay.

There must have been boys who saw them in both venues. Some kid who lived along Route 99, in Yuba City maybe. One night he was in a low-lit roller rink, holding the girl he'd waited all week to buy a soda for. The Golliwogs might have looked romantic then, even in their getups, as the kid's fingers interlaced with hers and he dreamed of the car ride after the show. The band was perfect for that moment. They were commanding and charismatic, they knew wonderful old music that still made girls move. But six months or a year later, after boot camp, there were no girls. Just a social function in the mess hall or an outdoor party to keep morale up, and in came the same four guys, still dressed ridiculously. They were wonderful back when that baby soldier's fear was far away, but the Golliwogs meant something different now, with a ball of adrenaline sitting in that soldier's quivering stomach. Now he heard the janky blues in their sound, and the desperation in that small singer's voice. He saw the way the singer always turned and faced the drummer when he took a solo. Like it was painful to face the crowd.

Many things separated the Golliwogs from the steadily growing music scene in San Francisco, and none more than this bashfulness. On those rare occasions when Doug and Stu could go up to the city and see Quicksilver Messenger Service or Moby Grape, they were amazed at how deep those bands sounded. They were so heavy and adventurous, touched by the same mind-expanding ambition that Graham brought to his venue. Those bands conjured a whole wall of rock and roll, which for Doug and Stu was more exciting than the ongoing lapping waves of the Grateful Dead, though they did enjoy Jefferson Airplane's confrontational psychedelia. None of these bands, which formed the pillars of Bill Graham's local roster, sounded much like the others, but they all shared a need to make their audiences feel, hear, and see. They offered their listeners a chance at shared transcendence.

Graham was the perfect ringleader for such a gambit. He was ultimately in the boundary-breaking business. He replicated the success of Appeal II by making the Fillmore into a collage of sensory experiences and further loosening the barriers between performers and audience, rich and poor, young and old. The decor combined every epoch and country. There were Formica tables at the edge of the main room, but a walk through the overpacked venue offered a maze of different social atmospheres, whether you wanted to dress like Indians and do acid, get your body painted so you glowed in the dark, or hang near the stage and talk to a band. There were hawkers and artisans selling and bartering for bags and leatherware. Some concertgoers were naked, hearing music in their heads and from a million different sources: Graham had installed microphones and speakers everywhere, rerouting people's overheard conversations throughout the building. Waves of sound washed over a scene of balloons, Frisbees, and men with foxes on their shoulders. Most magically of all, the audience was mixed, full of students, shopkeepers, bikers, and office drones. It reflected the Wild West, individualist's-haven character of the city, even if many of the venue's regulars were newly arrived. As for the music, Hendrik Hertzberg came to the city for *Newsweek* and said he heard a "Nitty Gritty Sound" in the Fillmore, "the newest adventure in rock 'n' roll. It's a raw, unpolished, freewheeling, vital, and compelling sound. And it's loud."

In May 1966, Andy Warhol's Exploding Plastic Inevitable arrived in San Francisco for the first time and played Graham's space.

It was advertised as a night of "light shows & curious movies" and looked like a photo negative of San Francisco's burgeoning peace and love movement. Warhol's show was a paean to deviance and disorientation. It offered a mix of stark German and offbeat American sensibilities: leather fetishism, cacophonous light and visual effects, and the Velvet Underground soundtracking it all with wails, whispers, and the monotonal tenor croon of their guest singer, Nico, a waifish model and actress from Cologne.

San Francisco didn't care for it. "Very campy and very Greenwich Village sick," wrote Ralph J. Gleason in the *San Francisco Chronicle*. Even open-minded Bill Graham regretted the tastelessness and felt the Warhol revue brought a "Perversion U.S.A. element" to the venue. The Velvet Underground's quaking, deafening tales of drug terror and sadomasochism may have scared the city with flowers in its hair, but the band had certain fundamental overlaps with the Golliwogs. They cribbed Black music and pop structures just as brashly: their song "There She Goes Again" contained a bridge taken verbatim from Marvin Gaye's "Hitch Hike." They weren't bluesy, but they understood the blues' ability to control time. They knew the messianic power of slow tempos and low drones.

And from a certain angle, Lou Reed, the Velvets' creative leader, was a Long Island Jewish version of John Fogerty. They were both self-taught savants who had studied the radio and thrown themselves into recording and commercial songwriting while still teenagers. Reed was a deejay, too, and, like John, thought in terms of records. As the Marvin Gaye homage showed, his taste was still fundamentally built on Black 45s from the 1950s and early '60s: doo-wop, Motown, Jackie Wilson. Late in 1966, Reed published a short memoir in an art magazine about his musical awakening. "The only poetry of the last 20 years was and is in the music on the radio," he wrote.

"It's the music that kept us all intact. It's the music that kept us from going crazy. Folk music. That's music on the radio. You should have two radios. In case one gets broken." He extolled the brilliance of Phil Spector and called Bo Diddley the "unheralded genius of our time."

For Reed, Warhol's overwhelming presentation was a way to heighten the emotional intensity of his own music and poetry, and an invitation to make his work as uninhibited as the community around him. The Velvet Underground played in sunglasses and black leather, as if to signal they were broadcasting from a different place than their audience. John only angled his face away a little, but it had the same effect. And to be truly welcome in San Francisco, you had to reach outward.

TEN

THE VALLEY OF
THE BLACK PIG

Ronald Reagan, the actor and GE spokesman, announced he was running for governor in the summer of 1966, and opened his campaign with a specific promise to "clean up the mess at Berkeley." At Santa Cruz, Doug and Stu had become enamored of *The Lord of the Rings,* and Reagan's ascension and rhetoric was like the Eye of Sauron narrowing its focus on youthful dissent. And then the ax finally fell for John and Doug: within days of each other, each received the dreaded envelope.

Now, in between gigs and practice sessions for their next single, "Walking on the Water," John and Doug tried every possible Hail Mary option to keep their military commitments to a minimum. Doug knew the family of a TV anchorman in El Cerrito who had gotten into the reserves, which was a known way to avoid immediate enlistment through the draft. But the Coast Guard Reserve, the anchorman's branch, had a three-year waitlist. So he brought Doug to the recruitment office and told a fib. He claimed that Doug was an all-city high school football player and would be an asset to the reserve team, which regularly played the other military branches. He was sworn in right there, with a pledge to start active duty in January 1967.

John, meanwhile, flailed around in a mad dash to find any reserve office within driving distance of El Cerrito, to no end. He lost his gas station job because he had to spend all his remaining time tending to this and nothing else. Martha, sweet Martha, eventually found an office with room on their register, or perhaps she just begged hard enough. The kind recruiter—John felt he was "soulful"—even backdated his registration so it looked like he was already enrolled when he received his draft notice. John was saved, at least from combat. For now. But boot camp awaited in the new year.

They pledged, after a gig in Davis, that this was not the end. There would be boot camp, then the guys would have a biweekly commitment for a few years. There was room to work in there. This did not spell doom. Not necessarily. They didn't speak of other possible outcomes.

What do young men do as they wait around for their lives to change completely? For Doug, he spent time with the San Jose State football team to get back in proper shape so he could fool his commanding officers come January. Doug was wiry back in high school, when he played three sports. With years since any competition, he wasn't exactly in dominating shape. So with his typical unquestioning intensity, Doug lifted weights, took hits, iced down, and subjected himself to the rest of the bruising routines of NCAA football—a boot camp before boot camp. He joined the team as a starting defensive back, leading them in interceptions.

He did all this while John tinkered with their recording of "Walking on the Water," which the Fogerty brothers had cowritten. Sonically, the song was the most powerful music the band had made to this point, a busy production and a rager. It had shades of R&B but a minor-key drama like the Stones' "Paint It, Black." After a fuzz-guitar intro, the band kicked into a sharp, quarter-note rhythm. John's singing had new contours and a wider range than before, and the lyrics spelled out a short, evocative scene where the singer is approached by a supernatural figure on the river near his house—a ghost story with Christian overtones, not at all like the love and heartbreak songs that John and Tom had defaulted to for years. John took a long guitar solo, played in high-treble distortion. It was a heightened, dramatic arrangement for a tune that had only one verse and lasted less than three minutes, but John had overdubbed a host of keyboards over the group, burying their instruments. As a finished product it was striking, but it was almost all him. The B-side, at least, "You Better Get It Before It Gets You," was a bluesy ballad that transformed into a big rocker in its finale. It was an altogether better showcase for the group's leaner live sound.

The ambitious single was released in December and once again, they failed to recapture the commercial success of "Brown-Eyed Girl." Despite the move to Fantasy's rock imprint Scorpio, despite the success of their previous single, the label had no real marketing budget or acumen. They were still known primarily for West Coast jazz, and for all Max's enthusiasm about capturing the youth market, he was a former plastics salesman in a Cossack hat and sandals with socks. He had more gumption than knowledge, and more clothes than gumption.

As if to mock them, the Monkees ended 1966 as the biggest band in the United States, which meant Bob Rafelson and Bert Schneider were suddenly moguls. Their breakthrough was to remove all compunction from teen marketing: unlike the Golliwogs, the Monkees were calculated to smother America's youth with their charm, across all the media platforms that these postwar kids were now accustomed to. Introduced in the spring, the band was instantly, accurately recognized as a knowing Beatles cash-in, a nonthreatening quartet of recognizable personalities and haircuts performing jaunty sing-alongs. They were silly, bright, witty, joyous, surrealistically rebellious, with no collective identity except "young." The TV show debuted in September, for which the group was sent on a whirlwind multicity media tour described by critic Vincent Canby as "an elaborate campaign designed by RCA and Screen Gems to capture the teenage imagination. The thoroughness of the campaign might prompt renewed debate on the age-old question of free will." By the end of the year, the group had the no. 1 song ("I'm a Believer") and album in America.

Rafelson and Schneider were ruthless marketers, but they didn't condescend. They weren't selling junk food to kids. The Monkees were a "fake band" but only in the sense that their recordings were boosted by some of the greatest session players in the world. And the producers didn't muzzle their musician-actors, which included Davy Jones, from the performance of *Oliver!* that appeared on the *Ed Sullivan* stage with the Beatles. In their first interview, with the *New York Times*, bassist Peter Tork even voiced opposition to the war in Vietnam.

The Monkees entered 1967 with plans to play San Francisco's 15,000-seat Cow Palace, the very venue where the Beatles played three years earlier. Meanwhile, the San Francisco scene that the

Golliwogs were attempting to enter had exploded. Graham began renting out the Winterland Ballroom, a onetime roller rink in Japantown, to hold even bigger concerts than the Fillmore could accommodate. His debut bill included the Paul Butterfield Blues Band opening for Jefferson Airplane. He partnered with Chet Helms, a lifelong Californian but new San Franciscan, who managed another rising local band, Big Brother & the Holding Company, and helped secure the much smaller Avalon Ballroom for additional gigs. The Golliwogs lost half their band to part-time military service. How long had it really been since "Brown-Eyed Girl"?

At least Doug and John would have company. By this point, most of the major US fighting units of the Vietnam War were already in country, and the reserves, as they saw, were brimming. At the start of 1966 there were 185,000 troops in Vietnam; now, at year's end, even as the Johnson administration was still hiding the real number from public knowledge, there were 385,000. A centerpiece of the recruitment effort was Project 100,000, designed by Assistant Secretary of Labor Patrick Moynihan to vacuum up and properly train that many men from the so-called subterranean poor, boys who wouldn't normally pass muster due to educational standards. But the special training never materialized for the vast majority of enlistees. Instead, the program shoveled poor young men into Asia after they'd already been designated unfit. The threat of service hung over every eighteen-year-old boy, but the actual experience of combat fell disproportionately on the poor and uneducated.

That year, President Johnson began having nightmares. Halfway between sleep and waking, he would imagine himself in a Da Nang battlefield with an American plane circling overhead. Then a gunshot echoed and the plane fell to the ground, bursting into flames. He claimed this was how he knew there had been more US casualties. The first lady, Lady Bird, quoted Yeats in her diary: "Now is indeed 'The Valley of the Black Pig,'" she wrote. "A miasma of trouble hangs over everything."

San Francisco was the agreed-upon national beachhead for anyone looking to postpone the miasma: dropouts, square-community escapees, art freaks, wannabe wanderers, and would-be communards. Haight-Ashbury was the center of it, a neighborhood that one of the Grateful Dead's associates felt might as well have had a welcome sign: "Come here and do whatever you fucking well please." There was "Superspade," a twenty-five-year-old Black pot dealer who only wore leather and a button anointing himself "Faster than a speeding mind." The streets were full of hippies, some of whom wandered with bowls dangling from their waistbands. That way they could stop for soup at the "Free Frame of Reference," the neighborhood's first free store, which operated out of a six-car garage and secured their wares through theft and donations. The city buses had been rerouted to Haight Street to accommodate tourists' interest in the hippies. One day in 1967, the Dead's guitarist Bob Weir grabbed the Chinese flag from the band's house stoop and took off with it, naked, sprinting next to a bus as terrified lookers-on recoiled.

On January 14, 1967, the neighborhood held its grand "Human Be-In," a daylong explosion of peace and love and do-whatever. The *Berkeley Barb*, one of a handful of new alternative newspapers in the country, proclaimed that "the spiritual revolution will be manifest and proven. In unity we shall shower the country with waves of ecstasy and purification. Fear will be washed away, ignorance will be exposed to sunlight, profits and empire will be drying on deserted beaches, violence will be submerged and transmuted in rhythm and dancing." An estimated twenty thousand people came to hear Allen Ginsberg and Gary Snyder intoning Hindu chants, and to hear Timothy Leary, intellectual leader of the psychedelic revolution, use his phrase "turn on, tune in, and drop out" for the first time. The event was a hallucinatory daydream: chemist Owsley Stanley delivered dosed turkeys to make sandwiches and another man in a white parachute fell from the sky and alit upon the crowd.

The event was peaceful, but the attention only intensified the movement of young people into the neighborhood, which was already stretched beyond its capacity to take care of them. Larry Beggs was a suburban preacher in his early thirties at the time. He left his congregation in 1967 to house wayward children in the Haight, a population that had grown so unignorable that the *San Francisco Chronicle* ran a series called "Runaway Girls: Life with the Hippies." Beggs's new shelter, Huckleberry House, opened that year, when running away was still a crime and mandatory reporters were required to turn homeless youth over to the police.

Judge Raymond J. O'Connor ran San Francisco's youth justice system at the time, and his solution to the runaway problem was to hold the kids in a barbed-wire warehouse, depriving them of toilets or adequate space. One boy claimed, "They get beaten up in the paddy wagon, then they get beaten up in jail . . . and then they get beaten up when they get home." Judge O'Connor was nearly sixty, gray-haired, and a father of seven. In 1967, his own teenage son ran away to Huckleberry House.

Despite the crackdowns and generalized local madness, the Golliwogs recognized that their band was being forcibly halted right as San Francisco became the most exciting place for young people in the world. This only made John's and Doug's heads hang lower when they reported for their ass-kickings in January. Basic training was a little looser than active duty; after some special pleading about their semiprofessional rock band, they received permission to keep their mustaches and sideburns. But they were not exempt from training's rigors. As ever, Doug's response was to break through every obstacle with charm and gumption. He was the first guy from his boot camp to make rank. Then he volunteered for colors, marching with the mounting flag. All of that for sideburns.

John's basic training took place at Fort Bragg, and he was initially devoted too. He took advanced individual training at the Quartermaster School in Fort Lee, Virginia, and was stationed at Fort Knox. His major duties were guard shifts, some as long as twenty-four hours. Yet he initially took to military life. His childhood home had been crowded, but a barracks was the exact opposite in every other way. Every kid in the same kind of bed, everyone nice and clean. He found it unusually comfortable, and even became barracks leader and an A-list rule follower.

After basic ended, Doug was most valued for his football. Manic and spry, he now tore through the field just like he did long Monkey Inn sets or midnight janitor shifts. He was still doing those shifts in his spare time and could complete his eight-hour duties in six. Having now fully dropped out of San Jose State, his life revolved around music, the military, and eking out a meager financial existence. He had no money except what he made himself. No family to rely on except the band, if they counted. His major duty on base involved dodging hits from linebackers. If he slipped, he could be sent up some Mekong inlet on a raft. His high school muscle returned, and he could feel it in his drumming. Doug, Cosmo to some, now played like his arms had outgrown him, a little ahead of the beat sometimes, though his swing was unbreakable. In life and on record, he always seemed to be midstride. Stay smiling, stay running, he thought, and you'll avoid the worst.

Neither Doug nor John could sustain this panicked sense of responsibility for long. When they began their monthly weekend duties, both, of their own volition, hatched the same escape plan: starvation. Doug's began as a simple matter of math: a man could not live his lifestyle and eat plentifully. The stress, the poverty, the constant working and driving, take your pick—none prioritized sit-down meals. El Cerrito to San Jose, he traveled it hundreds of times for practice. Then he'd head east to play gigs that always went late, so he'd drive to the base, sleep in the van, then wake up to go to work as a reserve guardsman. Doug grew convinced the sergeants were going to activate him, so he got down to about half a meal a day to stay weak. He kept playing all his gigs, though, and out of spite they made him cut his sideburns.

Now he was convinced they were trying to kill him. Two psychiatrists wrote letters to the military saying he was losing his mind. At one point he didn't shit for two and a half weeks. At the Army doctor's office, his body temperature was down to ninety-five degrees. The doctors put Doug in a bed and he finally felt victorious. He fought their pleas for hospitalization just to scare them. He wanted them scared.

After his initial charm offensive, John spent almost every day either attending to his military duties or approaching lawyers and advocacy groups for help liberating himself, all while his health deteriorated. First, he asked to rearrange his schedule to suit his music work on weekends, but when the sergeants wouldn't accommodate him, he began contacting his congressman, who involved himself in the matter just enough to rile the sergeants further. So

John stopped eating. Even at gigs. He lost enough weight that he had to drive into the city for an evaluation by Army doctors. To prepare him, Doug and Stu brewed him an herbal tea of unknown provenance and gave him a joint. By the time he got to the doctor he was shaking. He left with a diagnosis for dysentery.

John Fogerty lasted six months on active duty in the Army Reserve, most of which he spent desperately wrangling to leave it. But the experience matured him and shaped him—he was a different man when he came back, and not in obvious ways. He wasn't shell-shocked or maimed, and certainly wasn't indoctrinated with Army chauvinism. He was radicalized.

John arrived at basic training with his typical attitude of anguished self-consciousness. It hurt to have his name called out by a taunting sergeant, to hear the man mock it and repeat for everyone's enjoyment. In these moments John fumed with embarrassment. The unwanted attention burned him like a stove coil, and he resolved his approach for survival: stay in the shadows.

But ultimately the forced camaraderie expanded his range of feeling. John even spent time listening to contemporary music with his peers—LPs, not radio or singles. He heard *The Doors*, *Fresh Cream*, *Sgt. Pepper's*, even Jefferson Airplane's *Surrealistic Pillow*, which he adored. The songs, the playing, "Somebody to Love" and "White Rabbit," the intensity of it. But he also loved Marty Balin's song "Comin' Back to Me," which was the exact opposite, soft as dandelion spores afloat. That was the power of the San Francisco scene. The bands all had range.

John was not antimilitary by character. He entered the reserves with a general skepticism about the Vietnam War, mostly because of his age, but he was never going to be a flight risk or a conscientious objector. Then he heard his sergeants talking about suppressing the

antiwar resistance. He saw bloodthirst and illogic from authority figures who shared the same insane contempt as the cops who beat and
abused homeless kids. John's hunger strike was inspired, he felt, by
the people he saw on the news, putting their shoulder against the
wheel, refusing the war on moral grounds. There was no shortage of
such bravery at the time. Draft-card burning continued in the spring
of 1967, including a mass gathering for the cause in the Central Park
Sheep Meadow in New York. That same season saw the founding of
the Spring Mobilization Committee to End the War in Vietnam,
better known as Spring Mobe, a multiracial and interfaith coalition
whose leadership included Martin Luther King Jr. and Berkeley's
own Jerry Rubin, who had planned the recent Vietnam Day protest
that flooded past the Monkey Inn.

Twenty-two-year-old David Miller went to jail in April. A previously unknown Catholic pacifist, he became the first person tried
and convicted under the newly tightened Selective Service Act restrictions that forbade destruction of draft cards. Miller was a soup
kitchen volunteer living in New York just after college. He attended
an antiwar rally in the city and found himself overcome. He climbed
atop a truck and held up his card. He explained that his purpose was
to denounce the war as immoral, then he lit the card for all the cameras to see. He was sentenced to three years in 1966, and his appeal
was declined by the Supreme Court. Miller's jailing was supposed
to be a mounted head and a red line from the establishment to the
country's errant young: *Your country owns you, and don't pretend
otherwise.* But activists held a mass draft-card burn in San Francisco
soon after, and his sentence was stayed within months.

It took more time for John Fogerty to arrive at his own firm moral
resistance to the war in Vietnam, and ironically, he only got it from
basic training. He entered with a simple fear of death and a desire to

ELEVEN

FULL-TIME

It was as if Tom's hair grew on its own. Somewhere around 1966 or so, the old smooth pompadour fell away and his blond coils lengthened on either side of his soft face like spaniel ears. His eyes were fuller, too. It was like he couldn't hide them. Even with his new mustache, he had a face that gave you everything.

He was twenty-six now. Seven years into his career at PG&E, and like John, his time in the adult world had not made him more conservative. Those seven years had gotten him $1,250 worth of savings. He had two small kids and a house and worked a full-time job with little upward mobility. He willingly endured those grueling night commutes on weekends, freezing and prone for the chance to play music in revolting Technicolor costumes. And suddenly his little brother was a phone call away from a plane to Vietnam. Over the last few years Tom had seen Berkeley turn from a quiet university community to a hub of social unrest, and he understood why. He knew about Mario Savio and the Free Speech Movement. He was affected by the march to Oakland Army Base, too. He had wanted to be a musician since he was a child, but the band wasn't his indulgence. It was his work and his validation—his cause. The Golliwogs were on the edge of fame that could change his family's life. He had to believe this was true.

The songs were all still credited to "Rann Wild" and "Toby Green," but the movement of things was clear. John had no compunction about returning to the studio and adding what was needed, according to him and him only. If he didn't hear a place for Tom's rhythm guitar, it went. And as the reserve hiatus showed, the band couldn't function without all four members, and especially not without John. Tom's odds of making music professionally were higher if he fell behind his little brother. He couldn't challenge John too hard on the finer details of song arrangements anymore.

At one point Tom put his tie on and caught himself in the mirror heading out for the day. There he saw the utterly hopeless opposite of Tommy Fogerty, who used to make girls scream without even a microphone. In late summer, with John and Doug now both off active duty, he wanted to have a band meeting.

The setting of course would be the Shire, the house in El Sobrante where Stu and Doug were living. It was near the Berkeley Hills, so they named it for Tolkien and painted elvish runes on the mailbox. The Shire became the band's workspace, where they gathered to bash out the sound they were shaping. Thankfully, the couple in the next house down the dirt road, the only nearby neighbors, were forgiving. They had a young son who would occasionally ramble over and listen to the music, and they never complained about the noise.

One practice, at Tom's urging, they discussed the issue of time. As in time practicing, time honing their sound, time working. He felt they only had part-time hits because they were a part-time band. They'd been through enough now to place their faith in themselves. If they wanted the big prize, they needed to make the band their only job.

For Doug and John it was barely a sacrifice. They were adrift after a medical discharge and relief from duty, respectively. They *needed* jobs. For Tom it was a life-changing shift in commitments. And he doubled down, offering his full $1,250.

Stu had a choice, too. His father had cleared a path for him that few men have, and that few boys know the value of when they are only twenty-two. His life as a lawyer in that firm would have been more profitable and secure than any potential life elsewhere. And compared to life as a musician? It was like choosing to punish himself. But after Tom's gesture, Stu finally cut off the ongoing conversation with his father. He announced he was going with the band, not law school. And he bet big as well, selling the 1966 silver and black two-door hardtop Chevelle that his father had bought him. Even John admired him for that. The profits from a car sale and Tom's $1,250: that's what funded the Golliwogs' foray into professional music-making.

Tom, dutiful young man, gave his two weeks at PG&E. He finished out his final days on the job as his coworkers teased, "See you on *Ed Sullivan!*"

That meant a daily workday at the Shire, perfecting their songs and building up new ones. The newest was something that John had thought up while marching endlessly in those Army forts. John borrowed that strutting swing—*I don't know but I been told*—and started writing a little hook around it in his mind as he marched. Pushing in the direction opened by "Walking on the Water," he found a melody that wasn't quite a straight blues, and not a my-baby song. It was a character's recollection of a traumatic childhood. His father is thrown in jail and the boy is run out of their small town for being his next of kin. Delirious in the sun, John added little details and changed words until he conveyed that boy's perspective in a few verses and choruses. The lyrics evoked hanging, paternal sins, violence, and desperate escape. Tom, Doug, and Stu would supply the background vocals, barking out an unchanging three-word chorus, "I don't care," that sounded like the narrator trying to forget his own pain.

"Porterville," as John titled it, was partly autobiographical. He knew about the burning need to define himself outside a no-good father's travails. He was also developing a single-minded idea of heroism built on individual resistance to outside restriction. But most importantly, "Porterville" was a narrative. It put listeners in a specific place and made them see it through another person's eyes, beginning to end. In mood, theme, and even in its simmering, tragic southern atmosphere, the song resembled "Ode to Billy Joe," Bobbie Gentry's enormously popular debut single, released at the same time. Gentry was a bona fide southerner, Mississippi-raised, though she had been in California for years and spent time as a philosophy major, a conservatory student, a duet partner with her mother, and a model. She wrote "Billie Joe" herself, and the song was a sensation, a country crossover because it felt so free of country's template. Gentry's song had her husky voice and an R&B feel. It was an old-fashioned rural story song with a bit of Booker T. jerk in it.

The plan was for the Golliwogs to record "Porterville" and release it in November. Now John had every day to push the backing trio into shape, to match every detail he had all mapped out in his head. He didn't tell them what notes to sing, but he showed them where and how the background vocals went. He wore Doug out talking about tempos and timing. He was insistent that Doug couldn't find the true center of his songs, and when Doug finally grasped it, John gave himself credit for steering him there.

These two had a unique, difficult camaraderie. John and Doug were both underachieving little brothers who were now on their own, struggling and sprinting as hard as they could. Doug had discovered John and offered him his first opportunities to make music with people outside the house. They both made it out of difficult families, worked punishingly dull jobs, and were nearly swallowed by Vietnam. Then they destroyed their health. As this new era for the band began, with an even more grueling schedule and increased, self-applied pressure on John to lead them creatively, Doug was John's only competition, the only person he couldn't overdub or replace in the studio. Doug knew this, and was growing as a drummer, though he still yearned for John's approval. He wanted to make his band leader's songs better, and he wanted to be recognized for doing so. Neither of them knew how to get what they wanted out of the other, and they were tied to each other, tasked with making this band run.

Tom still handled their business matters. He collected money from promoters and advances from the record company and put everything into one band account except a small allowance: twenty dollars per man, per week. That was their salary as members of the Golliwogs, their first money as professional musicians. The rest went to gas, parking, van repairs, overhead. They mostly worked for the chance to keep working.

On Saturdays, the Fogerty brothers would go into San Francisco and have lunch with Max Weiss and Saul Zaentz. After a couple years working at Fantasy, John had come to admire Saul, and knew he was a better businessman than either of the Weisses. He started spending hours in Saul's office, listening to his stories and basking in his attention. Saul was born in 1921 in New Jersey and ran away at fifteen, during the worst of the Depression. He sold peanuts at ball games in St. Louis, won a little money gambling there, and traveled around the country, hitchhiking and riding freight trains. After landing in San Francisco, he served as an Army enlistee transport officer across Africa, Europe, and the Pacific during World War II.

After discharge Saul studied animal husbandry at Rutgers, worked on a chicken farm, and took a business course in St. Louis. He worked as a bookkeeper at a music publishing company, then as head of sales at Mercury Records. But restlessness drew him back to San Francisco in 1950, and in 1955 he was hired as a salesman by Fantasy. By 1967 he was the long-running director of sales and marketing. Add to that, apparently, a confidant to John Fogerty and vice versa. In October, after the session for "Porterville," John got a call.

"I just bought Fantasy Records," said Saul. With a small consortium of co-investors, Saul had gotten the company outright from the Weisses, and he wanted to talk with John about changes to their arrangement together. John was overcome. He knew Saul as a co-worker at Fantasy, a friend, even a father figure. Now that man was in control. The one with sense. As a goodwill gesture, Saul loaned the group $1,500 for a new amp for John's lead guitar. At the time, such a purchase was impossible otherwise. They had no money, "not even the ghost of it," as John said.

The Golliwogs' new contract was the same they'd had with the Weisses, just with a new name at the bottom. It was a seven-year agreement, the longest allowed by California law, and was not especially kind to the band, though few record contracts were at the time. It called for John to deliver twelve master recordings each the first and second years, and twenty-four for each remaining. The company retained the right to request up to ten additional masters each year. This set John up for an astonishing rate of productivity into the mid-1970s, assuming he still demanded that all the band's songs be his. But John felt he had every reason to trust Saul, who wasn't close to rich. He was risking as much as anyone; his first act as owner was to relocate the company to the cheapest part of Oakland to save on rent. And when the band asked, "What if we become huge?" Saul said, "I will tear this contract up." The starting contract was for a starting band. Hits, he promised, would change things. The group was convinced. They signed the contract as twenty-two-year-olds, under the impression that Saul Zaentz was on their side. He wanted fame for them, wanted to let them do their music on their terms, and he wanted to get them on radio and beyond. If they didn't achieve that, his new investment might not work out after all.

TWELVE

REVIVAL

J ohn, Tom, Stu, and Doug still had varying degrees of inferiority complexes about the city. The typical attitude held that the East Bay was more roughneck working class, if it was considered at all. The pithy, arch–San Francisco gossip columnist Herb Caen, for example, famously dismissed Oakland by saying "the Bay Bridge has to end somewhere." Thanks to the Be-In, the city was now gravitationally attracting young people from the world over, even just across the water. The Rollarena closed in 1967 and the East Bay rock and roll scene fizzled out with it, as all attention turned to the peace and love capital of the universe, "far and away the most turned-on city in the Western world," according to the *Village Voice*'s Richard Goldstein, who added, "The rest of the country will get the vibrations, and they will pay for them."

Since the Be-In, the Haight's population had increased fivefold. About a hundred thousand young people now squeezed into an area of less than half a square mile. By this point the neighborhood had become too "colorful" to sustain. Back in the spring, a sixteen-year-old runaway girl was picked up by a street dealer, drugged, and then repeatedly raped. This was "the politics & ethics of ecstasy," as some locals bemoaned. "Rape is as common as bullshit on Haight Street." On September 22, the Haight-Ashbury Medical Clinic, which was opened to confront the boom times, closed after treating thirteen thousand people since June.

In early October, beleaguered by the international attention and the overcrowding, neighborhood leaders staged a parade down Haight Street. Ron Thelin, proprietor of the famous Psychedelic Shop, staged a performance called "Death of the Hippie." Pallbearers carried a young man on a platform, trailing a coffin with the words "Hippie, Son of Media." The pallbearers held mirrors to face the crowd. The term "hippie" had come to the end of its natural use, they felt. It was a construction of older people and diminished the breakthroughs that residents were trying to make in the Haight. "We'd like to substitute 'free American' in its place," Thelin told the media.

Rolling Thunder, a Shoshone medicine man, lived with the Grateful Dead in their four-story townhouse on Ashbury Street, which also served as headquarters for the band's entourage and the offices of the Haight-Ashbury Legal Organization. He was moved by the Hippie's funeral. "What you people are going through is the same thing that we've gone through," he told his new brethren. "You're just getting your training. We'll help you in any way we can."

The Golliwogs missed the Monterey International Pop Music Festival, which featured Booker T. & the MGs backing Otis Redding, because it was gig night. Monterey Pop was held at a county fairgrounds two hours away from San Francisco, though most of the

West Coast bands on hand were from L.A., including the Byrds, the Mamas and the Papas, and the Association. Big-harmony bands. Redding's acrobatic howls and shouts bore no resemblance, but the California crowd was rapt, just as they were for Ravi Shankar, Jimi Hendrix's flaming guitar, and the Who's destroyed instruments. The unspoken theme was mind-expansion of all kinds, by all available means. And exposure to high-grade Memphis soul was certainly part of the experience for plenty of the weekend's attendees. The transaction went both ways, too. After arriving in the afternoon, the MGs had time to kill and walked around the flower children's playground. They had been to California before, around the time of the 1965 Watts riot in Los Angeles, but at Monterey, the concertgoers were building a new community from scratch. Jones and bandmates Steve Cropper, Donald "Duck" Dunn, and Al Jackson Jr. walked around the makeshift bazaar at the event's perimeter, where concertgoers sold artwork, diaphanous dresses, pottery, and pipes. There was no precedent for this in Memphis, but there was also little precedent for it in California only a couple years earlier.

Every other weekend of that summer, San Francisco was the mecca, not Monterey County. Things were becoming ideologically, even infrastructurally, unstable. Weekday traffic jams were a regular occurrence because of military burials at San Francisco National Cemetery. At the end of the so-called Summer of Love, police chief Thomas Cahill ordered a fourteen-officer raid of Haight Street that ended with the apprehension of thirty-two bedraggled kids, twenty-one of whom were sent to juvenile facilities.

That was in October, one of those months, so common then, when the country seemed perpetually on the verge of splitting across a giant chasm even if no one could tell where it might form. Everyone from every side warned of apocalypse. After the nationwide Stop the Draft campaign that lasted from October 16 to 20, Selective Service director General Lewis Hershey mandated universal fulfillment of conscription punishable by prosecution, for "the survival of the United States." Attorney General Ramsey Clark then revealed that a Justice Department Criminal Division special prosecution unit had begun targeting Selective Service Act violators, including those who aided and abetted draft dodgers. US attorneys urged local police forces "to vigorously prosecute violations of local laws" during antidraft demonstrations. Hundreds of young men were arrested for turning in draft cards soon thereafter.

On the local front, Haight celebrity Superspade was murdered. Oakland police attacked protesters outside a draft center, an event so brutal it was given the name "Bloody Tuesday." The *San Francisco Chronicle* reported that the cops swung their clubs "like scythes," cutting "a bloody path." All to silence resistance to a war that had already killed fifteen thousand young men and left seventy-five thousand more wounded.

Even protests elsewhere had the mystical, confrontational energy of San Francisco. The March on the Pentagon, held October 21 and coordinated by Spring Mobe and Jerry Rubin, featured a carnival atmosphere, the biggest draft-card burning to date, and a mass meditation meant to levitate the building. Rubin and Abbie Hoffman then set their sights on the upcoming Democratic National Convention, which was to take place in Chicago in 1968. Their partner David Dellinger said this event marked the antiwar movement's turn toward "active resistance."

A useful phrase. Late 1967 felt like something had snapped, like a mere defensive crouch would no longer do for the young and their heartsick comrades. It had been a decade since Elvis had given life to a teen market, almost that long since Berry Gordy and

Phil Spector had become impresarios by selling to it exclusively, and nearly four years since the Beatles' arrival in the States made that demographic the most powerful buying force in the world. The young people of 1967 had been shown a galaxy of possibility on television and radio for their whole lives, and now they were old enough to see how far the real world had come up short. They wanted life on the terms that art had set for them.

The Golliwogs did too. One of the band's stipulations with Saul called for a chance to rerecord "Porterville" at a more professional facility, so Saul bankrolled time at Coast Recorders rather than the outmoded Treat Avenue studio that Fantasy operated. They rerecorded "Porterville" and its B-side, a roaring Stax tribute named "Call It Pretending," at Coast as well. Both new songs were extraordinary. "Call It Pretending" was the ecstatic opposite of "Porterville," a breakup song that flew by in two minutes and begged for a horn section to drive its up-tempo chorus. With these two new tracks, proof of their growth and power, they agreed a new name was in order. And with it, greater autonomy for the band. Stu, who spent more time than the others in the city ballrooms watching the new generation of local bands, felt he was living a double life: his favorite groups had the acid-and-headband look, while he was stuck playing in that asinine Golliwogs getup. The band insisted there be no more hats or costumes. Saul hated all of it anyway, that was old Max's hacky gimmick racket. Consider it done.

They made plans to reconvene after they all gave thought to potential new names. The band pondered together. Stu had one: Hardwood. Not awful. Doug had another: Gossamer Wump. That didn't satisfy. John, a teetotaler but a showman, proposed Whiskey Rebellion. And Tom, borrowing the odd name of his South African friend, threw in a whimsical one: Credence Nuball and the Ruby. Somehow Deep Bottle Blue got on the list as well.

But none captured their sound, which by this point, after half a year's daily shredding in the Shire and regular gigs, had become a sinewy, irreducible blend of blues and early rock and roll. They hadn't invented something new, and even acknowledged their debts with plentiful covers in concert. But they played slower than most party bands, and faster than most blues bands. John's voice by this point didn't sound like suburban California, but it didn't sound like anything else either. There was something audacious and inspiring about the sheer spare power that he had sought out for them. His peers in the city were exploring feedback and chaos, and he wanted deep-pocketed rock and roll as sharp as pressed pants.

John held on to the odd name of Tom's neighbor. He had it in his head when he was watching television on the couch one night in December, home with Martha and their small son Josh. There was an ad for Olympia beer, focused relentlessly on the brand's natural, artesian water from the Northwest. "It's the water." Again and again against a nonstop background of golden bubbles and Pacific Northwest rivers: "It's the water."

What did "Moby Grape" mean, anyway? Or "Peter Wheat and the Breadmen"? It's just a band name. And Creedence Clearwater Revival—for a new beginning, for a new label, for a new year—sounded like a band name. It meant whatever you wanted. John pulled these words together and brought them to the meeting with Saul. Everyone had their little scratch pages with their silly ideas to proffer and defend. But John's came out first, and no more needed to be heard. It was perfect, which made John anxious. Now it was up to them to make good on their luck. So really, it was up to him.

THIRTEEN

STRIKE TIME

Redwood National Park was established on New Year's Day 1968, inaugurating a year of growing national attention to the environment. By October, Congress authorized another West Coast park, North Cascades in Washington, marking the first time in almost three decades when two new national parks were created in one year, a year that also saw passage of the Wild & Scenic Rivers Act to protect US waterways. Environmental concern was not new; in his famous 1966 address to Manhattan's Riverside Church, Martin Luther King began his public crusade against the Vietnam War by noting the United States' abuses of that country included environmental degradation. "We poison their water, as we kill a million acres of their crops," he intoned. "They must weep as the bulldozers roar through their areas preparing to destroy the precious trees." But environmental *activism* exploded in 1968, from the formation of new nonprofits like Friends of the Sea Otter to the alternative publishing projects like the *Whole Earth Catalog*, aimed at helping young people survive outside destructive modern civilization. *Life* followed its earlier Appalachian depiction with another photo essay depicting the pollution in the Great Lakes, in which was said that the Cuyahoga "oozes rather than flows" toward Lake Erie.

Edward Abbey—bearded, beer-guzzling, ornery, unsentimental—emerged as the fitting spokesman for the earth in an age of cataclysm. *Desert Solitaire,* his memoir of a year as a ranger in Utah's Arches National Monument, was published in 1968 and immediately adopted as a foundational text for those Americans, mostly young, who felt their defense of nature required "active resistance" akin to the antiwar movement. For Abbey, the natural world in late-'60s America was on the verge of extinction and demanded protection, not mere appreciation. "If industrial man continues to multiply his numbers and expand his operations he will succeed in his apparent intention, to seal himself off from the natural and isolate himself within a synthetic prison of his own making," he wrote in "Down the River," a *Desert Solitaire* chapter about his rafting trip in Glen Canyon before a dam was erected there. "He will make himself an exile from the earth and will know at last, if he is capable of feeling anything, the pain and agony of final loss."

The ascendant environmental movement was a victory for optimism during a time that otherwise rumbled with violence and attempts to crush dissent at home and abroad. In January alone, as Creedence Clearwater Revival released their first single and went back to the studio for their next, a Boston grand jury indicted a group including pediatrician Dr. Benjamin Spock for conspiring to undermine the Selective Service. By the end of the month, after "Porterville" / "Call It Pretending" failed to dent the charts, news came from Vietnam about a crushing counterstrike measure by the

North Vietnamese. The Tet Offensive, as the US media christened it, went on for weeks, demoralizing morale and further eroding support for the war at home. Protest, not love or dancing or even drugs, was becoming the common language of young people, at least those who took their cues from San Francisco.

Yet when the band returned to Coast Recorders, they brought along two songs that were a decade old. Bo Diddley's "Before You Accuse Me" was meat and potatoes for them, as it was for many real and aspiring bluesmen. The song is all shuffle and attitude, though the quartet had transformed it to a storming straight-ahead rocker that removed the blues affectations. It may have worked onstage as a pure burst of energy, but on record it sounded indistinct.

Next, they tried Dale Hawkins's old gem "Susie Q," originally recorded with James Burton, playing the ominously static melody on lead guitar and punctuating the drama with roaring distorted solos. This song entered the permanent Creedence repertoire in early 1968, when the band started a five-night residency at a Sacramento NCO club, "a toilet" in Stu's opinion. They were booked for five shows a night, and he recommended they reach back to the Hawkins standard to fill the endless stage time. The Hawkins version sounded almost Latin, with its sharp quarter-note beat and his drummer's ringing ride cymbal pattern. Creedence kept the minimal chord progression, the lyrics, and the melody—enough for anyone with a memory of late-'50s radio rock to recognize it instantly—but their small adjustments changed the song completely.

First, they slowed it down. Instead of Hawkins's herky-jerky tale of teenage obsession, the band held back the tempo just enough to replace the purposefully stiff feel with something just a little smoother and more swinging. Second, Doug switched the beat around. Instead of a quarter-note rhythm hitting every downbeat, he put the bass drum only on the off-notes. With this one small gesture, Doug opened the song up. The entire arrangement, including John's twangier version of Burton's lead line, now felt like it was perpetually tumbling forward, like it could go forever.

That was their third innovation. In the studio, the band recorded a version of "Suzie Q" (minimally but significantly renamed) that lasted nearly nine minutes, most of which was a showcase for John's guitar solos. The backing trio roiled along behind him, grinding their one-chord vamp into dust until John brought the song to a close with a descent to a dramatic E-minor resolution.

On record, this long, guitar-led journey sounded like the band nodding to San Francisco. John added feedback to match the sound of the Paul Butterfield Blues Band's thirteen-minute opus "East-West" and put a semipsychedelic telephone effect on his singing voice that they hoped would attract the city's far-out listeners. Once the band completed the basic track in a single take, John also completed the song's final mix himself, handling the studio's knobs and faders to weave in background vocals, backward guitars, and percussion into a long sampler of everything that Creedence—or simply John Fogerty—could achieve sonically.

Above all, they still wanted to have a hit on local radio, and John knew that the people wanted jams, explorations. Yet that very persistence of focus separated them from the groups that were making the city's name. Creedence Clearwater Revival were not natural improvisers. They were not mind-expansionists who made music as mercurial as Bill Graham's famous liquid light shows. They never dove into "Suzie Q" hoping to find some unexplored avenue in their sound or collaboration. Instead, they rehearsed it at the Shire every day for months, at ten- and twelve-minute durations that were always carefully plotted out beforehand. The song was a composition, as were John's solos. He still felt his playing and songwriting were more imitative than expressive, and "Suzie Q" made the most of that. It was a big, slinky epic made from old riffs, pre-planned solos, the hypnotic energy of San Francisco's ballroom scene, and John's own ambition. In all their years together, the band had never released an outright cover song before, but they'd also never made a record that sounded so different from their influences. With "Suzie Q," Creedence found the elemental connection between 1957 and 1968 for young people who had lived through both. In February, California labor leader Cesar Chavez began a nearly monthlong hunger strike for farmworkers' rights, and a civil rights protest at South Carolina State University ended with highway patrolmen killing three students and injuring twenty-eight—the first fatal gun violence on a US college campus. Somehow Creedence Clearwater Revival made a dusty AM staple sound anxious and disorienting enough to match this shocking new moment.

At the exact same time, they found their first home stage in San Francisco, Deno & Carlo, a little restaurant at 728 Vallejo Street in North Beach, miles from the Haight. Deno & Carlo opened in 1965 and hosted many of the city's musicians before they achieved fame, including Country Joe & the Fish, the Dead, and Janis Joplin. It was a tiny club—a long, thin rectangle with a narrow stage in the back barely big enough to fit Creedence's instruments. A local radio spot—read by San Francisco author Richard Brautigan—promised no cover and no minimum. Rather than their usual left-to-right stage setup, Doug was pushed way to the back just so he had room to move. The band started a Sunday night residency in early February. Other groups were performing new material or more recent covers, like "Purple Haze," but Creedence played their favorites from years past: "Walkin' the Dog," "Ninety-Nine and a Half," "Before You Accuse Me," "I Put a Spell on You." They were never paid by the venue; they made what customers dropped in the empty beer pitcher at the front of the stage, which often only covered the two-dollar parking and gas.

But it got them into San Francisco in front of paying audiences. After a few weeks, they achieved something they'd never had: fans. Seeing the same people coming back to Deno & Carlo week after week, new friends in tow, Stu suddenly recognized that they'd only played for captive audiences, whether soldiers, Berkeley partiers, or chaperoned kids. They were always the hired entertainment, pulling out of town before the amps were cold. Now they had a permanent spot in the city. Their little outpost to build on. Sunday nights.

Best-case scenario, word would spread to the deejays at KMPX, the city's leading underground station that just happened to broadcast out of a warehouse on Green Street a half mile east. In addition to the tried-and-true San Francisco bands with real records on real labels, KMPX played unreleased recordings from newer bands that hadn't even been signed. They had a library of unreleased recordings by Janis Joplin, Bob Dylan, Jefferson Airplane's Jorma Kaukonen, and more. John brought "Walking on the Water" to the station when the band was still the Golliwogs, and they played it a few times. He then brought "Porterville" in as well, though he never heard that one on the air. As the group settled into their Sunday night home, John knew he had their best song yet, and he gathered the strength to see what they thought of it. This song was the real debut of this new direction they'd forged, this country-groove thing he'd honed. In his head, everything was resting on the KMPX team's response. They would either validate the work or not.

John's worries were unfounded. "Suzie Q" was on the air that day. And KMPX became the first station to regularly play Creedence Clearwater Revival.

Like the single, KMPX was a mixture of old and new. The station started broadcasting in April 1967, right as the city's youth culture exploded into an unmanageable, globally notorious love circus. Veteran rock deejay Tom Donahue had logged decades in Top 40 programming, starting in Pennsylvania. He had last been at a station in Pittsburgh and relocated to San Francisco as a federal payola investigation got underway there in the early 1960s. He deejayed for KYA, the pop station that didn't interest the Blue Velvets at the time. In 1964, "Big Daddy" Donahue, as everyone knew him, cofounded a pop label, Autumn Records, whose roster included Bobby Freeman, of "Do You Wanna Dance." His debut for the label, an updated teeny-bopper R&B song called "C'Mon and Swim," was produced by Donahue protégé Sly Stone. Stone was something of a Black John Fogerty at the time, and significantly more successful. From his home base in working-class Oakland, he became a deejay at KSOL, a bandleader and regular at the East Bay Rollarena scene with his group the Viscaynes, an in-demand session musician, and even a local backing-band keyboardist for the bigger concerts produced around the Bay, including Dionne Warwick and Marvin Gaye.

In early 1967, Donahue tuned in to KMPX when it was essentially a public-access station. Programming blocks were given over to different ethnic minority and immigrant groups, many of whom broadcast in their native languages. The midnight-to-six shift, however, was the unofficial folk show, led by a young musician named Larry Miller. When Donahue heard Miller's eclectic use of the time, he approached the musician about his idea for an entire 24-hour station built on the premise of creative freedom for on-air talent.

Under this new format, Donahue and his comrades played long, uninterrupted selections from whole albums to make up for their lack of advertising. They had no budget, but word of mouth was strong. Within a single ratings cycle, KMPX became the leading FM station in the Bay Area among young men under thirty-five.

Nevertheless, the station wasn't a boys' club. As they started to grow, KMPX employed female engineers who were given opportunities they couldn't have received at other stations. They even hosted a weekly program, "The Chicks on Sunday," which became a venue for conversation about the emerging women's rights movement. The sales staff attracted traditional ad reps alongside pot dealers from the Haight, and they sought out youth-oriented local businesses like record stores, clothing stores, and outdoor-wear companies. One day the station announced a "PSA" that a marijuana delivery had been canceled. Deejays regularly flubbed their on-air readings and were accompanied by giggles from the "bird engineers."

When unions at the San Francisco newspapers went on strike in late 1967, the station invited local columnists and writers from *Ramparts* magazine to read the news on air. That strike lasted fifty-two days before ending in mid-February, the longest such effort from newspaper workers in the city's history. It clearly inspired KMPX's thirty staff members, who were disgusted with the station's owner, businessman Leon Crosby. Claiming that Crosby refused to buy new equipment or increase pay, that he regularly issued checks that bounced, and that he was attempting to stifle his team of popular provocateurs, the group met on Friday, March 16, in a staff member's apartment and planned their own wildcat action.

Donahue was technically management, but he couldn't resist the chance to support his team's independence and put on a good media stunt. He was also personally angry at Crosby, who would not let him maintain dual managerial roles at KMPX and another San Francisco station, KPPC. Other staff members had more experience with labor mobilization, including some who participated in the Family Dog collective, which produced early psychedelic concerts at the union-owned Longshoremen's Hall. It didn't take long to plan the effort. They were ready to walk off by Sunday night, March 18.

That meant the strike began on Creedence Clearwater Revival's Deno & Carlo night, and the band was keyed in, somewhat desperately so, to the workings of the station at that point. KMPX was regularly playing "Suzie Q," which the band had split into two sides of a 45. John, Tom, Doug, and Stu felt indebted to them; they wanted to help, so when the band finished their set and heard word of something big taking place, they drove over to Green Street, where they met a steadily growing crowd and a flatbed truck. The station employees were setting up a sound system. Creedence, still unknown to anyone around them, started unpacking the van.

Near 3 a.m., the KMPX studio was throbbing with James Brown and filled with guests and hangers-on, including Owsley Stanley, the Dead, and a dozen-odd lost-looking girls. At the top of the hour, KMPX chief engineer Abe Kesh, who went by Voco, announced on air that the staff was going on strike. Five minutes later, in front of a crowd that was now more than five hundred strong, John, Tom, and Stu's amps came on and Creedence brought the roaring 1950s to North Beach and Telegraph Hill.

Their typical venue was a tiny club, maybe the odd arena as openers. They'd never performed for an open-air ad hoc street mob before. But the band had already settled into an unchanging formation, and the particulars of any show, down to the guys' body language, never changed. Looking up at that flatbed at 3:05, San

Francisco's five hundred most dedicated radio fans saw Tom, Stu, Doug, and John, in that order, left to right. Tom strummed in jeans and a collared shirt and stood so still that his shoulder-length curls never wavered. Stu was a step back from him, in circular glasses, pounding the bottom end with a grin that was hidden by his drooping mustache. Doug's beard was now fit for Tolkien, and he wore sleeveless T-shirts so his brawny, thrashing arms could flail untethered. And then John, to the audience's right, nearly side stage, always with his face half-turned from the audience. When he didn't have to sing, he turned away entirely and faced Doug. All his solos were performed with that supposedly difficult, time-challenged drummer in view, and not even the band asked why.

Steve Winwood was playing in San Francisco that week with his new band Traffic, and he stood next to the Dead while the unknown East Bay band played. Eventually the police arrived and broke up the party, so the party moved to the water, Pier 10. Things fizzled entirely when it turned out that no one brought the amps to the new location. But Creedence Clearwater Revival, who were referred to as "the Creedence Clearwater band" in the next day's *San Francisco Chronicle*, had made their riotous, long-awaited entrance to the inner sanctum of San Francisco music: the street. The true home, the breeding ground of San Francisco rock, all respect to the ballrooms, was the outside party. The Dead's long, polyrhythmic explorations grew out of those long day jams. Since the hippie's literal and figurative death, there hadn't been as many calls to gather in the street. Creedence had finally led a block party, the kind that gets shut down by the police, the one Woody Guthrie would have played, the anti-owner walkout.

The hippie's death was a bit like the great early rock and rollers' sad fates ten years earlier: it left a hole. Young people formally, if kiddingly, rejected a name that older media makers had given them, and no ad-agency identity sprung up to take its place. Young people were losing patience with the abject insanity of their world. They were threatened and appalled by an escalating meat-grinder war and routine, horrific assaults on Black Americans. They were overwhelmed with disgust for the nation's level of poverty and by the inequities across every spectrum of society, from the bombing of civilians in Asia down to greedy management at the radio station. As the KMPX strike showed, young people were no longer content to be a shopping demographic and were now a self-appointed Movement. It wasn't as if every young person in the country was suddenly involved in direct action, but there had never been a group like the White Panthers, either, who formed in 1968 advocating "total assault on the culture by any means necessary, including rock n' roll, dope and fucking in the streets." Creedence finally achieved their spotlight right as the decade's rolling party became serious, even threatening. The stakes were becoming ever clearer, even for rock shows under the sky in San Francisco.

The KMPX staff, for example, didn't stop at one feisty concert. In the morning they were marching outside the station, holding signs for their newly formed "union," the Amalgamated American Federation of FM Workers of the World, North Beach Local No. 1f. Ralph J. Gleason called it "the first hippie strike" in the *Chronicle*, and with good reason. They decorated their membership cards with Aquarian imagery. The workers submitted their new contract on paisley-colored paper and specified that employees should be paid extra during solar and lunar eclipses. By the next morning, the strike was on television. A cameraman for KTVU captured footage of the bearded and bejeweled marchers while a straitlaced reporter, his hair tightly pomaded, marveled at "a picket line little like anything that's been seen on the labor front before." Interrupting a female marcher as she sang Woody Guthrie's "Jesse James" with an acoustic guitar, he asked if they intended to win their demands and she replied in the affirmative with an optimistic glow. Then she said there would be a fundraiser concert at the Avalon Ballroom on Wednesday.

Creedence would be there of course, as invited performers. On-stage again, in solidarity.

FOURTEEN

AN INCIPIENT FAD

The Avalon show went great. They all did now. If you spend every day pounding songs together like blacksmiths, you become consistent, if nothing else. And by now, Creedence was a cohesive unit that bashed through their setlist with insurgent intensity. Even their covers sounded transformed. "Ninety-Nine and a Half" didn't sound like Wilson Pickett, it sounded like John, Tom, Doug, and Stu. Same with "I Put a Spell on You." John didn't try to out-scream Screamin' Jay Hawkins, he just tried to rile his band, his voice, and his guitar to the most sinister racket they could make. It was more than enough for the Avalon. After fifty minutes of rapid-fire blues and blistering throwback rock, that room was positively adrenalized.

What a joke: they were a "real" San Francisco band now, after growing up forty minutes away. For Stu, who had lived there his whole life and seen more of old San Francisco than his bandmates, the city he grew up with was museums, stores, and Playland at the beach. Now he saw it all transformed. He liked the outgoing, positive environment, including the growing gay community. There wasn't much drinking, but there was an inexhaustible amount of mushrooms, LSD, grass, and hash. Looking around at the Avalon, he could see the lines drawn. Some people were taking the lifestyle deeply seriously, while others were there to watch. Stu knew he was the latter. He didn't trust strangers enough to lose his mind around them or join a commune. But he sure loved to take in the spectacle. He couldn't believe how many kids had arrived in his hometown just because of what they read in *Rolling Stone*, the magazine founded the previous year that was now the unofficial house organ of the new realm.

The Avalon was another of Bill Graham's antimacassar-strewn dream palaces, a 1930s hall filled with carpets, mirrors, and hanging lights. "Pure sensuousness," wrote Janis Joplin in a letter back home to her family in Texas. Another initiate said the place resembled "seven different centuries thrown together in one room." Like the Fillmore Auditorium, it was a second-floor spot in a poor neighborhood, up a flight of stairs from street level. Inside, near the stage, the strobes and liquid lights colored a spring-loaded dance floor. Creedence may have dressed relatively demurely, but they loved the place—the sound was good, as it always was in Graham's venues. When he sat between his friends' amps on a stage like that, Doug could hear the music differently. He could feel it in his guts and feet. It was another grueling physical challenge to add to his growing list of them. He was getting used to the frantic pace of a Creedence set and the high-wire energy of it. Once they kicked off, he spent fifty straight minutes pushing the train at maximum energy nearly continuously. And the Avalon had an extra ingredient he'd never seen before: a substantial portion of the audience were properly, out-of-body stoned. However socially conscious the Movement had become, however many childish things had been put away, music and drugs were nonnegotiable, and often inseparable. Deno & Carlo only served beer and wine, and the band had been in bars where an audience member or two got drunk enough to change the weather. At the Avalon, though, half the crowd, easy, was *flying*. Strange dances, glazed eyes, deep breathing—it was hard to tell if they were even hearing the music, but you couldn't say the audience wasn't engaged, in some way. That's what the Avalon promised: a density of feeling and experience. Reputations could be made there, and even the English bands knew. When the Animals came to San Francisco on tour, they offered to play the Avalon for free. Creedence was now Avalon-certified, even if they still didn't resemble the other groups around them. They didn't pack up their gear and return to the Haight or Heathrow; they went across the Bay Bridge and on to El Cerrito and the Shire. They weren't dressed for attention or subversion. John wore a flannel shirt.

That night, during sound check, John played a little guitar figure that felt new. It had a real mystery and that same repetitious power of "Suzie Q," but it wasn't as country. He mewled into the microphone and cajoled Doug and Stu to build a groove with him. It was just a little idea, something that caught him, and sound check only lasted two minutes. He filed it away for later.

John wrote songs that way more and more. He followed the ideas that came into his head, whether they arrived when he was playing guitar, watching TV, or driving. He liked guitar riffs. Short ones, one measure if possible. He liked good song titles that made you curious before you even heard a note. "Mystery Train." "Moanin' in the Moonlight." He kept a notebook that he filled with evocative phrases that came to him in dreams, from movies, or in memories.

When a good melody arrived, he paired it with a title and off he went. It wasn't a formula. He was at the mercy of this process, he wasn't rubber-stamping it. But it got him started. Once the ideas came, he could work on it from there, for as long as it took.

Saul Zaentz stopped in to hear a set at Deno & Carlo one Sunday. He knew the band was getting better, but even he was taken by the range and power they now expressed. John was still playing through the amp that he bought with Saul's loan, a Kustom, one of the new models with solid-state electricity. Most musicians hated the thing. They thought it sounded dead compared to warmer tube amps. But somehow John got his own irreplicable tone out of it. He pushed up the vibrato and made himself sound like Pops Staples on a motorcycle. He did that with a three-quarter-scale Rickenbacker, John Lennon's preferred guitar, that gave his small hands maximum control, from huge chords to screaming, trebly solos.

After the set, Saul approached the band excitedly. It was time to make a full record, an LP. They had more than enough material and the San Francisco scene was built on live shows and full-length statements, not singles. He didn't need to talk the guys into it. With the singles they'd cut so far, they were already halfway done.

They went back to the studio to fill out a full track list in late winter 1968. The songs for the first Creedence Clearwater Revival album were a hodgepodge of John's early triumphs like "Porterville," their gnarled oldies covers "Suzie Q" and "I Put a Spell on You," and a few new originals from John that weren't as immediately impressive. One new song, "The Working Man," was a twelve-bar blues with some clever turnarounds, and mostly a chance to ape a B.B. King–style call-and-response with his guitar. The lyrics, a funny tale about being "born on a Sunday, on Thursday I had me a job," were old-fashioned but nothing exotic; every San Francisco

band played some version of the blues. John's real breakthrough on
the debut LP, especially on this song, was the full display of his new
voice, which was nominally southern but didn't really match any
regional drawls from that territory. John pronounced "work" like a
Brooklyn deli owner: *woyk*. He dropped the last letter from "job."
"I was *woykin'* out on-a jo'" wasn't southern, but it fit the music
perfectly, this simple-sounding, clean recording of four instruments
playing together fluidly, carrying the songs in triumphant unison
from start to finish, evoking the blues and early rock without sanc-
tifying or undermining them. Unlike his steady, demure speaking
tone, John's singing voice was as active and unplaceable as the music he made. He could follow it now.

They finished the recording, kept at Sunday nights, and waited
once again. As the weather warmed up, Creedence played the newly
opened Deno Carlo Naval Base location, a more youth-oriented
program with psychedelic advertising posters. The party was held
out in Muir Beach, north of San Francisco. It was a hike to get out
there, but the band went about ten times in the first half of 1968.
They set up on a wooden porch stage connected to a private building and played facing the beach, running through their entire unreleased first record and a few extra oldies covers. The shows always
had a full day's worth of bands and an audience of hundreds, many
experiencing an outdoor LSD sense-journey.

The acid was simply unavoidable now, and it wasn't pretty up
close and through sober eyes. At a Grateful Dead show at Fillmore
West, one of the few such shows they attended purely as audience
members, the four of them were so underwhelmed by the psychedelic journeyers' playing that they stood together on the emptying
ballroom floor and made a pact: no drugs or alcohol while they
were making music. Everywhere around them were the dregs of

young people compelled to San Francisco because of the Dead's beautiful vision of communal freedom. These four locals may have been the only young men scared straight by their time in the city's ballroom scene.

The band joined the American Federation of Musicians union. They registered through the Richmond branch instead of San Francisco's because it was cheaper and didn't require an audition. Like good laborers they continued to meet at the Shire every weekday around 10 a.m. They had coffee and talked a bit about the day's songs, then got to work with their instruments. They spent all day cocooned in the knotty, rain-fed trees of the Berkeley Hills—far more time practicing and preparing than recording or performing. Waiting was nothing new for Creedence. They always knew how to fill the days: practice. And in the gap between their last recordings and their first album's release, the world shook loose at last.

In late March, President Johnson announced he was stepping down instead of campaigning for reelection, in large part because a youth-led coalition had emerged to back the vehement antiwar senator Eugene McCarthy. On April 2, British singer Petula Clark hosted a prime-time television special during which she touched the arm of her costar, Harry Belafonte—a gesture so fractious that it drew condemnation from the sponsoring Chrysler organization. Yet neither of these were any preparation for the tumult that erupted two days later, when Martin Luther King Jr. was assassinated in Memphis, at a motel that was a preferred haunt for Stax employees. Black uprisings followed in dozens of cities that night and across the following days. Even John's vocal and showmanship model, James Brown, was forced to make an uncommon change to his gig schedule and offer an onstage plea for nonviolence to his audience in Boston. It used to be that Brown kept as far away from politics as he could. But now "politics" meant people getting beaten at his shows. It was washing up on everybody's shores.

In San Francisco, the labor movement mourned King as one of their own. He was in Memphis organizing sanitation workers, after all. Bay Area longshoremen, warehousemen, and other unions stayed at home on April 9, the day of the funeral in Atlanta. The ILWU had made King an honorary member while he was still alive, and the union closed all West Coast ports as well, including the port of San Francisco. Throughout the month, the mail slowed, the trains slowed, offices closed. A whole city with sand in its gears, all from righteous collective anger. The injustice had grown so dire that everyone had to acknowledge it. Deejays became organizers, dance-band leaders became community figureheads, the underground became kingmakers, and public workers became resistance leaders.

Creedence's place in tie-dyed San Francisco was now assured, yet the mainstream still beckoned, especially with a record coming. And the national press was angling to cover just their kind of group. The *New Yorker*, of all places, hired a pop critic. A forcefully feminist woman, no less. Ellen Willis was a frontline Movement advocate who wrote about politics and gender in addition to music. A Bronx and Queens native, daughter of a policeman and a housewife, she went to Barnard, then to Berkeley, where she began a master's in comparative literature in the early '60s. She didn't finish. The changing state of the world agitated her too much. She wasn't meant to sit and study.

Willis returned to New York and found her written voice as an essayist in the burgeoning underground press. She could be smolderingly personal and shrewdly analytical whether writing about abortion or Bob Dylan, but in April 1968 she used her *New Yorker* column to cover less urgent issues, namely the release of two recent compilations, Columbia's 17 *King Size Rhythm and Blues Hits*, drawing from Cincinnati-based King Records, and Atlantic's four-record *History of Rhythm & Blues*. She heard rumors of an oldies tour in the works, and of a Mothers of Invention project involving the great AM radio drive-around tunes of their youth. "In England, where old rock records have become collectors' items, boys are trading in their Edwardian furs for leather jackets and greasing down their Beatle cut," Willis wrote. She didn't mention them, but Elvis Presley was planning a televised comeback special at this exact time and Jerry Lee Lewis had just reemerged from obscurity as a successful country singer. The Everly Brothers and Muddy Waters were making records with an updated, Fillmore-familiar sound and repertoire. "Fifties music is an incipient fad," Willis wrote.

But she did not dismiss the yearning that this fad revealed in young people. They were pining for their own simpler childhoods. Years that weren't even very far in the past now felt like eons ago. Willis saw chasms everywhere, whether between political factions or men and women, and she loved rock and roll because every song balanced rebellion and tradition. Its most brilliant artists bent the tradition toward themselves, which in turn showed their audience how to navigate their own path in the world and in history. "If the gap between past and present continues to widen," she warned in a 1967 essay about Dylan's winding artistic journey to *John Wesley Harding*, "such mediation may be crucial. In a communications crisis, the true prophets are the translators."

FIFTEEN

GRIEF

S aul brought Creedence down to L.A. for a showcase at the Cheetah, the closest thing that city had to the Fillmore. They arrived and learned shocking news: the opener, billed last, was Howlin' Wolf. Less than a year earlier it wasn't even guaranteed that John or Doug would survive, and now they were in Los Angeles on a bill with a founding father. The amazement was shortlived. Wolf wasn't friendly or near his best. By night's end they felt bad for headlining. How could they have taken top billing over a man who created the world they were trying to live in? How was that legend touring through ill health and money troubles even in 1968? It shook them.

Late in the month, San Francisco's most straight-and-narrow band was momentarily caught up in the growing anti-establishment furor. Rumors were still swirling that the Army Reserve would be used to suppress civilian protests, and John remembered his superiors nearly slavering for the chance. On May 22, Robert Kennedy arrived in Richmond ahead of the California presidential primary, and John made a map of the San Francisco–area locations where the candidate was visiting. The band spent the day running around the area hanging up posters decrying the military's "Iron Fist." The city was swarming with police, and when an officer discovered this young quartet with the seemingly anarchist message and a map of the day's most populous spots, they rounded up Creedence and held them in the station for a few hours. When they were let go without charges, the officers decried them as "liberal agitators," and one threatened to let them know what the "iron fist" was truly capable of.

Other than this small example of genuine street protest, the band hadn't changed their priorities. Their self-titled debut album went on sale on May 28, John's twenty-third birthday. It was also the exact day that the KMPX gang found liberation, if not victory in their strike. Donahue and his group began broadcasting on a new radio band, KSAN. Knowing they had fans and appreciators among the staff, John brought the tapes to the station before the full LP was printed. To that point, the band was known variously as Creedence, as "the Creedence Clearwater band," or just as the four shaggy guys with the affinity for old rock and roll who had played on the flatbed and one time at the Avalon. Here they finally were with a finished product and their name immortalized on an LP sleeve.

The packaging for *Creedence Clearwater Revival* was an obvious attempt to translate this "new" band to San Francisco, or at least to the San Francisco–inclined. The cover photo was shot in the knotty woods around the Shire. The guys were almost hiding behind the trees, like they grew out of the ground, too. John and Doug were both in mock soldier uniforms. Tom, perched on a tree limb in a sleek brown shirt, was the only one of the four whose eyes were halfway visible.

The cover, created by Doug's fiancée Laurie, nodded to the city's trademark textual design, not so much the lava-lamp style on Fillmore posters but a nearly Wild West script enmeshed in a beautifully ornate blue frame full of silhouetted animals, vines, and leaves. At first glance the cover looked psychedelic, but on closer inspection it was more like wood paneling.

Less fitting was the back cover, which featured a long Ralph J. Gleason essay. Born in 1917, Gleason was decades older than the typical San Francisco love child. He began his career writing and hosting TV programs about jazz, including the *Anatomy of a Hit* episode that inspired the Fogerty brothers to seek out Fantasy Records. By the mid-'60s, he was a renowned authority on that genre, but he recognized that the city's musical identity was changing, so he refocused his efforts as the foremost chronicler of the "American Liverpool." John even sent him a postcard every week to alert him of the band's residency at Deno & Carlo.

There was a self-serving element to Gleason's fascination with Jefferson Airplane, the Dead, Moby Grape, and the rest. If he could depict their work as world-altering, then he, as their best-known booster and interpreter, would be the acknowledged expert on this unfolding revolution. Securing his byline for the *Creedence Clearwater Revival* liner notes was a sign that the band were firmly established as a San Francisco group, but the notes themselves were largely a pocket history of the city's ballroom scene. Amazingly, Creedence wasn't even mentioned until the final paragraph, and then only as "an excellent example of the Third Generation of San Francisco bands" who "give every indication of keeping the strength of the San Francisco sound undiminished."

That judgment didn't help the band's ambivalent relationship to their ostensible hometown, even though they returned to the Avalon the week of the album release to open for Taj Mahal. There was the perceived slight of "third generation," for one, and beyond that, they were record and radio obsessives who had spent their whole lives in the Bay. They knew the region's R&B and garage band lineage better than anyone, especially a fifty-year-old jazz head. Did Gleason know about Spider Webb and the Insects? We Five? His history gave the impression that San Francisco was purely a West Coast jazz hub until the acid tests began. John, Tom, Doug, and Stu had a decade of devotion to the contrary.

They played three nights at the Avalon, then a month later, July 2, Creedence made their long-sought debut at the Fillmore. Creedence played with Steppenwolf, a leather-clad L.A. band who were just about to release their debut album, and It's a Beautiful Day, an arch–San Francisco group led by a husband and wife on violin and keyboards. It happened to be the final show at the venue before Graham relocated his business to the former Carousel Ballroom and renamed it Fillmore West to match a new outpost in New York City, Fillmore East.

Creedence played two new songs that they had worked up since finishing their debut LP in March. Both were originals by John and took the band even further in the direction spelled out by "Porterville." The first grew from that odd guitar figure he made up during sound check at the first Avalon gig. At the Shire they built it up slow and heavy, almost too slow for dancing. But the tempo allowed for greater space between the instruments and a real atmosphere when they played together—a perfect match for John's lyrics, which once again told a semiautobiographical childhood tale, this one about life in rural Louisiana.

It opened with the image of a father being dragged down by "the man" and warning his son, the narrator, to avoid the same fate.

But "Born on the Bayou" didn't have a narrative like "Porterville." Instead, it was a series of sensual remembrances—the family dog chasing "hoodoos," naked runs through the woods, and a steam train leaving for New Orleans. John had seen California's equivalent of this scene in the mossy Sacramento–San Joaquin Valley, but the specificity of this song was new, and entirely secondhand. He was inspired by Muddy Waters and Howlin' Wolf, whose very names evoked natural southern mystery, as well as the 1941 Jean Renoir film *Swamp Water*, which he must have seen on television during his own childhood.

"Born on the Bayou" was written and delivered as if it were straight autobiography, though so was "Folsom Prison Blues" and no one took Johnny Cash for a murderer. John Fogerty wasn't the first songwriter to make up a persona for himself, but he was the first to do so by conjuring a completely foreign atmosphere on his own— his vocal phrasing, his guitar tones, his production. James Brown showed you how hard he worked, whereas John reminisced about the place "he" grew up, even though he had never set foot there. He could remember the bayou, the hound dog, the Fourth of July, all from the media he absorbed as a kid. And he re-created them with an undulating, heavy-tremolo guitar tone that felt somehow humid.

The second new song they played at the Fillmore was a one-chord workout with a name taken from the silliest '50s tradition of nonsense rock and roll. Lyrically, "Keep On Chooglin'" made as much sense as "Be-Bop-a-Lu-La" or "a-wop-bop-a-loo-bop." But as a performance, it resembled Brown's "There Was a Time," which his two-drummer lineup was currently using to whip audiences into frenzies of Black pride and togetherness. While his band rode their single chord and skittering tempos, Brown narrated the history of Black American dance. Then he set his band free to blare wildly as he twirled from the mic to demonstrate the moves himself before reigning it all back in for the next chapter. John wasn't so ambitious. "Keep On Chooglin'" was merely a feel-good song. To choogle meant to "ball and have a good time." But the song was sinister, the Velvet Underground at double speed, and Creedence was considerably harder than them, if not as ominous.

The structure of "Chooglin'" was simple. A couple verses, then John got to business. A guitar solo followed by a harmonica solo, then back to guitar. "Chooglin'" was designed to be a showstopper. At the Fillmore, they used it as their dazzling closer. It didn't appear to have any greater meaning beyond blowing the stoned audience away. The hippies and dance hall freaks wouldn't have remembered that the same nonsense word appeared in the set opener, "Born on the Bayou." In that song's remembrance, the steamer is "a-chooglin' on down to New Orleans." Neither song was terribly complex or subtle on its own, but they reflected each other. They formed a little world.

Robert Kennedy's California sojourn turned out to be the final trip in a life increasingly defined by movement. On June 5—a week and a day after *Creedence* went on sale and only two months after King was murdered—he won the California primary and was assassinated while leaving his victory party. The band, especially John and Tom, who were Catholic, revered the Kennedys, even if they never thought much about politics per se. They had seemingly nothing in common with the Boston scion, though Kennedy made uncommon efforts to know fellow citizens beyond his privileged circle, especially in his final years. In 1968 alone, he traveled to Appalachia, to Black ghettos, and to Cesar Chavez's side as the organizer's hunger strike ended. Robert Kennedy was a symbol of bleeding-heart white people's best intentions in the 1960s, and his sales pitch was a government that finally acknowledged and united the disparate pockets of consciousness in the United States. While campaigning for president, he told British journalist David Frost, "I think there has to be a new kind of coalition to keep the Democratic party going. We have to write off the unions and the South now. And to replace them with negroes, blue-collar whites, and the kids. We have to convince the Negroes and the poor whites that they have common interests. If we can reconcile those hostile groups, and then add the kids, you can really turn this country around."

Like his brother's, and like King's, Kennedy's optimism was met with a bullet. And like them both, his death elicited a national spasm of grief. On June 8, Walter Cronkite once again presided over a special report, this one from St. Patrick's Cathedral in New York, where Kennedy's funeral mass was held. Andy Williams, the powerful corn-fed belter and variety show host, sang "The Battle Hymn of the Republic," Kennedy's favorite song, before the senator's body was transported by train to Arlington National Cemetery near Washington, DC. Hundreds of thousands of mourners lined the tracks as the train passed by.

John watched it all on television, of course. Most Americans did. He often had a guitar in hand on the couch with Martha and Josh, even during these live-television events that were becoming more and more routine—announcements of tragedy followed by days of suffering and ritual. At night as his family slept, John sat up in their apartment and stared at the undecorated white wall. A nondescript surface in his hometown, a literal blank slate. His mind was full of Bill Graham circuses and mass mourning, half-remembered old movies and thoroughly memorized 45s. With those examples guiding him, he fashioned his own little world of mystery and insinuation. He wrote more songs that related to each other in a network of marshy crime and humid labor. The music in his mind was so boiled down it was like tar. There was nothing extraneous or extractable from Creedence's sound or John's songs at this point, nothing hidden. His strange invented South was convincing because his music didn't strain to explain itself. He never seemed like an artist that was trying to put one over.

Doug got married. He and Laurie had no money whatsoever, so they planned a honeymoon at Doug's aunt's house. The whole band attended the ceremony, and before the newlyweds set off over the mountains, Tom pulled Doug aside to give him twenty bucks.

"I already got paid this week," Doug told his business manager, his reason for playing music for ten years now.

"How often do you get married?" Tom asked, then sent him on his way with a brotherly smile and a pat on the back.

Halfway up the Berkeley Hills, the car radio was turned to KYA, not KMPX for a change. This was the AM pop station—the mainstream, not the underground. And for the first time, Doug heard them play "Suzie Q." The deejay even complimented John's "good country pickin'" on the track. Doug gripped the steering wheel and looked at Laurie.

"We won't have to live this way forever," he told her. And this time it was a promise, not a wish.

SIXTEEN

A CRIME TO
BE YOUNG

Doug moved into an El Cerrito house with Laurie with the intent to start a family. Stu, now the only unmarried member of the band, had no interest in keeping the Shire for himself, so he moved into the city and lived in North Beach, then Western Addition with friends from Deno & Carlo. But he blanched at the house-sharing vibe, so he relocated to his father's condo on Lake Merritt in Oakland. They came to loggerheads almost instantly. Herman made it clear that either Stu or his marijuana had to go. Stu moved out the next day. He went first to his brother's house, then finally got himself a small house in northwest Berkeley, one that had no band practice space. Without any other options, their only available practice space was the backyard shed behind Doug's rental house.

This was a step down. The shire was an Eden. They featured its land on their album cover, as if it was literally the soil they'd grown from. Doug's little shack was only 120 square feet, and he covered the walls and windows with carpet to muffle the sound. Things were worst for Doug himself, since he was the only band member who didn't smoke. The other three puffed cigarettes and left them burning in their ashtrays in between run-throughs of "Keep on Chooglin'." Doug tried keeping the doors open, but even with that he ended up coughing and shouting. At one point he stormed out, fuming about the working conditions.

"It's a goddamn factory," he screamed, and the rest of them took their next drags and laughed at him. Eventually he calmed down and got back to work. When he showed up for the next rehearsal, Tom had painted a sign and attached it to his shed: "THE FACTORY."

The Band's *Music from Big Pink* came out in July, and like Creedence's debut, it represented a shift. That quintet didn't bother with psychedelia either. Their songs and harmonies, even their instrumentation, recalled older eras and hand-worn artistry. The trend had been inaugurated, of course, by *John Wesley Harding*, which dribbled into stores between Christmas 1967 and New Year's 1968. Like Creedence, the Band had lived through a decade-long swing from roadhouses to heady freak-outs, but the Band had been to realms that the El Cerrito boys could only dream of. They had prowled North America's backwoods bar circuits while touring with Ronnie Hawkins as the Hawks. All but Levon Helm accompanied Dylan on his first, fabled electric tour of England. Then, with Helm onboard again, they recorded sessions with Dylan in upstate New York that were widely bootlegged and fabled for their depth of oblique historical exploration. *Music from Big Pink* was a debut, but the Band were already royalty, and their music felt appropriately stately. "Tears of

Rage," the opener, and "The Weight," the lead single, crept by like drifting clouds. By comparison, Creedence was an upstart band. And their South was borrowed from television and records, not Faulkner or lived experience.

Fantasy released the "Suzie Q" single, with parts one and two on alternating sides, in August. It went to no. 11 nationally thanks largely to airplay on two stations: KMPX and Chicago's WLS. The first was understandable, but Chicago was no accident. Saul got them booked at the Cheetah again, and this time he accompanied them to L.A., summoning a table's worth of record promoters to join him for the set. One of those was Bill Drake, a known "breaker," someone whose endorsement could give bands a foothold in markets around the country. Drake was fond of "Suzie Q," and after seeing the group rip through their airtight fifty minutes, he became the first person to commit to building a Creedence audience outside the Bay. Chicago was his first success.

Heavy Chicago airplay in August 1968 meant that "Suzie Q" bubbled up into the white-hot national center of political chaos. The Democratic National Convention was in town, attracting a throng of leftist revolt and ensuing police retaliation. Jerry Rubin was there as promised, leading the Yippies, an increasingly theatrical protest group he founded with Abbie Hoffman and others. They deemed the gathering the National Death Convention because the presumed party nominee, Hubert Humphrey, was insufficiently antiwar. Hoffman staged a counter-event in the street at which they nominated an actual pig for president. All week, downtown Chicago swirled with an ebb and flow of marchers and riot cops. It was "a crime to be young," as one such criminal put it.

Ellen Willis was there, on assignment as usual. She reported that the experience was "an emotional marathon; between bouts of rage and fear, exhaustion and boredom, pessimism and euphoria, we slept little and badly." Her dominant sensation, however, was that Chicago functioned like an overnight network of peace signs and racial harmony. "Never had I been so conscious that what I was involved in was a rebel community," she wrote, "whose emotions and sensations had a collective life of their own." And if any member of that community retreated to a comrade's apartment or car and turned on the radio, they had a better chance of hearing "Suzie Q" than any other song.

The single peaked on the charts in September, the same month that Creedence made their Hawaii debut, playing in Honolulu with Vanilla Fudge on a bill arranged by Dick Clark Productions. They got two encores that night and could have taken three if not for deference to the other bands' time. Instead they took a bow, grabbed their instruments and came offstage. As he passed beyond the curtain holding his bass drum, Doug felt someone grab his arm. He turned to find one of Dick Clark's guys, middle-aged in a suit, who told him one piece of information without a hello or goodbye: "You're in the big leagues—you don't touch your instruments unless you're playing."

A review of the show in *Billboard*, which appeared next to a picture of the Monkees receiving an industry award, praised the band for offering "oldies updated and dressed in new grooves." They brought wives and kids for the occasion, then returned to San Francisco for a weekend of shows with Albert King, one of John's guitar heroes, at the Fillmore West.

The success of "Suzie Q" validated John's expanding vision and control over the band's direction, but the sensation was short-lived. Rather than worrying that the band would never make it, he now began worrying again that the group would be lost to history like one of the regional R&B singles he listened to as a teenager. He took stock of their situation and still felt desperate. They had no real manager, no publicist, their label boss was still operating on a shoestring and even looking to John to help establish things. He was expected to lead his band to stardom without any of the tools that stars had at their disposal. The stress in his life made success feel like a burden that could break him. And John was not one to share his burdens. As ever, he just tried to outwork them.

The Beatles had established a pattern of double A-side singles, so that became John's standard. Never mind that they had three world-class songwriters and he was just one man. Booker T. & the MGs were in the middle of a nonstop working period that their label had deemed the Stax Soul Explosion. The quartet recorded on most of the twenty-eight albums that Stax produced in eight months starting in 1968, a grueling schedule by any stretch, but at least the band members weren't writing all the material. John was setting himself up for an expectation of superhuman productivity, comparing himself to these contemporaries and even Elvis. He convinced himself this was simply good business: corner the market with songs, and don't let them forget you.

He stayed up until nearly dawn many nights and didn't even need a guitar to write. Plenty of times he'd sit with only a notepad and pen. He knew what all the chords sounded like in his head anyway. The real work was building the imagery with his words and building the structure of a hit song, piece by piece. A little intro with a catchy guitar riff, verse, chorus, bridge. Put those in the right order and give them the right words. It wasn't rocket science, but it had the same power.

As Creedence prepared for their New York debut in October, John took stock of the songs he'd written so far. By his count, they had another album ready. And not every track was a slippery blues throwback like "Born on the Bayou" or "Chooglin'." He had another one ready by that point, something that was just as simple as those, though more melodic. It fit into their same Southern mystique. But this one, he thought, was catchier.

SEVENTEEN

DISHARMONY

"I Put a Spell on You" / "Walk on the Water" (the latter re-named as a Creedence song) came out in October and stalled at no. 52 on the national charts, which dampened everyone's excitement and only increased John's fear of underdelivering. Nevertheless, they flew to New York for a stint at the Fillmore East, Bill Graham's attempt to export San Francisco's ballroom madness to the East Coast. The first night, they opened for the lushest harmonies in America, the Turtles and the Beach Boys. The second night was an East Bay reunion, with Oakland's own Sly & the Family Stone.

Sly's group was his only focus now, after spending the past half decade producing and playing for others. Onstage they were a neon multiracial coalition of funkateers in blown-out Afros, bubbled sunglasses, bell-bottoms, and denim vests—quite simply the most turned-on people alive. The septet sang big churchy harmonies in front of blaring horns and Sly's amazing hooks. They played a little blues, but mostly focused on huge repeating beats and chest-thumping pop. Sly wrote songs about people coming together, and the songs themselves offered the occasion. They were self-fulfilling calls for utopia. That night showed New York that the East Bay could rival anywhere for musical range. Creedence showed their mastery and creativity with sounds from the past, while Sly & the Family Stone showed the future that might be. Their respective records did the same. John Fogerty wrote imagined reminiscences and rescued old covers from obscurity. Sly, on the group's 1968 LP *Dance to the Music*, wrote boogie-down songs to match anyone's but also concocted a studio-born audio epic of his own, "Dance to the Medley," which incorporated a capella chants, white noise, and tape manipulation.

Creedence went to RCA Studios in Hollywood to record their second LP. The sessions were bankrolled by Fantasy but John was the producer, and the material was his newly completed Southern song suite. Creative control was the trade-off for being on a tiny label with no clout at all. John could dictate this release with as much artistic freedom as Sinatra so long as he put songs on the charts.

His focus was on getting a clean sound that felt like four people in a room. He took pains to preserve that, and Doug, Stu, and Tom hit their marks and never cluttered the takes. John's writing was getting more tasteful, too. He hadn't composed anything as cinematic as Robbie Robertson's songs for the Band, but the new one, the catchy one, was as calm and content as anything that Creedence had ever recorded. It grew from a few different unfinished water-themed tunes in his mind named "Rolling on a River" and "Riverboat." John combined them with a third, "Proud Mary," named for the vessel that the song described, and the whole thing finally made sense. It was a love song, addressed to a means of escape.

"Proud Mary" was a product of that summertime creative spark that John experienced in the days after Robert Kennedy was killed. He got his Army discharge in the mail while home in El Cerrito, and the joy exploded out of him. He radiated with relief. Within a few minutes he had a first line, "Left a good job in the city," which came close enough to fitting how he felt. The rest was a Mark Twain daydream about floating down the Mississippi on a barge, creating his own life between the sun and the water. "Proud Mary" was simple and universal enough to feel wise, though John was just trying to approximate Booker T. and his group. The solo on the song was his attempt to channel Steve Cropper.

"Rollin' on the river." Doug didn't hear anything special. It sounded like mid-tempo album filler to him, not a single. But the chorus was catchy. After they laid down the basic rhythm tracks, the three background singers took their places around a mic in the vocal booth. "Rollin'," they sang, "rollin' on the river." Again. "Rollin'." They had sung it onstage and a dozen times in Tom's shed, "the Factory." But that day it wasn't jelling, apparently. John couldn't be pleased. So they left and went to dinner, and John said he was going to close some things up and meet them there.

About forty-five minutes passed before John joined the others at Two Guys from Italy, the kind of place where candles melted onto chianti bottles. They had a booth. Things were tense. The "Proud Mary" harmony fight seemed ridiculous. As ever, they went into these sessions well practiced, even over-practiced. They didn't require more than a take or two to track anything. In Creedence, every decision was already made before the tape was rolling or the show began. A take or a concert was a simple matter of execution.

But John sat down with other decisions on his mind. He steered things from celebratory to serious, and said he wanted to discuss band roles now that they were making their biggest statement yet with original material. Stu listened with growing concern. "Band roles"? John seemed to be delivering a practiced monologue, but none of the other three knew where it would lead, and the possibilities could alter everything.

John said that he'd scrapped their "Proud Mary" vocals and rerecorded them by himself. Just a chorus of Johns backing up John. That was how it would be from then on, too, at least on record. Starting with this LP, he would handle all studio background vocals. On the debut, he had already shown that he was comfortable adding percussion and other textures to complete his arrangements. He sometimes played rhythm guitar instead of waiting for Tom to join a session, and of course he sang every lead, wrote every original tune, and played every solo. Now Stu, Doug, and Tom had to sit in a dark restaurant booth and listen to John explain that, for reasons of strict quality control, he had no choice but to strip them of one last means of contribution. He laid out that he had the vision and that he was writing the songs, so he was going to say how everything went. He had one other stipulation, too. No one could bring any original songs to the table. On the debut, only Tom's cowritten "Walk on the Water" challenged that rule, so this was effectively just another wall around his older brother's ambitions. But John felt it needed to be said out loud: *Don't even try.*

In John's mind, this was only the cost of success. He saw no other way to respond to the challenges in front of him, especially after years of false starts. A misstep here meant the previous decade had been for nothing. He didn't want to go back to the gas station. He was making a sacrifice by taking so much on for the sake of his band.

Nevertheless, blood boiled, as John must have known it would. For Stu, it felt like a coup. John was angling for power. For Doug, it felt like punishment—John could never give them credit as musicians, and now he was just finding new ways to emasculate them. And for Tom, nothing was so simple. Here was Johnny, his kid brother. His co-harmonizer at the family piano, his awestruck admirer when Spider Webb and the band came around the Fogerty home. Tom had been a singer before John could hold a guitar, then he supported his younger brother's every move and laid a garden path for him to follow. When John learned to sing, Tom moved stage right and picked up the guitar himself. He put his entire savings on the line. And hallelujah, John's singing brought them to the center of the musical world at last. And instead of sharing the experience—its spoils or its difficulties—he shut his friends out of it. He shut his brother out of it.

John was insistent that this only applied to studio efforts. It was not going to change the dynamic that the band had onstage or at practice. They would still collaborate and build things together, and everyone should feel free to provide input. But why should the other three bother voicing any opinions about songs now? John had made clear the songs were his, and he had final decisions on potentially everything but drums.

Doug stewed. These decisions didn't make sense from any side. Musically, you make harmonies as a group, mixing your voices together. He and Stu weren't natural singers, but Tom had proved himself beyond any measure. Anyone sane would want to feature him, not cut him out. Yet he was becoming a touring sideman in his own band.

Doug alone observed John's retreats back to the drums during guitar solos. John didn't dance or strut onstage, and he didn't coax or lead the audience. If he wasn't needed at the mic, he turned toward

Doug and even made eye contact with him. He never lost himself in soloing, he kept eyes on his drummer so he could adjust the volume and intensity of the group in real time. And when Doug was pissed, he didn't return the stare. He left John hanging, trying to connect with eyes that weren't there. In the restaurant booth with the candles, Doug knew he'd be avoiding eye contact for a while.

They finished the L.A. sessions and returned home to practice for a November trip through the Midwest. With kids at home, Creedence decided on a touring schedule based on short bursts rather than endless road-dogging. After Utah, Minnesota, and Chicago, they played another stand at the Fillmore East in December. By this point they were playing half the songs from the upcoming record, which had been named *Bayou Country* and set for a January release.

The biggest-selling albums of 1968 were the White Album and the Stones' *Beggars Banquet,* both of which showed the top artists in the Western world pushing past their established sounds and reconnecting with their roots. Albums where screaming fuzz-tone solos and lilting acoustic ballads both had their place. Even the Monkees, who had been lab-born as a goof on those bands back in simpler times, were now certifiable experimenters. *Head,* their first foray into film, produced of course by Bob Rafelson and Burt Schneider, was released in November. The Monkees' trick was always to beat the stuff that they spoofed—their songs were catchier than most of their peers' and their TV show was funnier than most sitcoms. They didn't quite achieve that with *Head,* which was no cinematic masterpiece. But it was instantly a new urtext of psychedelia, the first studio film to embrace that aesthetic authentically. Its writer, Jack Nicholson, had most recently acted in *Psych-Out,* a straight crime drama set in squalid San Francisco that delivered a tragic antidrug message about youthful lives lost. *Head* was a whoopee cushion in comparison. A whoopee cushion that belched pot smoke.

Creedence Clearwater Revival hadn't made much of an impact in such a year. It received scant attention in the important underground press. *Kudzu,* one such paper in the South, did review it, though not kindly. At one point the reviewer asked, "What It gets down to Is: Can music that shows no originality be considered good?"

At a Fillmore East show on the day after Christmas, a Dadaist anarchist collective called Up Against the Wall Motherfucker attacked Bill Graham, breaking his nose. Things were not getting calmer, or more fun, at the Fillmore scenes or elsewhere. No one's temper was going down anymore. They couldn't afford to.

What kind of music fits that tension? In Chicago months earlier, "Suzie Q" was the soundtrack. Now as Creedence prepared for 1969, the biggest song in America was "I Heard It Through the Grapevine," a new version by Marvin Gaye, slower and moodier than Gladys Knight's recording the previous year. Somehow it was Gaye's first-ever no. 1 song. It fit that pleading, churchy voice of his so well. And the rumbling drums resembled a march, too, like those taking place at San Francisco State College through the late fall. A professor was suspended for comparing contemporary Black people to slaves that needed "to kill their slave masters" and implying that Black students needed to bring weapons to campus to protect themselves against the administration. The entire student body went on strike to protect his free speech rights, then the college president closed, reopened, and closed the school again.

January would bring the biggest test of John's wits to date. Among everything else, he remembered that Saul had promised how things would change once real money started coming in. "Proud Mary" was going to be his first completely original single, not a cowrite or a cover. The first test of his total abilities. If the other guys didn't understand that, he couldn't worry about them. They couldn't appreciate the level of responsibility that fell to him every day. "Proud Mary" had to be perfect, and he could manage that. He just needed everyone to get out of the way.

EIGHTEEN

ROLLING

As 1969 began, the US government was launching 1,800 B-52s a month into Vietnam from bases in Thailand and Guam. Seventeen thousand American men had now been killed in action. The sheer scope of senseless death was altering young people's philosophical assumptions. When Gallup polled students about the war in 1967, they found 35 percent identified as "doves" and 49 percent as "hawks." In 1969, the doves swelled to 69 percent.

On Haight Street, former aorta of the counterculture, more and more houses were boarded up. It was rumored that neighborhood drug addicts were eating stray cats. San Francisco police pulled over a twenty-three-year-old who was driving a stolen black Volkswagen and claimed to be in the middle of an eighteen-month-long acid trip. There was an arm in the back seat, wrapped in blue suede, which was found to belong to the car's owner.

For those still coming of age, the tenor of American life had grown more brutal and shocking every year since 1965. Dispatches from Operation Rolling Thunder or the Edmund Pettus Bridge, for starters, were unignorable and transformative for most people who saw them, but neither the Vietnam War nor the assault on Black rights slowed at all in response. In fact, the two conflicts merged: Martin Luther King became an outspoken antiwar voice, for example, in part because of the disproportionate number of Black soldiers fighting and dying in Asia. His assassination was just one enormous tragedy in a cascade of them throughout 1968. It was like everyone in the country held their breath going into 1969, waiting to see whether the previous year of multiple assassinations and Nixon's victory was a nadir or a new phase of horror.

Into this darkening, uncertain world, the "Proud Mary" single arrived on January 9, a double-A with "Born on the Bayou." *Bayou Country* was released the same month. The song debuted at no. 62 on the *Billboard* Hot 100 in the final week of January, between James Brown's "Give It Up or Turnit a Loose" and "Sweet Cream Ladies, Forward March," the newest single from young Memphis soul-rockers the Box Tops. A week later, Creedence sat atop Johnny Cash's "Daddy Sang Bass" at no. 55. Then the explosion happened. By late February the song was in the Top 10, and by early March, only six weeks after its release, "Proud Mary" was the no. 5 single in the country, behind four songs that had all been on the charts for months: "Crimson and Clover," "Build Me Up Buttercup," "Touch Me" by the Doors, and, at no. 1 since overtaking Marvin Gaye, "Everyday People" by their compatriots Sly & the Family Stone.

Like their respective bands, "Everyday People" and "Proud Mary" were inverses of each other. Both were bouncy, droning sing-alongs; Sly's tune only had one chord. Their choruses were retorts to the grim, unsure atmosphere of early 1969. The Family Stone sang theirs as a unit, per custom, building the verses around individual statements of racial and cultural harmony before exploding into a joyous, collective mission statement: "I am everyday people." We are all—Black ones, white ones, long-hairs, short-hairs—the salt of the earth.

"Rollin' on the river" seemed less immediately revolutionary. John's narrator left a menial, laboring life for a career on a riverboat. Like "Everyday People," the song was an outright celebration. The floating life is a rebirth. He only sees "the good side of the city" when he cruises out of it on the Mississippi. By the third verse, he's a proselytizer: "You don't have to worry 'cause you have no money / People on the river are happy to give." These are everyday people, too.

The songs' differences were just as obvious, of course. "Everyday People" was an urban dance anthem, and "Proud Mary" was a southern-tinged pastoral. Sly's song featured a half-dozen voices, male and female, taking turns with the verse melody and gathering for it on the chorus. Creedence's harmonies, as only they knew, weren't a group effort at all. John's song was about self-actualization, about a man finding himself in a community of exiles afloat. It wasn't about the community.

They may not have sung the background vocals, but Tom, Doug, and Stu provided much of the song's drama and character. Tom's clean, steady, rhythmic strumming evoked the big wheel turning, while Stu wandered up the neck of his bass to lead into every gospel-style chorus. And for such a loping groove, Doug's drums were busy and fluttering. His stray snare hits and fills complemented the narrator's youthful adventurousness, like he was finally set free and fully alive. *Bayou Country* and the "Proud Mary" single were released simultaneously with a drilling explosion off the coast of Santa Barbara,

California. It was the largest disaster of its kind in US history: twenty
thousand gallons of crude oil gushed into the water over January
and February. America's rivers were oozing, and most, the Mississippi included, were increasingly dammed. But this new band was
named for healthy water and "Proud Mary" truly flowed. Lyrically
and musically, it felt like a wide river pushing down to Louisiana,
carrying fortunes and dreams.

The single peaked at no. 2 but stayed there for weeks and eventually sold a million copies, a genuine phenomenon. Just like their
honeymoon experience with "Suzie Q," Doug and Laurie knew the
exact moment when the winds changed. They were having dinner
at the apartment of Laurie's best friend and her husband. It was
the night when KFRC, a local Bill Drake station, was doing their
weekly Top 10 countdown and the quartet had champagne waiting
on ice just in case. "Proud Mary" was on the national charts, but it
still hadn't appeared as the countdown drew close to the end. Finally, the deejay announced, deep and formal, "And number one
is 'Proud Mary' by Creedence . . . Clearwater . . . Revival," and the
couples all screamed and hugged like mad. No one would misstate
the band's name anymore, least of all around the Bay. The cork flew.

Whatever their frustrations with his methods, the Creedence
rhythm section had to acknowledge John's talent and canniness
at this point. For Stu, *Bayou Country* showed that John's anal re-
tentiveness didn't hinder his imagination. His friend's songs were
catchier—and more successful—than ever, yet they were also more
mysterious. There were no easy clichés on the LP and no mention
of the many headline issues of the day. The band's name didn't even
appear on the cover. Instead, it was another group photo in a forest
scene, this one deeper green and shot with a distorted lens. John
never spoke of it this way, but Stu recognized that *Bayou Country*

was a song cycle, almost a concept album—*Sgt. Pepper's* recorded in a raised wood cottage.

Starting with "Born on the Bayou," it went into "Bootleg," a song about whiskey-making driven by Tom's insistent acoustic guitar and sung in the voice of a backwoods distiller. "Graveyard Train" was a crawling Howlin' Wolf tribute filled with deathly imagery. "Good Golly, Miss Molly," a Little Richard cover, and "Penthouse Pauper," another of John's workingman vignettes, were relative filler, but they made a place for the straight twelve-bar blues in an album that was otherwise made of skeletal riffs and drones. The cycle closed with the life-giving bounce of "Proud Mary" and the chugging stomp of "Keep on Chooglin'." It was a tour of southern myths and archetypes delivered in thirty-four minutes and seven songs. It didn't remind Stu of Booker T., or of San Francisco. It wasn't just a pop album, it was world-building. It reminded Stu of Tolkien.

Creedence followed the album release with a show in Portland, John's first trip back since his transformative summer. They then returned to San Francisco and played two nights at the Fillmore a few weeks later. In February they played at Fillmore East, in San Diego, and in Hawaii. Their entourage, such as it was, remained remarkably small, limited in most cases to a couple roadies and their friend and road manager Bruce Young. Advertising, too, was almost nonexistent. *Rolling Stone* was always fat with full-page, color ads for bands whose records and singles hadn't come close to Creedence's chart success, but Saul Zaentz made no such push for his new standard-bearers. "Proud Mary" was a breakthrough by any stretch, and especially for a record label that was barely scraping by and previously best known for cool jazz. It was purely a radio success, too. Other than the few thousand total people who had seen them live, listeners had no preconceptions of who this band was. Was Creedence Clearwater the singer? Was he white, Black, southern? The album cover offered few answers. There were no Ralph Gleason ruminations to contextualize them. Listeners requested and bought "Proud Mary" because they loved it.

The band knew this, and it pleased them. All four held it as a point of pride that you didn't need an opinion on Vietnam to like "Proud Mary." They thought of their music as a universal plug-in. Equal parts rock, soul, and country, it could work on any radio dial that adopted them. They had followed an unlikely path toward this moment, and now Creedence knew that their music could be adopted by rednecks, hippies, military, young people and old. At practice and among themselves, they would repeat a little slogan, "Creedence is like burgers." They built this into a whole series of inside jokes comparing every group they knew to menu items, all of which were more acquired tastes. But Creedence Clearwater Revival was for everyone. They insisted on it. And now they had the proof.

There was a built-in trade-off to this attitude: even well-made burgers are easy to take for granted. When the reviews came, they were positive but always hesitant. *Stereo Review* called the record "a synthetic but spirited rehash of early rock." *Rolling Stone*'s Ray Rezos gave credit to the rhythm section and even noted John's zealous control over the arrangements, writing, and production. "He probably swept out the studio when the recording was finished, too," Rezos wrote. He praised the big hit and a few others but ultimately said, "A few more fresh ideas would be helpful." The single was successful enough to garner notice in *Life*, where critic Albert Goldman gave perhaps the most positive review of all. But even Goldman, a man so arch he made Ralph Gleason seem like Jerry Garcia, viewed Creedence as fundamentally derivative. He hailed their "mastery of the black idiom" and their ability to "manipulate an alien tradition," adding that their songs "burn through the trash being spewed on the radio today."

The band now had money. For all but Stu, it was their first experience with it. They went to a local auto dealer owned by the father of their old Portola friend Jake Rohrer, who worked as a salesman. Rohrer was a couple years older than the three youngest members, though he was a frequent companion to them in the Blue Velvets days; the trio even played his high school graduation party, and he got them gigs when he went to college. Now that they had cash to throw around, they went to him and each took home a Peugeot. John also indulged himself with some new recording equipment and a record player, though the bounty disappointed him. He'd learned his trade on borrowed tools and by making the best of his limitations. With a sudden raft of brand-new equipment, he lost some of the basement-dweller resentment that made him so hungry and driven. The high-end stuff broke too easily and couldn't be fixed. So John returned it all. He wanted only to get back to work. Thankfully there were more song titles in his notebook.

NINETEEN

RISING

Johnnie Taylor, a slick blues guitarist for Stax, performed at Nixon's inaugural ball, though the much greater number of Creedence's fellow travelers were gathered elsewhere in Washington, DC, that day. There were protests representing every wing of the Movement. Every anti-Nixon young person hated him for the war. From there they all had their own pet causes and specific disdains. At one of these events, Ellen Willis saw men screaming at female speakers. Not just hooting and cat-calling either. It was violent, vile abuse like "Take her off the stage and fuck her!" Willis had spent so many years writing and thinking about "women's issues," which was often to say male violence against women, but this one aggressive act knocked her back. Even among the so-called enlightened, this was what women had to deal with. Men who bullied women and others who let them. Up until that day, Willis wrote later, she assumed "women's liberation was part of the

radical movement, that one of our essential functions, in fact, was
to bring masses of women into the left. Washington has destroyed
that illusion."

In February she founded Redstockings, a confrontational feminist group, and led a protest on a New York State expert hearing on
abortion. The event featured mostly male speakers appearing before
a panel of fourteen men and a nun. Florynce Kennedy, described
by reporter Gloria Steinem as "a lawyer and black militant at whose
name strong white men shake," offered a counterproposal to the
state's punitive, eighty-six-year-old laws: "Why don't we shoot a New
York state legislator for every woman who dies from an abortion?"
Willis's own accusatory speech supplemented a pamphlet distributed by the collective Women's Liberation that she excerpted in
the *New Yorker*: "The only real experts on abortion are women," it
read. "Women who have seen their friends dead or in agony from
a post-abortion infection. Women who have had children by the
wrong man, at the wrong time, because no doctor would help them."
The appearance created an uproar in the courtroom and compelled
one male legislator to feebly plea, "Won't you act like ladies?" Another simply screamed, "Lesbians!" Steinem, writing in *New York*
magazine, noted that the cops "resorted to the rather feminine tactic
of hair-pulling."

Back in El Cerrito, the band's focus was, one could say, smaller.
A friend of Stu's father tipped them off to a property in Berkeley's old
warehouse district. They went to see it and found an empty stucco
building with upstairs offices on Fifth Street, perfect for a business
headquarters and practice space. On the lower level they covered
the greater part of the square footage in lush red carpet and wink-
ingly hung blue velvet drapes along the back wall. They added a
basketball hoop and Ping-Pong and pool tables for their occasional

breaks, but they spent most of their time on the carpet, hammering away like always. They called their previous shack the Factory and that turned out to be prophecy. This new place was near the race-track. The practice room abutted a foundry that could drown out the band when it was fully operational. This was their true Factory, no sarcasm needed.

Upstairs, one office belonged to John and a second had a phone that the others shared. Neither room was decorated. Bruce Young got his own space behind a windowed door where he hustled hotel and flight deals. They also employed two roadies, Ray Francoise and Bruce Koutz, and a lighting man, John Flores, but they weren't in the office every day.

John had his men working on a couple new songs, "Bad Moon Rising" and "Lodi," that he wanted to cut for their next single. They were both stylistic curveballs. "Bad Moon Rising" had a Texas two-step country beat with a little Sun Records bomp in it. "Lodi" was a straight folk-rocker like something the Byrds might adorn with high harmonies and a twelve-string. But John didn't change the formula. His vision was still focused on four instruments and one voice, well separated. He was still driven to see what he could achieve with that limited, powerful concept.

His influences had always been the oldest, grittiest bluesmen and early rockers, but after *John Wesley Harding* and *Beggars Banquet* and the White Album, there was a more general trend toward stripped-down sounds. All kinds of bands, from the whispering to the bludgeoning, simultaneously arrived at the same basic idea: simplify. Between 1967 and 1968 the Byrds lost the twelve-string and turned to traditional country. Neil Young, whose 1968 solo debut bore a heavy hippie influence, spent early 1969 on tour with a raw L.A. trio called the Rockets. Elektra Records signed the MC5, who

were effectively an offshoot of the White Panthers, with that organization's hatred of injustice and subtlety. Elektra also signed their
fellow Detroiters the Stooges, whose melodies, to speak of simplifying, were practically simian. Iggy Pop was the anti–John Fogerty.
He stalked the stage and drooled and bled, forever shirtless, barking
and howling. Guitarist Ron Asheton used a wah pedal and more
reverb than John would ever try. But every Stooges song was essentially a wilder "Keep On Chooglin'." Iggy ooga-booga'd and Ron
wailed, chasing a pummeling catharsis. John, being responsible for
both roles, played his song by going dutifully from one to another,
and he cared more about getting the take or ending the show on the
best possible note. He put on new guitar strings before every gig, and
played so gently that they never broke or snapped.

Over the same period, Lou Reed took the Velvet Underground
from anti-melodic swarms to shuddering close-mic intimacy.
White Light/White Heat pushed the art affectations of their music to the fore in 1968. That record wasn't psychedelic, just sonically abrasive, and brilliantly, multifacetedly innovative on that
account. Reed and his group turned amplifier feedback into the
basic ingredient of their sound, then were forced by John Cale's
exit and the theft of their instruments into a complete reversal late
in the year, when they recorded an album of near lullabies. *The
Velvet Underground*, out in March 1969, was a quiet record of soft
strums and stunning ballads. It sounded like Reed was singing on
the couch next to you.

Creedence was built from the same influences and enthusi-
asms as these bands, so they sounded a little like all of them. A bit of
twang, heavy distortion, soul harmonies, boyishness. Mix and match
those and you could cover most of the bands in mainstream rock
in 1969, at least the men-only kind. Hard rock, the writers called

it. And Creedence, along with Steppenwolf, was its vanguard. They played the first songs of this drawly, power-chord genre to explode on the radio—and television. On March 9, Creedence made their first appearance on *The Ed Sullivan Show*, playing "Proud Mary." Sullivan's was still the biggest stage in the United States, watched by tens of millions. There was no making it beyond this.

At the theater in Manhattan, all four were more nervous than they'd ever been. They were set up on the customary massive stage, floating apart from each other like separate moons rather than packed tight like they knew best. Morning rehearsal took ninety minutes, and the producer told them that if the big man liked you at rehearsal he would call you over to learn more. After playing their song, they got the gesture from Sullivan. The quartet walked over and stood with their knees locked as the most famous television host in the world went through the cue cards with them and learned their names. Then Sullivan went off for lunch. The production geared up, eventually the doors opened for the audience, and by the time the band saw Sullivan again at taping, he was as drunk as a Berkeley fraternity brother. After "Proud Mary," they alit from their massive risers and met the host at the front of the stage, where he threw his arms around them like an old uncle and called them all the wrong names. When they finally made it offstage and into their fifth-floor dressing room, they exploded in group laughter from excitement and embarrassment. It was less than eighteen months since Tom's PG&E coworkers had laughed at the very idea of his appearing on *Sullivan*. The show ended with a performance by the headliner, Topo Gigio, an Italian puppet mouse and one of Sullivan's favorite returning guests.

John didn't want to lose such a privileged view from the top. It was time to get back in the studio and back on the charts. And this time the band didn't even need to go to L.A. to make the record. Wally Heider, a renowned producer and engineer in L.A. since the 1950s, opened a new studio at 245 Hyde Street in San Francisco. Heider had worked sound at Monterey Pop and recorded Bay Area bands for the big labels. In 1965 he became one of the first producers to go independent and open a private studio, and he modeled it in more of a San Francisco style. No strict working hours and office-style session behavior like at the corporate facilities. Instead, he let his artists have their run of the place and create whatever atmosphere was necessary for their music. Drugs or odd schedules were not a problem. It was only good business to establish an actual San Francisco outpost.

The Hyde Street building was previously used for 20th Century Fox storage. After moving in, Heider constructed rooms based on measurements he learned from the famed Bill Putnam, "Father of Modern Recording." Putnam was the mastermind at Hollywood's United Western Recorders, the magic rooms where Sinatra and the Beach Boys and a hundred others had made their breakthroughs. Wally Heider Studios in San Francisco had the best equipment in town and a spiritual link to the most cherished pop recordings in American history.

An item in *Billboard* in early 1969 announced the new facility with fanfare, touting Heider's huge outlays for sixteen-track mixing boards and consoles, recreational space, and echo chambers. The final paragraph listed the staff, all of whom were poached from other recording institutions except the very final name in the final sentence, Russ Gary, "who moved up here from Heider's L.A. studio." Russ was a Virginia boy originally, suburban all the way, and loved microphones and rock and roll. Lloyd Terry & the Victors, Russ's earlier band, had cut a record at Heider's Los Angeles studio in 1965, with Wally himself behind the boards. But Russ was drawn to that side of the glass. He took his first job apprenticing under a former mixer for the iconic Gold Star Studios, then came under Heider's wing. He only came to San Francisco from L.A. to help wire the place but was soon installed as a full-time recording engineer.

Russ was standing in a hallway among the studio's barely un-packed gear and cables when he saw a short guy in a flannel shirt come into the building alone. Russ assumed he was a worker. In-stead he introduced himself as John Fogerty and asked to have a look around. He played in Creedence Clearwater Revival. Russ was grateful to see someone equally unassuming. He was no match for San Francisco's musical, wardrobe, and lifestyle requirements, and it appeared John wasn't either.

John gave away nothing as he cased the facility. A quick thanks and he was gone. Russ forgot about him. A few days later, Fantasy called to book three hours for Creedence. The day of, the band's roadies arrived an hour beforehand and set up the gear in Studio C. Then, just a few minutes before start time, a limousine arrived on Hyde Street and the band emerged one by one. Doug sprung out like a golden retriever, the happy-go-lucky one. Stu's glasses gave him the air of a professor. Tom, Russ quickly noticed, was the most sensitive of the four. He was always alert to others' unease. And John, though inscrutable and reserved, was clearly the leader.

It was one thing to arrive on time, but Russ noticed another immediate distinction between these guys and the Bay Area groups he was just getting to know. As they got ready to play, the only sub-stances on hand were cigarettes, coffee, and root beer. Before tap-ing, Russ took note of the group's setup. Doug's gear was particularly odd: an enormous snare drum, big enough for a marching band, and eighteen-inch hi-hats, four inches wider than the usual. The sound would be massive, especially since John was asking for echo on the snare. So Russ took a minimalist approach. He put two microphones on the snare to control its tone, one mic above each cymbal to control their volume, then another mic six feet behind Doug for ambient noise. The other instruments were extremely close-mic'd, including John's solid-state Kustom and Stu's heavy-bottomed bass amp. Russ also took some little creative liberties. He put the mics just off-center on the amps' vibrating cones, thinking it could cut down on treble.

The session produced two instrumentals, "Glory Be" and "Briar Patch," that neither the band nor the label had plans for. It was not a complicated day. The band required little postproduction, so Russ gave it a quick mix and handed the tapes over. Once again, John's thoughts were completely unreadable.

A few days later, Fantasy called again. This time it was for an actual session, the new single. Russ had passed the audition and now Creedence Clearwater Revival was dropping the follow-up to "Proud Mary" at his door.

This time was just like the first. The band was all business, devilishly prepared. Nothing required more than a couple takes, and those were just for safekeeping. After the full group got the full rhythm tracks on tape and left, John came back by himself to sing and add background touches like the acoustic guitar on "Lodi." Russ could see that John had it all in his mind. He wanted a little slapback effect, so Russ jerry-rigged a whole setup in an echo box. John would sing or add his parts, then run back into the booth and stand beside Russ to twiddle knobs until all channels were balanced perfectly. John had found a way to bring such incredible space to his records. No instrument stepped on any other.

The songs, too, were undeniable. "Lodi" was a Pete Seeger version of a bluesman's road song. It turned the lonely troubadour into a symbol of grinding labor, and it had the attentive detail of Chuck Berry or Tom T. Hall. John made the endless parade of gigs in small, sad, undifferentiable bars in front of their disinterested patrons sound like punching a time card. Like "Proud Mary," it was a strumming song played entirely on the end of the neck. Anyone could play it, just like anyone who tried to make a career from such a trick could turn out like the self-pitying narrator—lost, ignored, and poor. It was a teary bar song that was produced one degree tighter and shinier than Bob Dylan.

But "Bad Moon Rising" was the shocker. It was nearly a sequel to "Proud Mary," something like its evil twin. Another strummed intro, more outdoors imagery. But instead of escaping, the narrator is awaiting destruction. An apocalypse is brewing and he can only accept it. It rolls in. The best comfort he can offer his listener: "Hope you are quite prepared to die."

John wrote the lyrics based on another old movie, *The Devil and Daniel Webster*, in which a terrible storm destroys a farm. And plenty of bands were singing about incoming calamity in spring 1969. Creedence, though, was different from the Velvet Underground, who sought mystic darkness. Creedence didn't have the Stooges' primal nihilism, either. They were not the Rolling Stones, who, with characteristic nuance, were now channeling Satan. Creedence were never looking for trouble. They were squeaky clean. Even their devil-minded song bounced like old country.

But John's very naive earnestness was his gift. His singing was committed, and his lyrics were life and death. The band captured the feeling of something good turning bad, the bad moon on the rise. Starting with this song, Creedence became the musical encapsulation of their age group's increasing sense of betrayal and disappointment. They captured the anger of watching the world go wrong—the exact feeling Ellen Willis experienced watching wretched men spew bile at a dais full of brave women. Mark Rudd, a militant leader of Students for a Democratic Society, heard the song playing during a June meeting when one of his conspirators agreed to leave that group. The Movement was becoming factionalized. All progress seemed fragile. John had a knack for refining such feelings in just a few words and this moment was no different. "Looks like we're in for nasty weather" might as well have been a bumper sticker.

Of course "Bad Moon Rising" didn't *sound* apocalyptic. It was meant to be a dance song, meant to be for everyone. John's songs might have seemed a little bubblegum to certain audiences, but he was mastering a very specific niche at its moment of highest need: feel-good tunes for feel-bad times.

TWENTY

SMOLDERING

ete Hamill's "The Revolt of the White Lower Middle Class" was published in *New York* magazine, the April 14 issue. The essay was a long first-person tour of the laboring white man's plight in postindustrial America. It was simultaneously protective, defensive, judgmental, and condescending toward its subject, New York's underemployed "working-class whites." Hamill described them as overworked, desensitized by television, and undereducated, with no complex feelings about the world. "Most of them have only a passing acquaintance with blacks, and very few have any black friends," for example, "so they see blacks in terms of militants with Afros and shades, or crushed people on welfare." Hamill shared another secret about his typical joe: "When he gets drunk, he tells you about Saipan. And he sees any form of antiwar protest as a denial of his own young manhood, and a form of spitting on the graves of the people he served with who died in his war."

"Their grievances are real and deep," Hamill wrote, "their remedies could blow this city apart."

Ultimately, Hamill looked to his own class of literary people to take note of the white working class. "Our novelists write about bullfighters, migrant workers, screenwriters, psychiatrists, failing novelists, homosexuals, advertising men, gangsters, actors, politicians, drifters, hippies, spies and millionaires; I have yet to see a work of the imagination deal with the life of a wirelather, a carpenter, a subway conductor, an ironworker or a derrick operator."

As it happened, a debut novel was published to some renown in that same season, rectifying the situation slightly. *Fat City* was written by a thirty-five-year-old named Leonard Gardner and depicted life on the lower rungs of the central California boxing circuit. Its two heroes were Ernie, an eighteen-year-old comer, and Billy, a welterweight in his late twenties on a downhill slide. They drank and tended fitfully to their romantic relationships and traveled the long, punishing roads around Stockton, picking fruit alongside Mexican laborers between bouts. *Fat City* was set in the late 1950s, but its rhythms and angry longing felt attuned to the Vietnam era. Gardner's description of the Central Valley working class was beyond cynical, it was hellish. He described "countless lives lost hour by captive hour scratching at the miserable earth."

The book was set largely in bars in Stockton, perhaps on the same strips where the Golliwogs played. When John, Tom, Doug, and Stu were first learning how to move an audience, they were playing to ruined men like the antiheroes in *Fat City* and Merle Haggard's new hit, "Mama Tried." Those two visions of the place were enough to make life in central California feel like a death sentence in 1969. The double-A single of "Bad Moon Rising" and "Lodi" bound that landscape to apocalypse once and for all. After the single went to no. 2, Lodi, where Leonard Gardner once lived, was now a stock image of depletion and dereliction. On the country charts, pop charts, and in book reviews, it was decreed. Though a decade older than the Creedence men, Gardner resembled them too. He told *Life* magazine that his book's title was lifted from "Negro slang" for the land of milk and honey, "a crazy goal that no one is ever going to reach." He also shared their disillusionment with American creeds, saying that he grew up with a sense that "America was granite. When I realized that the country was coming apart it came as a shock."

For their similar uprightness, Creedence were sometimes called "Boy Scouts" by the Fillmore crowd. It was said mostly in jest, even in envy, given their newfound fame. Paul Kantner, Airplane guitarist and Tom's old St. Mary's schoolmate, teased them most obnoxiously of all. But everyone noticed that Creedence stuck to beer, if that, and only after performances. The Dead were always trying to dose them unsuspectingly. They got Doug once. He poured a cup from the wrong Fillmore coffeemaker before a set, then went down the hallway to the bathroom. The toilet began spinning, then he ran to the sink and saw the muscles of his face in the mirror. He played the set white-knuckled, biting the insides of his cheeks to stay balanced.

"The Boy Scouts of Rock and Roll," then, because now all four were married—Stu to his girlfriend Jacalyn in 1969—not explorers of consciousness or communards in kaftans. Most people meant it well, but the El Cerrito boys were predisposed to take these comments too seriously. They played the ballrooms in San Francisco and they knew people respected them, but there was never going to be a place for them in that scene. They'd often see Janis Joplin in the halls of Fillmore West, where she was invariably teetering and clutching a bottle of Southern Comfort, accompanied by two enormous Hells Angels who steered and cleared the way for her.

"I love y'all," she told them once, with real joy. "You're never playing that stupid psychedelic shit." She promised to come see them anytime they played in town if she wasn't touring. Her word meant something; it seemed that at least half the times they went on-stage in San Francisco from that point on, they saw Janis. But what were they going to do, party with her? Any time they saw her, they were hours late to the party anyway.

The person they most related to was Bill Graham. They gave him no trouble and they met their obligations, just as the cantan-kerous German liked. He expected artists to show up on time, to be in shape, to deliver what the people bought their ticket for. For that attitude alone he could have been a fifth member of the band. As Creedence became more comfortable with him, they would visit in his office sharing stories and philosophies. It reinforced the band's way of thinking to see that they shared it with the most successful promoter alive. Graham would tear into artists for slow-walking their way through the night due to fatigue or, more likely, drugs. He com-plained about Hendrix in particular. In March, Creedence played a four-night residency at Fillmore West and came out for four cur-tain calls each night. Sixteen encores in the city's sacred room, and the Dead still wanted to act like the cooler older brothers? Graham bought them all engraved Omega Seamaster watches and paid them cash bonuses.

They played Fillmore East that month, too, with the Aynsley Dun-bar Retaliation. The *New York Times* sent a reporter, who took note of their "hard, firm rock in a traditional style." After taking a swipe at psychedelic groups, the reporter praised Creedence's "easy-rolling

dynamic rock similar to a lot of early rock." There was nothing Creedence could do to telegraph danger, it seemed. All of John's hoodoos
and haunted swamps, his lost men and oncoming revelations—it all
felt traditional and comforting. A warm blanket.

When they started work on "Green River," John's new song,
it was immediately clear he'd made another beast of a tune. This
was his most aggressive yet, and "Commotion" was even deadlier.
"Green River," however, had a hard, rolling bounce, almost a snap
to it. The melody was snaky and insistent. And the lyrics were more
riparian coming-of-age recollections. By now it could be said that
John had a formula: moody reminiscences about earlier times with
complicated father figures, lived among the marshes. In "Green
River" his narrator recalls another liberated time among bullfrogs
and catfish. He had a rope swing and friendships with the area's in-
digent, left-behind men. The kind who build the rails and the kind
who ride them. The narrator knows them from "Cody's camp,"
where Old Cody Junior confides in him, "You're gonna find the
world is smolderin' / And if you get lost, come on home to Green
River."

Through their first two albums, Creedence played songs onstage
before releasing them. Since "Bad Moon Rising" and now "Green
River," they made the recordings first, which meant John thought
as an arranger instead of a performer. He added acoustic guitar and
a little shaker under Doug's giant swishing hi-hats just for added
swing. Slapback on the vocals. There was no unnecessary feedback
or reverb in his productions. Everything was dry.

Lyrically, John wrote within the formal restrictions of the blues,
and kept his descriptions as skeletal as possible. The wisps of physical detail in the new song could be read as a horror story or a bucolic romance. John insisted that Green River was just the name of

a soda. But the song did grow out of his own real California child-hood. His parents had taken him to Putah Creek, near Winters, between Sacramento and Napa. He might not have known a labor camp on the premises, but "Green River" was, compared to "Born on the Bayou," a personal statement. He'd been somewhere and was thinking back on it, recalling it as a place to come back to when the world was on fire.

He could've used such a place himself. John made his living with a guitar, but he felt like a mug on a factory floor. He'd backed himself into sole responsibility for every aspect of the band's success with minimal share in the rewards. How could he not be nostalgic, even for leaner times? Everything was too complicated now. And he was not prepared for this moment. There were never any records or songs about contracts and business management when he was grow-ing up. He was at sea, even as his greatest successes came.

Around this time, Kathy Orloff, an L.A.-based music writer for the Toledo *Blade*, was invited to see the band's show in Anaheim. She loved the music, but Orloff was even more struck by the men themselves. "From the records, I had the impression they were go-ing to be Mick Jagger and the Rolling Stones—very nitty gritty, tough, above the whole scene," she wrote for her paper. The Stones were in fact preparing their first tour of America since 1966, since Brian Jones's death. Based on their recent preoccupations, it prom-ised to be a Dionysian assault, demonic and sexual. The Stones were committed to that bit now, they always had to up the ante. But Creedence, to Orloff's surprise, were nothing of the kind. "Berke-ley's *Daily Californian* was right when it said they are 'a credit to the business.' They're both, great musicians and beautiful people. Creedence Clearwater Revival is four very nice, personable, articu-late and interested young men. The kind you think you remember from high school when they played all the sock hops and sports nights. They did."

John was mystified. How could he sound like Mick Jagger, feel like a Pete Hamill schlub, and come off like Beaver Cleaver? However it happened, he'd found the perfect combination to prevent anyone from taking him seriously. And he was the only one of the four that critics respected.

TWENTY-ONE

AT THE FEET
OF THE GODS

May brought new milestones. Sales of the self-titled album and *Bayou Country* eclipsed a million dollars each, and Creedence was breaking their own attendance and ticket sales records with seemingly every show. Early in the month they played the Anaheim Convention Center in front of 9,000 people, grossing more than $43,000. Only three weeks later they sold out the 13,000-seat Long Beach Arena and grossed $62,000. They demanded a minimum of $15,000 per concert and 60 percent against the gross, and still had gigs lined up through the summer. Saul Zaentz was fielding regular offers to buy the band's contract. Some offered to buy the entire label. In interviews, he claimed he wouldn't take $6 million for the group. "We have turned down much higher offers than that," he bragged.

These numbers testified to the band's explosive live act and their power as a band. They didn't simply re-create their songs note-perfect onstage—they increased the energy, the volume, and the tempos. Especially after John's tightened grip on the arrangements and recordings, the live show was where Stu, Doug, and Tom got to exhibit their contributions to the Creedence sound. John still sang at an angle to the crowd and still stepped away from the front of the stage to solo. Even though their songs were mostly his, the full effect of their stage show relied on Tom's unwavering rhythm, Stu's smiling enthusiasm, and Doug's thunderous, athletic bashing. They approached live performance like the singles chart: awe the audience, overwhelm them, leave no doubt about the band's dominance.

And yet those perfect songs were beginning to pay off in their own right. The same month that Creedence continuously crushed their own attendance records, Solomon Burke, the big baritone journeyman soul singer, released a new LP for Bell Records, *Proud Mary*, named for the Creedence cover that opened side one. Musically, Burke didn't change too much from the original except to add a blaring horn section, but he added a brief spoken intro explaining that his "forefathers" could only work on a boat like the *Proud Mary*. They were "stokers, cooks, and waiters," not liberated voyagers. "I made a vow that when I grew up I'd take a ride on the ol' *Proud Mary*," Burke intoned before kicking off the first verse. He turned his own singing into an act of historical reclamation; John's song, released only four months earlier, was now a gesture to Burke's ancestors. Burke performed the song on *American Bandstand* and released it as a single, marking the first time John made money from someone else's performance of his song.

Burke was not the only legend who embraced the group. In the spring they went to Nashville's Ryman Auditorium to tape an episode of *The Johnny Cash Show,* which had yet to begin airing. Cash's *At Folsom Prison* album, released the previous year, had made him a revered figure even among rock fans, and the band was indeed starstruck. When they met, John could only get out a single stuttering sentence: "I love you, Johnny Cash."

The big man put his hand on John's shoulder.

"I know, son," he said.

Backstage, big-bellied virtuoso Tut Taylor showed John how to play the dobro. A group of other musical guests comprising Carl Perkins, Roy Orbison, the Statler Brothers, and Minnie Pearl sat around reminiscing about Elvis and old days on the road. John was sitting at the feet of his gods, hearing the origin stories of modern American music.

Flush with growing confidence and newly aware that his songs, not just records or concerts, had a value all their own, John began questioning the contract they still had with Saul. They were receiving 10.5 percent wholesale royalties—a small share even by the extortionate standards of the day—and only half that on tapes. They didn't own their songs at all, which was more typical, even though songs (as opposed to live shows, merchandise, or even record sales) were fast becoming their most valuable asset. For Doug and Stu, the answer was simple: just withhold product. A labor strike, like KMPX. They had the company by the balls. It was nothing without Creedence's songs, John's songs.

But John couldn't imagine staying off the charts that long. They were on a run—how could they stop? They'd been working for ten years for this exact moment and he was already planning their next double-A. By himself, he went to Fantasy to renegotiate the contract, with an eye toward getting ownership of his songs. Saul didn't want to relinquish that, but he offered something else more lucrative, certainly more innovative: a stake in the company.

Ten percent, in fact. No small amount. To be split among the band and cashed out, or not, at each member's sole discretion, in perpetuity. So as their band's success helped the label grow, including through song royalties, they'd all get a piece. Purely monetarily, this was a different kind of contract for a recording artist in 1969. But then John never thought purely monetarily. It didn't give him ownership of his songs, so he walked.

Saul countered with a different arrangement, devised by an attorney in Chicago. In this, the contract was not with Creedence but with "King David Distributors Limited, a Bahamian corporation," an overseas shell company that the band would own. With taxes sheltered from Uncle Sam, Saul explained, the band would effectively receive a one-third increase in royalties.

They signed this one on June 5. The revenue stream made sense, keeping taxes low made sense, so their money was redirected into Fantasy's tortuous new hoarding scheme. And Creedence was now locked into a devastating reality. Instead of a fresh start befitting a band who had conquered the world, the nuts and bolts of this revised contract looked horribly similar to the same straitjacket Saul had tied for them in 1967.

Article 7 of the new document, for example, specified that the band's publishing rights would remain under Fantasy's control through 1970. Only beginning in 1971 could Creedence songs "be assigned by Artists or their respective successors in interest to a publishing company or companies of their choice." Further articles limited the band's cassette and single royalty rates beneath even their previous miserly levels. And Fantasy's lawyers specified that the new royalty rates were based on net profits rather than gross—a classic entertainment industry side step, since it only took a little inventive accounting and investing to reduce net profits to zero on paper. John still didn't own his songs, and he agreed to receive less for the ones that he'd written already. And the most debilitating part of their original deal—the number of recordings owed to Fantasy per year—remained in place. They owed twelve masters in 1969 and 1970, and twenty-four every year after that through 1974. Along with the clause that allowed Fantasy to demand an extra ten masters per year, they owed a potential 180 songs to the label in that time, and if they fell behind then the required tunes would follow them into the next year.

John was still their only business manager. For a twenty-four-year-old with only a high school education and the added stress of writing and recording all their material, he managed some success. In May, for example, he signed a deal with Associated Booking Corporation, an industry-leading company that could get them into venues throughout the world. But the outcome of this so-called negotiation with Fantasy was an utter disaster. John's negotiating tactics were as blunt and desperate as a child's, as was his rage at Saul for breaking the gentlemen's agreement they made back when the Creedence era began. As far as John was concerned, he was being betrayed by a man who he admired like a father.

He wasn't wrong. Doug, Tom, and Stu tried appealing to Saul for mercy. They explained that John was stubborn but didn't speak for all of them. They only wanted what they'd been promised: to rip up the old contract now that they were an established, money-making group. But the fact remained, John was the manager, the

Doug (*left*) and Stu in the 1959–60 school year, when they first began playing seriously with John. *(Courtesy El Cerrito High School Archiving Project)*

John (*back row, second from left*) in the Bass Clef boys' choir during the 1958–59 school year at Portola Junior High. *(Courtesy El Cerrito High School Archiving Project)*

CAPWELL'S

A continuing stream of customers pours into El Cerrito Plaza for opening of Capwell's great department store.

A corner of the Plaza, with wide walkways and planted areas to invite the customers, here heading for restaurant.

Where El Cerrito Plaza now stands, Don Victor Castro more than a century ago built an adobe home for his bride. Bricks from this home have been preserved in a monument at the Center which now covers the land where cattle once roamed and the Don strolled with his bride.

Things have changed since the days of the Dons! Today action on the North Bay Empire scene is kaleidoscopic. New bridges, new highways, new factories, new homes, new people by the thousands all provide new business opportunities. Investigate this great new trading center now.

A few of the thousands of cars parked at the Plaza. Hourly turnover is exceptionally high.

An announcement for the opening of El Cerrito Plaza in 1958, the year that Doug and Stu first met at Portola Junior High. Note the advertisement for Capwell's department store, where Doug's mother worked, and the sly reference to El Cerrito's mafia history: "Things have changed since the days of the Dons!" *(Courtesy of the El Cerrito Historical Society)*

A detail from a collage in the Portola Junior High 1960 yearbook shows Doug on the drums. *(Courtesy El Cerrito High School Archiving Project)*

By 1962–63, their senior year, the boys were looking more grown-up. *(Courtesy El Cerrito High School Archiving Project)*

FALL Student-Body OFFICERS

"El Cerrito's first classes built its spirit to legendary heights, and this spirit has been sustained by each succeeding class. We can insure the superiority of El Cerrito in the future only by working for improvement as we maintain El Cerrito's tradition of spirit."

Bruce Jones, President

President, Bruce Jones; Vice President, Ed Newlin; Secretary, Jan Pezzaglia; Commissioner of Finance, Ellengale Toki; Entertainment, John Fogerty; Publicity, Beth Eaneman; Athletics, John Merit.

John was even a class officer for entertainment. *(Courtesy El Cerrito High School Archiving Project)*

The true face of youthful Southern soul: Booker T. & the MGs during a promotional shoot in the "Green Onions" era. *(Courtesy the Stax Museum of American Soul Music)*

Music played an essential role in protests like the Berkeley Free Speech Movement, which overlapped with Blue Velvets' tenure playing fraternity parties at the university. Above, students play in front of Sproul Hall in November 1964. *(Courtesy the Bancroft Library, University of California, Berkeley)*

THE GOLLIWOGS CIRCA 1965
AKA THE VISIONS

The Golliwogs, suitably dapper for the post–British Invasion era. They had yet to don their tall hats and goofy patterns. *(Getty Images/Michael Ochs Archive)*

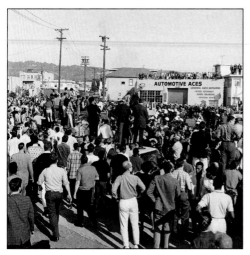

The October 1965 Vietnam Day Committee protest brought thousands out to march from Berkeley to the Oakland Army Base. The group walked past the Monkey Inn during Golliwogs gig night before being stopped at the Oakland line by police. *(Harvey Richards Media Archive)*

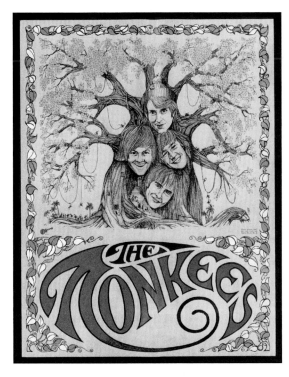

A 1967 promotional item for The Monkees, then the biggest American band in the country, shows that the "prefab four" were embracing a San Francisco aesthetic. The debut Creedence LP, released the following year, had the same woodsy design with hippie affectations, including barely legible font. *(Library of Congress)*

Poster for Creedence's August 1968 appearance at the California State Fair in Sacramento. *(Courtesy of the Special Collection of the Sacramento Public Library)*

KMPX
ON STRIKE

amalgamated american federation of international fm workers of the world ltd.
NORTH BEACH LOCAL No. 1   PHONE — 989-6396

NOTICE

COMMENCING MONDAY, MARCH 18, 1968 — AT 3:00 AM, *AMAL-GAMATED AMERICAN FEDERATION OF INTERNATIONAL FM WORKERS OF THE WORLD, LTD.* (NORTH BEACH LOCAL NO. 1) IS ON STRIKE ! ! !

A.A.F.I.F.M.W.W. IS STRIKING FOR ARTISTIC FREEDOM AND IN THAT INTEREST DEMANDS THE FOLLOWING FROM *CROSBY-PACIFIC BROADCASTING*, OWNERS OF *RADIO STATION KMPX*.

I. That there shall be wage increases commensurate with the increase in station profit, and immediate wage increases to be agreed upon (including wage increases for full-time announcers earning $125.00 per week or less).

II. That the employees shall share in the increase in profits of the radio station.

III. That Harry Rogers, attorney at law, is to have no authority over or supervision of any of the employees, directly or indirectly.

IV. That Tom Donahue and Milan Melvin be reinstated.

V. That Tom Donahue shall have complete control of programming.

VI. That Milan Melvin shall have complete control of sales.

VII. That Paul Boucher shall have complete control of engineering.

VIII. That Harriet Blue shall have complete control of traffic.

IX. That no employee shall be discriminated against for reasons of union activity.

X. That employees shall be paid in full for time on strike.

XI. That all the conditions named herein shall be agreed to in writing before the strike shall be considered settled.

The strike demands from "Amalgamated American Federation of FM Workers of the World, North Beach Local No. 1," i.e., the staff of KMPX, printed in the *San Francisco Express Times* on March 21, 1968.

The American Indian Movement arrives on Alcatraz Island, November 20, 1969. Creedence paid to replace this barge when the US government seized it. *(San Francisco History Center, San Francisco Public Library)*

Ellen Willis in the era when she considered Creedence "the only 'serious' post-Beatle band to deliver one hit single after another, playing classic rock and roll without ever sounding archival." *(Courtesy of Ellen Willis's family)*

Creedence outside the Duck Kee Market in Oakland, play-acting as "Willy and the Poor Boys" for the cover of their third LP of 1969. *(Getty Images)*

Jack Nicholson in Bob Rafelson's *Five Easy Pieces*, dressed in the same working-man outfit as John Fogerty. *(Getty Images)*

Bill Graham at work in May 1971, only months before Creedence closed the Fillmore West. He once gave watches to all four band members, and clearly knew how to pick them. *(Center for Sacramento History)*

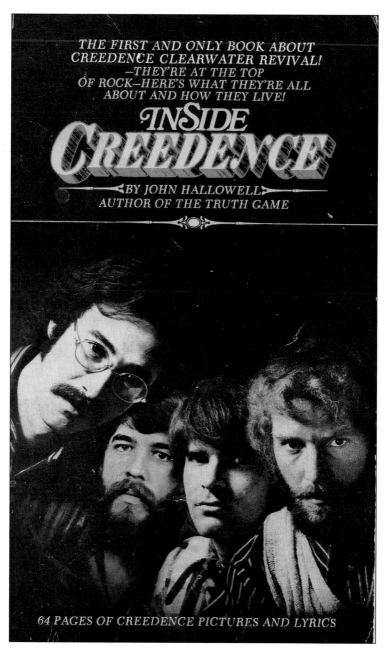

Inside Creedence shared a cover image with Pendulum and was the first CCR product to fall short of expectations.

The trio's final appearance together in public, at the 1993 Rock and Roll Hall of Fame induction ceremony. Tom's son Jeff Fogerty represented his dad, who died in 1990. *(Ken Levy)*

negotiator, and the sole decision maker. And now they knew that Saul was a shark who was willing to exploit John's every tactical weakness, former promises or no.

His bandmates were mystified as to why John wouldn't hire real representation. It was as self-defeating as his insistence on writing every song and handling every creative decision. Doug felt only anger at John's irrational demands for control. Stu felt a bit more sympathetic. To his mind, John was still living in that damp basement in the flatlands. Afraid to have friends over. Afraid to show fear. Stubborn, desperate, and ambitious. And perhaps talented enough to overcome it all.

Meanwhile, Bob Rafelson and Bert Schneider, who started as actual schlockmeisters in the thick of the corporate entertainment world, were now at the bleeding edge of artistic and financial innovation. *Head*, their 1968 psychedelic free-for-all, ended their relationship with the Monkees and they moved full-time into feature film production. They put up $350,000 to finance *Easy Rider*, a new motorcycle picture from Dennis Hopper and Peter Fonda, with Columbia Pictures handling distribution, as with *Head*. They had seemingly cracked the code: creative control with the weight of Hollywood behind them. With a new distribution partner in the mix, Stephen Blauner, they rechristened Raybert Productions as BBS Productions and prepared *Easy Rider* for Cannes and a summer theatrical release.

The film was more than just a druggy happening. It had a point of view and a philosophy. Hopper and Fonda played bikers making their way through the American West for a drug deal. The plot was just a means of getting these men from one place and social setting to another, an odyssey through the fringes of American life. The actors smoked real pot on-screen and cinematographer László Kovács shot parts like a documentary, and others like an experimental western. But most importantly, it had music, an endless stream of it. Like *The Graduate* two years earlier, it revealed its characters' feelings through pop songs, though nothing like the cherubic yearning of Simon and Garfunkel. The movie's soundtrack was a roundup of 1967 and 1968's hard and heady rock standards: the Byrds, the Band, Hendrix, the Holy Modal Rounders. "Proud Mary" would have fit perfectly among them, maybe, but even without their presence on the soundtrack, the movie shared Creedence's preoccupation with lost innocence. "This used to be a hell of a good country," one of the bikers tells the other at one point. Their trip through the cleansing desert ends inevitably in gruesome tragedy, which of course set a new standard for on-screen violence.

"Bad Moon Rising" was high on the *Billboard* Top 10 as *Easy Rider* mania peaked in the summer. Other bands had bigger hits, and the Beatles and Stones were still guaranteed to chart with anything they released, but by summer 1969, Creedence Clearwater Revival already looked like an institution. This song epitomized American mainstream rock as well as any, and no band was sending so many beloved tunes up the chart so reliably. "Bad Moon Rising" wasn't as immediately new or revelatory as some of *Easy Rider*'s songs were, but not every young person—not even every transgressive young person—was looking to strike out on a chopper for free love and existential exploration. Some feared the oncoming storm.

Many, for example, were moved by the Vietnam Moratorium Committee, which began in June 1969. This group had its roots in the Clean for Gene movement, which supported antiwar candidate Eugene McCarthy for president in 1968. That year, young canvassers went door-to-door in suits and skirts to put a mainstream, nonthreatening face on the antiwar movement. The Moratorium Committee vowed to continue that work during Nixon's administration. The co-founders shared a belief that the Movement was growing too divisive and violent. So many sects and causes were becoming militant and independent. Stokely Carmichael was head of the Student Nonviolent Coordinating Committee, Redstockings was planning their next protest event, and even as the Moratorium made its own pact, another group was gathered in Chicago at the Students for a Democratic Society convention, writing the tenets for the Weathermen, a self-proclaimed "clandestine revolutionary party." They set their sights on a previously unseen form of protest, a mass action in a major city, bent on property destruction. Whatever it took to show the extent of their moral objection to the war.

The Moratorium leaders ultimately wanted the same kind of revolution, and they weren't simply squeamish about violence. They just felt it was ineffective as a political tool. Their goal was to appeal to nonradicals by rejecting, or at least minimizing, the more incendiary and visible elements of confrontational leftism. They sought a "broad-based" antiwar movement that didn't feature Viet Cong flags or seek to freak out mainstream society, including labor. As Pete Hamill showed, this was not a population that wanted to hear about moral objections and civil unrest from hairy young men who'd never served. David Mixner, one of the cofounders, had family who had served in Vietnam, including some who died, an experience that put him in league with an increasingly high number of Americans. Their pitch was appealing: middle-of-the-road progressivism. And they knew it would work. They began planning an October event of their own, this one big and peaceful rather than subterranean and dangerous.

In June, as these two operations began, Creedence made their first-ever trip to Memphis. A show at the Mid-South Coliseum opened another of their short travel bursts, this one to Houston and Dallas with a white soul band as openers, Butterscotch Caboose. They arrived in Bluff City a day early to make two pilgrimages. For the first, they got to the gates of Graceland but were told, like many Elvis fans before them, that the King was not at home, whether that was true or not.

At the second, however, it was just another workday at Stax Records. Creedence's reputation preceded them by this point, and of course the label and their effective house band, Booker T. & the MGs, knew the songs that everyone else did. But the Creedence guys felt humbled before them. They knew how many uncredited sessions the MGs had played, how many immortal hits they solidified. Stu and Doug knew Duck Dunn's and Al Jackson Jr.'s playing down to the note. They were north stars while the Blue Velvets and the Golliwogs wandered all those many years, trying to find their style.

Jim Stewart, Stax's president, came out to greet them in the lobby, expressing his thanks and excitement. With their label worries front-of-mind, the band joked about jumping ship, knowing Saul would never free them. Stewart took them around, showed the band everything on the premises, before dropping them off at the studio, where all but Al Jackson Jr. were present and working.

"Me and Cropper were driving down the highway in our Cadillac listening to 'Born on the Bayou,' trying to figure out where in Louisiana you were from," Duck told them. "When we found out you were from California we broke your records." He laughed like mad. They felt like family with him instantly.

Steve Cropper and Booker T. Jones were by the mixing board. They were equally friendly but couldn't match Duck's unflagging energy. Few could. Jones, the nominal front man though he never sang, was some kind of savant—barely older than John, Doug, and Stu, he became famous by writing and recording "Green Onions" when he was still a teenager. Then for four years he split his time between weekends at the Memphis studio, playing Hammond B-3 and arranging songs like Carla Thomas's "B-A-B-Y," and weekdays at Indiana University's famed music program, where he learned transcription, notation, arrangement, music theory, and most important of all, respect for regimen. As if that weren't enough, he matched that with a military zeal, having served as battle group commander in a student program at Booker T. Washington High School. He never saw combat, but he could dismantle an M1 blindfolded by the time he recorded "Green Onions." Like John Fogerty, he had a knack for every aspect of music and an accompanying perfectionist's streak. Unlike John, he had the educational rigor to back it up, though that wasn't their biggest difference. That rested in Jones's studio approach. He was a leader but not a dictator. He left room for the others' contributions, from writing to solos. And of course, most of his work, certainly his most lucrative work, came as a sideman. He was also a stoically handsome guy who never lacked options for women. He had plenty of ego, but he never brought that to his music-making. It made him just as happy to arrange someone else's song as it did to play his own.

When it came time to leave, Doug tried to hide his disappointment at not meeting Al Jackson. The band walked out to the parking lot in the middle of a rainstorm, just as Jackson pulled in. Doug ran up to the man's car with rain pouring down his enormous beard and yelled, "You're my idol! I've been borrowing from you for years!" He had spent so much of his life running toward his dreams that he'd

TWENTY-TWO

SONGS FOR
EVERYONE

"Newport '69," as its organizers called it, had no relation to the long-running Rhode Island jazz and folk festivals with that name, and it didn't even take place anywhere called Newport. The event was held in the Devonshire Downs fairgrounds in Northridge, California, just west of Van Nuys in the San Fernando Valley. The Jimi Hendrix Experience were headlining for a rumored $100,000, more than one-third of the total expenditures for bands. Their presence alone ensured that tickets would sell out. But the nation's concert promoters and producers were crazed with ambition during this spring and summer. Though the social and political movements of the time were splintering, commerce was booming, and a whole economy grew from the goal of herding young people around stages for days. Music fans were willing to come from everywhere to attend these massive druggy be-ins, and enterprising promoters in every city could potentially assemble a couple days' worth of bands; scrounge together enough parking, toilets, and water for a miniature city; and hang on for dear life.

Newport '69, held June 20 to 22, wasn't the first festival of the season, and in fact a similar event, the Miami Pop Festival, was held in December 1968. Monterey was still the model, with its international sounds and peace-flag aesthetic. Newport heralded the new era at hand, however, one in which crowds seemed to grow beyond any existing capacity to serve or even entertain them. Creedence headlined Saturday, when the party was still relatively under control. They were just one fifty-minute gunshot among a three-day bill that made Bill Graham's Fillmore marathons seem muted and restrained.

The music began with Love Exchange, and then proceeded through a cross-genre roundup of bands big and small unlike anything seen in rock, at least not on the West Coast. Southwind. Albert Collins. Friends of Distinction. Jethro Tull. Charity. The Rascals. Jerry Lauderdale. Three Dog Night. Spirit. The Womb. Booker T. & the MGs. Flock. The Grass Roots. Buffy Sainte-Marie. Love. Poco. Lee Michaels. Steppenwolf. Taj Mahal. Sweetwater. The Ike & Tina Turner Revue. Joe Cocker. The Chambers Brothers. The Edwin Hawkins Singers. Brenton Wood. Eric Burdon. The Byrds. Marvin Gaye was supposed to play but missed his plane.

Even with tickets set high—$7 per day or $15 for the whole weekend—the crowd grew beyond capacity. Parking was minimal. The promoters, who had already botched multiple previous smaller concerts, didn't provide enough toilets. Large portions of the crowd couldn't hear the music at all. Gate-crashers made it over the reinforced hurricane fencing or simply toppled it. Teens below driving age made it to the event, where they met an atmosphere of free acid, free love, and car campers. The weekend attracted a rumored two hundred thousand people over the course of the three days, and the goings-on also included prowling gangs and sexual assault. Friday night, after a lackluster Jimi Hendrix performance, someone in the crowd shot a flare at a circling police helicopter.

On Saturday, the most punishingly hot afternoon of a brutal weekend, wild-eyed and boiling concertgoers roamed the area around the fairgrounds, stepping on residents' flowers gardens and swimming in their pools. Some of the feistier, younger contingent found a nearby shopping center and stole food and broke windows. Others threw rocks at police, who responded by grabbing any young people they could catch and beating them with nightsticks. Most attendees weren't even aware that such bedlam was taking place. Plenty had driven in from far away bearing peace signs and wanting only to swim in the mega-sized vibe cultivator, the latest "biggest rock festival ever."

Creedence had played an event called the Garden State Rock Festival in May, appearing with Chuck Berry as one showcase night of five. But Newport '69 was Creedence's first experience with the new colossal event trend. And they delivered, ending day two on a familiar positive note, playing all their hit singles so far and a few requisite oldies covers. There were more than fifty thousand people in the crowd, an unimaginable number for any band on their own. John, Tom, Doug, and Stu could barely see the full audience while they played, and god only knew how many could even hear their set. But they learned quickly that you can *feel* the presence of fifty thousand people, even if some are nodding off or tussling with the biker gang security a half mile away. Even in the dark, under the California sky.

Sunday, things finally got out of hand. Now the teens threw rocks at the Don Ellis Orchestra, a progressive big-band jazz group, and the cops responded brutally like always. Overall, the weekend saw nearly two hundred arrests, dozens of injuries (including police), tens of thousands of dollars in property damage, and massive losses for the organizers. The biggest concert ever was an unmitigated disaster—even *Rolling Stone* said so. But the summer of rock couldn't be stopped.

On June 27, Creedence played the Denver Pop Festival, which was at least held in Mile High Stadium rather than a semirural suburb. Once again they headlined, going on well past midnight on Saturday after Tim Buckley, Johnny Winter, Poco, Zephyr, and Aorta. And once again the event devolved into violence. Municipal police were hired as security. When the fence-hopping began during the afternoon before Creedence's set, the cops used tear gas to keep order. At Newport, the weapon of choice was a nightstick, but in Denver, the wind swept up the gas and moved it through the festival crowd, choking and blinding the tens of thousands of attendees. Things cleared by the time Creedence performed their fifty minutes that night, only to devolve again on Sunday, when thousands of young people outside the gates began tossing beer bottles and rocks at police inside during Jimi Hendrix's performance. A riot nearly followed their set as police set off more gas. Hendrix and his group were hustled into an empty van for safety, only to have the vehicle set upon by hundreds of gas-fearing young people who climbed atop and nearly crushed it. It was a crazed end for the Jimi Hendrix Experience; shortly after the festival, bassist Noel Redding returned to England and declared the trio was over.

Another week, another messy try for collective musical transcendence. The Atlanta International Pop Festival started on the Fourth of July and was another instant sprawling cacophony. The event took place at Atlanta International Raceway outside the city and advertised as "More Blues/Psychedelic/Soul/Jazz/Rock Legends than ever assembled before anywhere." Creedence headlined on Independence Day, playing after Dave Brubeck with Gerry Mulligan, Johnny Winter, Canned Heat, and others, including their friends Booker T. & the MGs. It was a bluesy, soulful lineup, but the afternoon was a logistical disaster. There were no trash cans, no chairs, and too little food. Eventually the organizer began giving away watermelon, the dust-covered rinds of which soon littered the grounds. Vendors loudly sold drugs. "Acid, acid! Get it while I'm here!" one shouted. Hours before Creedence performed, keyboardist Al Kooper took the stage with his own announcer and a conductor-led horn section. His set included a cover of "Proud Mary."

This was all a long way from Deno & Carlo, Creedence's home base barely a year ago. They had tried for ages to get into the Fillmore or on KYA, then it took barely a full turn of the seasons to get a spot on *Ed Sullivan*. A few months after that and they were playing for the largest music crowds ever assembled. Certainly John's productivity helped matters. He had wanted radio success since middle school, and now he had it. But he was prolific at the right time, too. The music business was moving at a different pace and on a different scale than even just a few years earlier. A headlining spot at Newport, Denver, Atlanta, or Woodstock, still being planned for August in upstate New York, was an accomplishment that didn't even exist when the band took shape and began working. It didn't even really exist when they released their first album. Now they were playing to audiences that big every week.

Even out on their own, without dozens of other bands, their crowd sizes were seemingly multiplying every time they left for one of their quick road jaunts. Playing the ballrooms wasn't even really possible anymore; they had outgrown that scene as fast as they'd entered it. But Creedence was capable of filling basketball and hockey arenas that held tens of thousands of people. On one midwestern swing they played Cleveland's Public Hall, which held ten thousand, then Detroit's Olympia Stadium, which held fifteen thousand. These crowds weren't diffuse and embattled like the festivalgoers, they were enthralled. The Beatles didn't perform any more and the Stones hadn't been stateside since 1966. Dylan was in seclusion. After *Music from Big Pink*, the Band played their first shows in spring of 1969, though they were still more beloved as a living rock and roll myth than a charting pop band. Other groups on their festival bills—from Ike and Tina Turner to Booker T.—were older or more influential, but no band was bigger or had more momentum than Creedence as they stormed through July 1969, the month that "Green River" began its march to the Top 10.

They also found a hungry audience overseas: "Proud Mary" only went to no. 8 in the UK, but for a time in summer 1969 it was ubiquitous in London, floating out of bedroom windows and transistor radios. One music writer marveled, "It's years since any one number has been so pervasive." The song was a Top 10 hit in Germany as well. In their earliest practices together a decade earlier, their biggest possible notion of fame was a single on the radio and a 45 in the record store. But they had instead become the poster children of the superstar-band era. Their music summoned crowds of hundreds of thousands and filled Bahamian trusts. People *needed* them. At one of their increasingly rare shows at the Fillmore East, a young man was hanging around near the back of the venue, talking guitars with John and questioning him about gear, recording, all of John's real lifelong obsessions. In a moment of unprompted and uncommon generosity, John gave the kid the Rickenbacker that he used to record "Suzie Q."

Maybe he was grateful for the momentary connection with a stranger. Every other relationship was strained. The second quarter of 1969 was four times more successful than any previous quarter for Fantasy, yet Saul was hardly the garrulous patriarch that he had once been. There was too much money on the line, and John was growing suspicious about the fate of his songs. Worldwide fame didn't guard John from the difficulties of young fatherhood and marriage, either. He came home from his record-breaking tours and still found himself struggling to keep things happy at home. He took no breaks. When he wasn't traveling, he was writing, and Martha felt understandably cast aside. She took the kids to her mother's.

A phrase entered John's mind: "I wrote a song for everyone, and I couldn't even talk to you." He thought of those metastasizing crowds, the journalists and reviewers who covered his work like he was reconnecting American young people to their own history, the icons—Solomon Burke, Al Kooper—who found personal meaning in his songs. And yet his own wife, mother of his children, was tired of the single-mindedness that made it possible.

"Wrote a Song for Everyone," the tune that emerged from that paradox, was the first ballad that John wrote, and the slowest, longest song on the LP that they finished at Wally Heider Studios that summer. The song's most prominent instrument was acoustic guitar, and John even tempered his raring drawl to something like a croon. It felt and sounded like personal songwriting, not only a well-made record. But even in this semiautobiographical mode, John reached beyond himself. As in "Lodi," he sang from the vantage of a much less successful person. His narrator is on welfare, scared of being sent to war, on the cusp of jail time. And though the final lines of the third verse reference "pharaohs" leading the country into carnage, John ultimately felt sympathetic to the people in power who were unable to communicate with their own sons and daughters. He recognized that he was better equipped to speak for strangers than to speak for himself. He couldn't help but reach for universality.

Green River was released in August, just after the moon landing. For the third time, a Creedence album cover featured the band posing in the woods, though this time everyone was clearly visible, especially John, who stood in front of the others with an acoustic guitar. Of course it went to no. 1. In the middle of that month, they went to Hollywood to tape a performance on *The Andy Williams Show*. Williams was synonymous with the mainstream at this point. He would showcase young bands, but he was just as likely to have on Bobby Darin or Dick Van Dyke. The staging for Creedence's performance of "Green River" reflected the producer's assumed audience. Coming back from commercial, a large, young dance team moved through the crowd and onto the stage, dressed as a marching band, complete with instruments. A toothless flower-power anthem played while off-screen women sang, "In this world of troubled times, we all want survival / One solution seems to be—Creedence Clearwater Revival." When the smoke from the fog machine parted, there was John and his flannel shirt, accessorized that day with a fringed brown suede vest.

The band perfectly re-created "Green River" while the dancers remained posed and unmoving around them. John seemed positively loose by comparison. He had actual charisma in that vest. Creedence's television performances were also chances to see the band's musicianship up close, and for a band on the heavier side of the pop world, they played their instruments almost delicately. Perhaps it was a habit from their years in small venues. You had to find the nuances of your own playing when your music was ringing off the nearby walls and everyone around you was screaming. It gave them such focus, and you could see it on a TV soundstage the same way Russ Gary saw it at Heider Studios, the way they stood glued to their marks, effortlessly assembling the swing in "Green River" as every instrument fell into place behind John's melodies. The song faded out on record and the band re-created that effect, becoming quieter and quieter as the stage lights dimmed until one final down-beat signaled that the audience could clap. The entire performance was barely three minutes including the surreal opening number. It was watched by millions, by people who otherwise watched *Andy Williams* to see the Osmonds.

Creedence left on a red-eye to New York, where a few cars picked them up for a drive into the Catskills. They slept a few hours before a private jet took them the final leg into Bethel for the Woodstock Music and Art Festival, which was predicted to be the grandest of all such gatherings. Approached from above, the crowd was like a wonder of the world. Biblical, Tom thought. The lack of police helped keep things relatively subdued. There was no property or stadium to protect, just a massive field with an estimated half-million young people who, perhaps because of the summer's earlier calamities, were intent on keeping the vibes peaceful, druggy, and communal.

Creedence was the first band to sign on to the festival. Back in April, before their rate and popularity truly exploded, they agreed to a one-hour set for $10,000—the most money they'd seen up to that point for a concert. They arrived early on Saturday, which was almost a San Francisco showcase. Santana, Janis, and the

Dead were scheduled to appear before Creedence, and Sly & the Family Stone and the Jefferson Airplane were due on after. When Creedence arrived, they found the Dead and Santana were already into the acid, so instead they connected with one of Bill Graham's assistants, who prepared them a dinner of steak and wine in a secluded trailer.

They played their set after the Grateful Dead, who unsurprisingly went long but surprisingly never hit the instrumental peaks that they were known for. Their set was also halted by malfunctioning amps. It was well past midnight by the time Creedence took the stage—the darkest part of night, in the country, after the audience had been sapped by two days of sun and hallucinogens. It appeared that the kings of Haight Street had just lulled the entire crowd to sleep. Creedence saw nothing from the stage and could barely hear a soul clapping between songs. John's guitar and Stu's bass crackled and went silent at different points, and John didn't feel the set met their standard.

He might have been the only one with that opinion. This was not a band that had off nights. Not anymore. They weren't going to play "Born on the Bayou" perfectly seven hundred times in a row and then fall apart on the seven-hundred-and-first. And they did not do so at Woodstock. On the shaking plywood stage, Stu's bass was a giant, steady force moving through John and Tom's guitars. He played melodies on the neck of his bass occasionally too, including some that John wrote into the songs. Tom had become a truly artful rhythm guitarist, with a style that was specifically built for the band—his upstroke attuned to Doug's snare, his downstroke connected to Stu's bass. He knew how to disappear into their songs so the band members all sounded like one thing. Wherever a song structure went, he was underneath, deepening it and holding it together. And though he'd get no credit for it, he filled the songs when his brother took his solos and screaming guitar runs.

John's solos at Woodstock were a copy of the recorded versions of his songs, if a bit faster and, thanks to the band, more forceful and insistent. His showcase, still, was "Chooglin'," which ended the proper set before they played "Suzie Q" for an encore. After the intro riff established the band's tempo and feel, he sang the title phrase, the first verse, the riff, the second verse, the title, and began a solo. The solo as always started with a triplet lick done twice, then two more times an octave higher. By now the band was a massive crashing wave behind him: Stu's one-note thud, Doug's ringing cymbals, and Tom's unceasing, unsettling major-seventh chord played as a backbeat throughout. When John finished his guitar workout, he put it down and grabbed a harmonica. The groove kept on, so unflaggingly insistent, as John poured a wild four minutes' breath through that harp and into the microphone on its other side. Then he picked up his guitar again and shrieked on its highest frets for another couple minutes before returning to the mic. After a final chorus, the band ran the song off into the stratosphere, racing it fast enough that they eased unavoidably into white noise. A more heavily drugged band, a more committedly exploratory band, a band who enjoyed each other's company more, even just a band that wanted to cherish the sensation of performing for a half-million people—any of them might have dragged out their set a few minutes longer than usual given the circumstances. Not Creedence. When those four got onstage, you got no fat.

Creedence had come to conquer the charts so quickly that it was easy to take them for granted, and Woodstock was the biggest showcase they'd ever had for the other side of their work, the live show. Creedence's performance at Woodstock, whatever John felt about it, left others starstruck. Leslie West, who played earlier in the day with his band Mountain, marveled as the El Cerrito guys moved from one wildly popular song to another like a self-contained jukebox. Back-to-back, their run of hits was a pure rush. John Sebastian, ringleader of the Lovin' Spoonful, couldn't believe what a solid, tight four-piece force they were onstage.

The Who were on hand as well, preparing to play after Creedence, between Sly and the Airplane. Two years earlier they had rolled into Monterey and delivered a blitzkrieg of souped-up R&B that climaxed in a fury of destroyed instruments. In 1969, they were touring something even more ambitious: a fully composed two-LP rock opera, *Tommy*, that they played in full every show. Singer Roger Daltrey no longer dressed like a swinging London dandy. He had grown out his blond curls to shoulder length and wore outfits that exposed his glistening, muscled chest. He was a superhero, a self-styled demigod—how else could he deliver *Tommy*'s challenging, epic narrative? At Woodstock Daltrey wore a fringed white leather jacket that made him look like a glowing white dove in the stage lights. But it was a long, exhausting, uncertain day before he took the stage to deliver the Who's boundary-breaking artistic statement, a day full of waiting and boredom. The fog lifted momentarily as he stood in the wings watching Creedence tear through their customary setlist, from "Born on the Bayou" to "Keep On Chooglin'." His own four-piece band was pushing rock music to the furthest reaches of artistic seriousness and wild showmanship, but of all the music Daltrey heard that weekend, none hit him so hard as the quartet from the East Bay playing bluesy rave-ups in the still of the night.

TWENTY-THREE

THE ACCEPTANCE
OF DEATH

Stu Steinberg arrived in Vietnam in September 1968 as a volunteer, not a draftee. He'd been in the Army for two years and spent the previous six months at the Dugway Proving Ground in Utah, a major testing site for chemical weapons and nerve agents. Right before Steinberg left for the war, this unholy place was the site of the infamous "Dugway sheep incident," in which thousands of animals died from chemical exposure on farmland well outside the base. He was among the first on the scene, taking stock of an endless expanse of rotting animals. After a week on the cleanup team, picking through the remnants of a mass chemical livestock die-off, Steinberg was ready for a change. Any change. Even Nam.

He was aware it would be terrible. Khe Sanh was in the news, and Tet was still a scar in the nation's psyche. Soldiers reported to

Dugway after serving in country, and even if they didn't share much about the experience, the numbers were staggering. By the time Steinberg got his orders, thirty-three thousand US troops were dead. But Dugway was a kind of living death, so after saying goodbye to his family in Virginia, he left on a military plane from San Francisco and landed in Quy Nhơn, where US forces had installed a giant naval base on the South China Sea.

When he arrived in Vietnam, Steinberg didn't think it was possible that he could be killed. He was young and invincible, for one, and since he was familiar with chemical and biological materials, he was placed on the bomb squad, Explosive Ordnance Disposal, or as that prideful, death-defying community referred to themselves, "E-O-fucking-D!" They performed one of the most dangerous and respected jobs in the entire military: detecting, defusing, and detonating enemy bombs. Obviously some of them died, but to perform that task you nevertheless had to bet on your fearlessness and education against your own common sense, every time. Stu and his team trained with nerve agents and chemical gas. They exposed their skin to poisons just to know what the reactions looked like. And this was only their lab training. In the field, EODs worked without flak jackets. Those only made it harder to move. And if you messed up, there wasn't a jacket in the world that could save you anyway.

Steinberg was a rocker. He arrived with the debut LPs by Savoy Brown and Cream in his bag and quickly discovered that every other guy brought their own records as well. EOD crews were tight bands of ten, and you build intimacy in a hurry when your work involves the constant possibility of instant death. When they weren't out in enemy territory, they were back on base, listening to the R&B and soul that the Black guys brought. The soldiers in Vietnam were the first fully desegregated military force in US history, and notably younger than those in previous wars. Music was a shared language, essential to everyone, and a way to fill the frequent long waiting periods between missions. And the musical scene had changed significantly since the first US troops in Vietnam blared Pat Boone in 1965.

At first Steinberg's group didn't have stereo equipment. They listened to the radio. But the post exchange, the PX, had a huge record and electronics section. Soon he had an enviable hi-fi, all Pioneer gear, including a reel-to-reel, great big speakers, receiver, and a new-model record player. He went regularly to the PX with his closest friend Roger and never left without buying. One trip in early 1969, he got a typical haul: another Savoy Brown album, one by Hendrix, one from the Stones, and the tree-lined debut record from Creedence so he could have "Suzie Q," which he recently heard on Armed Forces Radio. Only a few months later, Creedence was everywhere on that station, as they were stateside.

In 1969 and 1970, US troops purchased half a million radios, 178,000 reel-to-reel tape decks, and 220,000 cassette records. By 1969, about a third of troops—and half of those who were still teenagers—listened to music more than five hours a day. The military stocked LPs and stereo goods in every PX to keep troops from growing depressed or even mutinous. As in California motorcycle chop shops, some soldiers even made a sport out of building sound systems piecemeal from elements purchased or swapped on base. Music was the primary driving force of social life for everyone.

Creedence's musical and production styles, even their lyrics and song titles, were perfectly suited to all the typical musical settings in Vietnam. The radios often sounded small and tinny. Usually you'd hear one blaring from someone's bag as you entered a tent, or from above a bar in the PX. Creedence sounded great on those things. Their melodies cut straight through any conversation, and the rhythm was distinct enough that it didn't get lost either. On nicer equipment you could pick up the delicate mixing or John's guitar tones. Or maybe in the bush at night, alone with only nine other guys and your tape deck, maybe with an enemy afoot, those songs could make you feel strong. At least one tank crew christened their vehicle "Proud Mary." Other squadrons had theme songs, like one who called themselves the Buffalo Soldiers and blasted "Bad Moon Rising" into the dark jungle before their attacks. Plenty of the fan mail that showed up at the Creedence headquarters, the Factory, came from military addresses in Asia.

Creedence joined the highest pantheon of Vietnam music. Like Jimi, Aretha, and Marvin, they defined the aesthetic of the war. Like those others, John Fogerty's voice was pure honesty. He took no shortcuts. His songs were made from simple parts, but that only made the final product more incredible. He made music worthy of those moments in the jungle with just a joint and a tape, pretending Creedence or Hendrix was with you, waiting for a possible explosion or ambush, unsure if you'd ever see another sunrise.

In the cities, in less perilous moments, you might see an incredible cover band, all women, playing American and British songs. The famous Seoul Sisters, in Long Bình, were one such group, and played the Ventures, the Supremes, Johnny Cash, and Creedence, whose major hit made their accents unavoidably indelible: "Lollin' on a liver." Other bands came from the Philippines or Korea just to entertain the Americans. Often they spoke no English and learned songs phonetically. But the bands were phenomenal. GIs rarely performed for each other in clubs; they couldn't do better. For most of them, music was a soundtrack and an escape, not

a pursuit. Every day, men in Vietnam heard bands or songs, sometimes unconsciously, in a field or a tent or a bar or a chopper, and
anointed them with the emotional intensity of their ongoing reck-
onings with mortality and broken trust. Music colored the whole
demonic world.

These men were already in a state of escalating faithlessness
about the war by the time Creedence's music appeared in PX record
bins. Polls showed collective idealism about the US presence col-
lapsing simultaneous with Creedence's rise in 1969, and the band's
music even reflected the soldiers' attitude. It was direct, unromantic,
brotherly, and haunted by visions of a world in decay. In other sur-
veys, soldiers increasingly equated maturity and poise with an "acceptance of death." Creedence met that challenge directly: *Hope
you are quite prepared to die.*

Stateside, many people were having similar epiphanies. A Gallup poll in 1969 found that, for the first time, most respondents felt
it had been a mistake to send troops into Vietnam. Here too, Creedence captured the era's sense of betrayal and disappointment, the
anger of recognizing a world gone wrong. And nothing embodied
that feeling more than the war.

The draft was still in effect, and thanks to bootstrap-government
initiatives, was still pulling more Black and poor white boys than
ever out of their towns and families, into a war that was not getting
less deadly. After so many years there was no longer any kidding
about the lopsidedness of it all. Across the United States, local draft
boards of "upstanding citizens" decided which boys effectively lived
or died. Barely a handful of these upstanding souls were nonwhite.
The southern boards were known for special cruelty, as when civil
rights activists Bennie Tucker and Hubert Davis filed to run for city

offices in Mississippi and got their draft notices shortly after. When another leader in similar circumstances reported for his physical a few minutes late, he was given a five-year prison sentence.

Boards arbitrarily granted deferments for only some fathers and hardship cases, but for all who were rich enough to attend college. Even jobs with Lockheed and Dow Chemical—even Honeywell, making ovens—were considered exempt out of "national interest." It was no secret where those companies got their workforce, either. Throughout the 1960s, about three thousand men graduated every year from Harvard, Princeton, and MIT. And through the whole decade, fewer than twenty died in Vietnam. It was all so glaringly *unfair*. That was the feeling that tightened people's skin. *New York Times* columnist James Reston wrote that the Selective Service was "a system whereby poor boys are selected to go to Vietnam and rich boys are selected to go to college."

In the summer and early fall, the band practiced and recorded an instrumental that John was calling "Fortunate Son." John had them hammering the music down for more than a month before his lyrics came. He wanted the bass to pound and the guitar to snarl. Creedence worked at the Factory and played the odd sport complex during the earliest months of growth and planning for the Vietnam Moratorium Day movement, which inspired protest events in thousands of communities, including Muskogee, the small town that Merle Haggard had just made synonymous with hippie bashing. More than two million people participated in these marches altogether on October 15, the largest antiwar protest to that point.

John wrote the words to "Fortunate Son" quickly, even by his standards. Twenty minutes, he said. The entire band read the fan mail they received from Vietnam. The letters weren't written by private school boys from Sacramento. They weren't even by El Cerrito Highlanders. Being who he was, having experienced an actual training camp and known the kind of guys who ended up in those caskets on TV, John didn't need a spur to write about these feelings, though the television images of Julie Nixon and David Eisenhower, two dynasts in love, left him enraged. That made the words flow.

"Fortunate Son" went to no. 14, an underperformance for John, but that only made it a relatively countercultural commodity. The civilian antiwar movement adopted it as a standard anthem, of course, though it wasn't technically an antiwar song. Not a word of it concerned anti-violence, or even Vietnam. Ultimately it was a working-class song. It was about rich boys getting away with things and poor boys getting punished. Just like "Born on the Bayou" or "Porterville."

But the song made perfect sense in Vietnam. Anyone in country could sing "Fortunate Son" and mean every word. To sing "It ain't me" in the jungle was to tell the war to fuck off while still doing your duty. The narrator of "Fortunate Son" doesn't contemplate draft-dodging, not that the listener knows of. He'd probably fight if asked. He would learn the same lesson that Stu Steinberg and his E-O-fucking-D crew learned. The same lesson taught by the "I-Feel-Like-I'm-Fixin'-to-Die Rag" in Country Joe's mordantly sarcastic manner, and by "2 + 2 = ?," the terrifying antiwar track on the Bob Seger System's 1969 debut, *Ramblin' Gamblin' Man*. He would learn the acceptance of death.

Stu lived. He was in Vietnam just under two years. Things did not improve. Not in general morale, not in Stu's own mental health. Not in the American goals for the war, either. He was sent into enemy territory and bomb-filled caves. His close friends died. In December 1969 he watched from two hundred yards as a group of soldiers

TWENTY-FOUR

TOGETHER
AND APART

"Fortunate Son" was a bolt of anger. Its flip side, "Down on the Corner," was the exact opposite, and more popular. It had a bouncy, near-calypso beat and lyrics about a group of small-town buskers, Willy and the Poor Boys. It wasn't an obvious musical direction for Creedence. Even snappy "Bad Moon Rising" was heavy by comparison. This was John leaning into the cornpone in his world-building and his voice, then adding a beat and a hook that a baby could play. Simply put, another dance song, Sly Stone a little slower and mellower. It went to no. 3.

"Down on the Corner" was one of John's old-time fantasias, like a scene that the riverboat rider from "Proud Mary" would stumble onto if he disembarked at the next port town. John wrote it while the band was in Los Angeles for the *Andy Williams* taping and based all the characters on the four Creedence members. There was Willy, the dancing leader, clearly John himself. Then Blinky, a play on Stu's glasses and nervous nature. Poor Boy was Tom, since John felt he could be self-pitying, and Rooster was Doug, who John felt was a strutting, cocksure bantam. John even repeated the earlier song's free and easy attitude about money matters: "You don't need a penny just to hang around / But if you've got a nickel, won't you lay your money down?" John's utopia was a place where people shared money for camaraderie's sake, a poignant photo negative of the societal sketch in "Fortunate Son" where everything was hoarded.

After a summer of festivals and more hit songs, Creedence was wealthy enough to justify splurging on their own tours and gigs. Standard procedure now included a chartered flight to the next city, solo hotel rooms for everyone, and individual limos to and from the venue. They kept to their no-drinking policy before gigs, but there was plenty of beer afterward. In addition to their sound crew and road manager Bruce Young, they now employed Jake Rohrer, the former auto salesman, as a publicist and media manager. Rohrer brought in his sister Mary to serve as a secretary, and it was her idea to inaugurate *The Fifth Street Flash*, a quarterly fan club newsletter.

This was mind-bogglingly opulent living by the standards of their R&B and rock and roll legends, not to mention every band on earth except the Stones. The sports arenas offered excitable screams and rapturous, huge crowds, but they lost the boundaryless interplay between backstage and audience that defined their earliest experience with live gigs. When they weren't playing, the band was tucked away, sometimes underground, in the makeshift greenrooms among the arenas' lockers and offices. Before their concerts, they could feel and hear the crowd growing above them like a fulminating storm. Then after the set, that same twenty-thousand-person thunder returned, begging for an encore.

No one disliked the limos and the hotels, yet these encores were the band's true reward for the work of the past ten years. Now that the creative decisions were entirely under John's control, the stage was the only time that Tom, Stu, and Doug could show their audience exactly what they brought to the band. They sang the background vocals, they determined the tempo, they followed John but also prodded the songs upward, toward a louder, faster, more muscular sound than anything they could have accomplished in the studio. They toured infrequently enough and were a fresh-enough commodity that their audiences were filled with people seeing them for the first time since they exploded. By late August 1969 they had a career's worth of hit songs to bring those audiences to hysterics in under an hour. The encores were the backing trio's confirmation that they played a role in those hysterics. The crowd shouted for Creedence Clearwater Revival, not just John Fogerty.

In the final days of August they had a swing through the Midwest. In Minneapolis, the set was their usual face-melter, and the band finished and went back underground with their adorers rumbling and shouting above. Doug was on a high, toweling himself off and asking his friends what the encore would be when John made what he assumed was a joke.

"No encore tonight," John said. He was sitting on the floor next to Stu. Their backs were to the wall and both were incredibly still. Doug's adrenaline was rushing. He could hear the pounding of twenty thousand fans in his chest and his own throbbing heartbeat in his ears. He waited for John to announce he was sarcastic.

"We're not doing an encore," John explained. "From this moment on, Creedence Clearwater Revival will never do an encore." They were fake, he explained. An encore isn't special if it happens every night.

Doug blew past him. "Which are we gonna do?" he asked, referring to the three rotating songs they played when crowds inevitably demanded it. The crushing noise from the crowd surrounded them. "You're gonna let 'em bleed?" Doug asked. But John didn't reply.

Doug turned to Tom and Stu.

"C'mon," he said. "Let's go back out. If we do, he'll have to." But their heads just fell, and Doug realized that he'd lost even this small, occasional control over the band's music. He could feel a rage rising in him and when he opened his eyes, there was John, now standing near a massage table, wearing what Doug read as a small smirk.

Out of body, Doug grabbed the table and upended it. His bandmates stood frozen, shocked by the violence as the table landed on the floor. The relentless crowd noise still swallowed the room as the four men stared at each other in frightened silence. Doug looked to John with a beating fury in his chest. He didn't see the smirk any longer, didn't even see the cool, composed face that his boyhood friend wore in the studio. Instead, he saw, for the first time in ages, the same face that he first encountered in 1958, in the Portola band room. A shy face. John looked scared. But the argument was lost.

"Beer in the dressing room," Doug said. It was a demand, a last defiant acknowledgment that John had won. The others took their limos back to the hotel. Doug stayed as the colossal crowd emptied, surely disappointed, and his own heart rate settled. At the next show, there was beer backstage before the gig.

Despite that olive branch, the no-encore policy stayed, and Doug wasn't the only one who took issue. On September 19, Creedence played the Phoenix Memorial Coliseum with Poco as their opener. They were paid $32,000 to play for forty minutes, "a lot of bread for less than an hours [sic] work," according to an unimpressed writer for the underground paper *Rebirth*. "They left the stage even though 14,000 plus of their brothers and sisters were screaming for an encore. The entire crowd kept their plea up for almost ten minutes. In addition to the crowds [sic] screams for more, the promoters of the show asked them to go back on stage and do one more song. Creedence stated that they had done their gig and owed the people nothing else . . . It appears to me that Creedence has forgotten about the people who made them who they are; and support them by buying records and tickets to their concert."

John's argument for artistic purity didn't match the situation that the band found themselves in. Creedence was a phenomenon. Their crowds wanted encores because the band had become the most consistent soundtrack to late-'60s youth culture in less than a year. Their arrival in new cities was an event. Five long, hard years after the guitar-quartet dam broke, young people were fighting a war of attrition against a world that seemingly wanted them quiet, obedient, or dead. Music was an essential component of that battle, and in 1969 Creedence made the most essential music of all. Whatever old bluesman's standard of artistic purity John created in his head, his decision left thousands of people deprived of a greater communion with him.

For ten years they had resolutely focused on the same shared junior high notion of success. Ten years traveling from basement practices and school assemblies to frat parties and doo-wop sessions and awful uniforms. A long enough journey that the entire musical world had shifted and grown in the meantime. Mainstream radio play was all they yearned for at age thirteen, and now they were twenty-four and bands were expected to find their place on independent radio, play colossal concerts, and engage in a symbiosis with fans who insisted on the sanctity of the environment, world peace, cosmic consciousness, and the independent soul. Creedence was helping to create this world. They were its biggest sensation. But the shared work of music-making had kept them young in bad ways, too. They still clung to early-teenage dramas and squabbles—who could play what, how they delegated responsibility, and most of all, how to retain their camaraderie now that John's role had outstripped all the others'. Onstage and in the Factory, they could operate as a single four-part brain. In almost every other way they were stubborn adolescents, full of raw nerves and unacknowledged personal gripes. John wrote songs about utopias while wresting power away from his brother and his bandmates at the moment of their crowning glory. Doug was furious, Stu and Tom were hurt and resigned, and none of them could live without the others. Their fans heard and saw a uniquely dialed-in group with uncanny musical communication and sympathy. They didn't know about the bone-deep codependency, forged in childhood, that flowed underneath and threatened their future.

As ever, the roiling interpersonal drama and distress had no effect on the band's popularity. The *Green River* LP was selling millions, "Down on the Corner" and "Fortunate Son" were still charting, and even in their encore-less era, they had gigs booked for months into the new year, including their first European tour scheduled for the spring. Perhaps more importantly for the band, they had earned the respect of elder statesmen. Solomon Burke was only the first artist of 1969 to cover "Proud Mary." He was followed by Conway Twitty, Gary Lewis & the Playboys, Junior Walker & the All-Stars, and the

Checkmates Ltd., whose version was produced by Phil Spector. Creedence's performance on *The Johnny Cash Show* aired in September, the final episode of the year. The ballyhooed first episode had featured Bob Dylan, making his return to public life after a few years away from touring. Dylan himself said that "Proud Mary" was his favorite song of the year.

Given the requirements of his contract, John might have saved songs for the future. He had already fulfilled his duties to Fantasy for 1969 in terms of delivering masters. But now "Down on the Corner" was a hit, and he was still writing at his usual manic clip, creating the most diverse set of songs he'd yet made. His new ones included "It Came Out of the Sky," a science fiction farce about an outer-space arrival that spirals into an international race to capitalize on it. John's swipe at governor "Ronnie the Popular" Reagan, who suspects "a communist plot," was the first-ever mention of the former actor in a song. "Feelin' Blue" let the rhythm section shine with an insistent, laid-back feel that sounded like "Born on the Bayou" with better posture. Then there was "Poorboy Shuffle," a little acoustic country number that helped expand the world that "Down on the Corner" created. In the subdued, bouncy country tune "Don't Look Now," John admonished the young, himself included, for their political complacency. "Effigy," a long, minor-key dirge, was directed at Richard Nixon, slaughterer in chief. The lyrics were spare and spooky, depicting a fire spreading from a palace to the countryside, and the arrangement matched it. The chords descended as John moaned and took a heartbroken guitar solo between his verses. With this song, John married his apocalyptic preoccupations to his sense of social injustice, and gave Creedence the material for a third album in the calendar year.

They recorded everything at Wally Heider with Russ Gary manning the boards. Business had picked up considerably at the studio. Jefferson Airplane, Quicksilver Messenger Service, and Crosby, Stills, Nash & Young all recorded albums at the San Francisco facility in 1969. Creedence may have tripled the output of those groups for the year, yet they still didn't really think in terms of LPs. "A single means you've got to get it across in a very few minutes," John told *Rolling Stone*. "You've got to think a little harder about what you're doing." To the notion that AM radio play was beneath a serious artist, he blamed "a built-in uptightness" in the new breed of bands. "'Singles is what I dug when I was little, therefore I have to change now. I've grown up, I don't like top-40' . . . which is dumb. Why not change top-40?" That was still their goal, and accordingly, they remained the most businesslike band in the city. They would stop in at the studio every few weeks to record a new double-A and rarely took longer than an afternoon. They almost never recorded anything that wasn't meant to be released. When they had enough songs to make a record, they came back to cut the rest of it in similarly truncated fashion. Their 1969 albums had no real outtakes, no guest musicians, no gatefold sleeves or obvious studio trickery—none of the expansive concepts that their contemporaries were indulging to push the LP format forward. Creedence wasn't concerned with that. The most overtly experimental gesture they made was a brief overlapping fade between "Poorboy Shuffle" and "Feelin' Blue," which closed side one of *Willy and the Poor Boys*, as they named their fourth album.

On September 19, Fantasy ran a small ad in the *Los Angeles Free Press* that led with a question: "Do you need $500? Are you a starving artist?" They were soliciting visuals from fans for this upcoming record, offering to pay $500 "to the artist whose work is judged by our prejudiced staff as being the best representation of where Cree-

dence Clearwater Revival is at. The winner's work will be Creedence's next album cover. Any medium may be used: crayon, coal,
watercolor, oil, wood, metal; anything that suits the artist's psyche.
Submit a photograph of the work to the address below, and we will
then ask finalists to ship their entry to us, to be returned if not selected as winner." The notice closed with fair warning: "Fantasy will
positively not reply to any bitching from losers."

The openness to outside collaborators—not to mention the
goofy humor—was a change of pace. And sure enough, the plan was
scrapped. The eventual cover for *Willy and the Poor Boys* showed the
group playing in character in front of Oakland's Duck Kee Market.
Doug was on washboard, Stu on gutbucket bass, Tom on acoustic
guitar, and John on harmonica—a scene that John felt channeled
Alan Lomax. Some neighborhood kids wandered into the photo
shoot and ended up on the album cover too. This was no stranger's
notion or crayon sketch. Everything, from the idea down to the crop-
ping of the photo, was John's call. He had the right to demand such
oversight, perhaps, yet it was hard to see how John benefited from it.
He was bitterly at odds with his label boss and vastly overmatched as
a would-be businessman.

The band brought their families along for a vacation in Hawaii
after an October gig in Honolulu. They went to Hana Ranch, a
secluded cattle farm in Maui where each little group could stay in
their own cottages and the entire "Creedence family" could eat and
play together every day. It was idyllic, and a welcome, needed re-
spite after the most insane summer of their lives. The setting was
perfect for a reset. The band members could reconnect with their
wives and children and hang with each other outside the constant
din and churn of touring, travel, and practice. Or so it might have
been. John spent nearly every day in the ocean, swimming alone.

TWENTY-FIVE

AN ARMY GROWING IN YOUR GUTS

I n October, the Weathermen tore through Chicago in a multiday campaign of destruction and antiwar speechmaking. Their campaign was christened the Days of Rage, and it cost the city $200,000 in property damage and police overtime. Following the unrest, *New Left Notes*, the newsletter of Students for a Democratic Society, informed their readers that "FROM HERE ON IN IT'S ONE BATTLE AFTER ANOTHER—WITH WHITE YOUTH JOINING IN THE FIGHT AND TAKING THE NECESSARY RISKS. PIG AMERIKA—BEWARE: THERE'S AN ARMY GROWING RIGHT IN YOUR GUTS, AND IT'S GOING TO HELP BRING YOU DOWN."

It was an age of manifestos. When the Stones' greatly awaited tour arrived in San Francisco in November, audience members distributed copies of an anonymously written flyer: "Greetings and welcome Rolling Stones, our comrades in the desperate battle against the maniacs who hold power," this one began. "The revolutionary youth of the world hears your music and is inspired to even more deadly acts. We fight in guerrilla bands against the invading imperialists in Asia and South America, we riot at rock 'n' roll concerts everywhere. We burned and pillaged in Los Angeles and the cops know our snipers will return."

These were frightening promises, but they reflected ongoing violence elsewhere. That same month, journalist Sy Hersh broke the story of the My Lai massacre, a horrific act of civilian terror perpetrated by US troops in Vietnam. The timing was propitious. A significant follow-up to October's Moratorium events was long scheduled for the next day, this one was called the March of Death. Beginning on November 13, nearly 50,000 people walked single file from Arlington National Cemetery with names of the US dead on placards hanging around their necks. When they arrived at the Capitol the next evening, they laid the signs on the ground to compel Congress to end the war. Concerts and speeches continued for the next two days, drawing a crowd of about 250,000. A similar event took place in San Francisco, one of the largest gatherings in the city's history.

Within a week, the city was once again an epicenter of rebellion. Members of the American Indian Movement arrived at Alcatraz Island in San Francisco Bay. Calling themselves the Indians of All Tribes, they announced their intention to reclaim the land for Native populations, and naturally explained themselves in a public letter. "We moved onto Alcatraz Island because we feel that Indian people need a Cultural Center of their own. For several decades, Indian people have not had enough control of training their young people. And without a cultural center of their own, we are afraid that the old Indian ways may be lost. We believe that the only way to keep them alive is for Indian people to do it themselves." The leader acknowledged that their "Red Power" uprising was inspired by the growing Black Power movement. They positioned their effort as a retaliation and reclamation after years of broken treaties and land theft by the United States. Most of the occupiers were college age, including leader Richard Oakes, a Mohawk who first came to the city to enroll in San Francisco State's recently established Native American Studies program. He and his followers initially used a small barge to bring food and supplies to the occupiers, but the government soon seized it.

The occupation attracted the attention and support of a few Hollywood celebrities including Jane Fonda and Anthony Quinn. Creedence stepped in as well, alone among their cohort of local bands. In an increasingly rare moment of total unity, they quietly purchased a boat to replace the lost one and furnished the occupiers with food and supplies as well, an investment totaling about $10,000. The band may have had a reputation for being square or insufficiently radical, but this was a cause that spoke to all four of them. They had an instinctual support for underdogs, in John's case gleaned from his early exposure to folk music, and this was a perfect example of concrete political action, not simply the dropout ethos he saw in so many of his peers. In "Don't Look Now," he had asked, "Who will put his back to the plough? / Who'll take the mountain and give it to the sea?" The Alcatraz occupiers had done so. They christened their new vessel *The Clearwater* in tribute to the band who recognized their sacrifice.

These acts of collective disobedience, like the huge concerts that preceded them over the summer, were natural media events. No news camera could resist the sight of crowds mobilizing or marchers disrupting normal life. The organizers of the 1963 March on Washington understood this, and every social movement since had similarly attempted to hold the media's attention long enough to make a widespread impact. The Alcatraz occupation was a local story, covered by the underground *Berkeley Tribe*, but it had national ramifications and was monitored by the Nixon White House. *Time* ran a cover story later in the year on "the Electronic Front Page," meaning television. Citing Morley Safer's reportage from Vietnam, the writer concluded that "as a result of its extraordinary impact, TV news has become a powerful force encouraging social ferment."

Right on cue, Creedence returned to *The Ed Sullivan Show* on November 16 to play "Fortunate Son." Performing on a dark stage set made to look like an abandoned farmhouse, the band performed almost solemnly as the camera slowly wound a tight circle around them. Doug was high up on a riser, Tom was seated near John's feet, and Stu was angled over his shoulder. It was a stark, visually arresting performance for a prime-time variety show, and it made Creedence look like four men on the outskirts of civilization. That fit the tenor of the song, which was angrier and musically heavier than any protest pop of the time. Only four days after the revelation of My Lai, John Fogerty was in living rooms around the country proclaiming, "I ain't no military son." He made no drug references of the sort that got Jim Morrison in trouble with the show two years earlier, and the group was too stoic and dark to make teenage girls scream. The more conservative viewers might even have enjoyed the blues riffs in between the lyrics, which perhaps they couldn't understand through John's signature yelp-drawl. Young people knew the song, however, and knew the lyrics well. They understood it as another manifesto.

On November 29, Creedence played the Inglewood Forum in L.A., a sellout crowd of 18,300. The promoters said there was

enough interest to fill a second night too. A few days later, December 3, they were back home for a rare show at Fillmore West,
a benefit for the community-funded Pacifica station in Berkeley,
KPFA.

"The crowd had come, virtually to a man, to see Creedence
Clearwater," wrote *Rolling Stone*'s Alex Dubro, who guessed that
most of the "overwhelmingly suburban audience" had no idea what
KFPA was or what it stood for. The night was truly surreal for the
Fillmore: an audience of "clean-cuts and bouffants waited through
several hours of barbiturate-rock," until the Bay Area's biggest band
took the stage.

Creedence Clearwater Revival, known from the radio, from TV,
from the PX, everywhere, had apparently grown a bit stale for the
arch–San Francisco audience of *Rolling Stone*. Dubro felt their set
was by-numbers. John dedicated "Bad Moon Rising" to "R. Milhous
Nixon," the only deviation from his routine song-title banter. The
teenybopper crowd seemed pleased as the set proceeded, if a little
staid themselves. When Creedence finished after their usual tight-
fifty, though, they wanted more. "The crowd nearly became dangerous," Dubro wrote, "when Creedence refused to do an encore, and
left in a bad mood."

John, Tom, Doug, and Stu had started as total outsiders in the
San Francisco scene, then, in a period of about eighteen months,
gone from its dorky newcomers to its grandest success, too big to
play any show but benefits. To an outsider it appeared that they
achieved this by reining in the scene's excesses and making everything about their operation—production, arrangements, entourage,
song structures—as streamlined as possible. So streamlined, in fact,
that even their enormous mainstream audience now felt they were
stingy. They were so locked into the format that made them famous

that they couldn't even enjoy the spoils of their fame. They could sell out any venue of any size, but no crowd, no matter how big, small, or hysterical, could get them to vary from the strict parameters that John had set for a Creedence show.

They were different in this way from the Velvet Underground, who returned to San Francisco just a week earlier for two nights starting on Thanksgiving eve. The deafening, sensory-experiential band that scandalized even Bill Graham in 1966 was gone. They no longer traveled or collaborated with Andy Warhol and the Exploding Plastic Inevitable. John Cale, their most schooled and experimental member, had left the group, as had Nico, the German with the voice like dark beer. That left sole creative control to Lou Reed, the Booker T. & the MGs fanatic and former songwriter for hire, and the band's sound changed significantly. In late November, they performed at the Matrix, a former pizzeria about the size of Deno & Carlo, and the guitars rarely wailed. Instead, Reed led the group through two sets a night of largely distortion-free grooving and mid-tempo R&B-style rock.

His songs now sounded more like John's—or more truthfully, like the '50s influences they shared—though his approach couldn't have been more different. He changed his lyrics from one set to another and led the band through long improvisational journeys. A song might be two minutes long or thirty-five. Feedback, formerly the underlying force of their sound, was now essentially gone. They played more traditional rock and roll now, including a new Reed original called "Rock and Roll." Even though they still played "Heroin," his musical depiction of a transcendent high from the Warhol days, and even though he played guitar solos that went beyond John's for sheer atonal string-warping and drones, Reed gloried elsewhere in understatement. Their rave-ups resembled James Brown's

Famous Flames more than the Grateful Dead: insistently rhythmic, defiantly unchanging. But their ballads were tender, and Reed was a proper deadpan comedian onstage, like Buster Keaton with songs and solos instead of stunts. Their first night fell on the day that President Nixon signed an executive order that ended the tiered draft system. The Selective Service was now a randomized cattle call, anyone's number could come up at any time. "We're your local Velvet Underground," Reed greeted the small, quiet crowd. "We're glad to see you, thank you, but we're particularly glad on a serious day, like today, that people could find a little time to come out and just have some fun and listen to some rock and roll."

December 6, just days after the Matrix shows and Creedence's KPFA benefit, was the day of 1969's final megafestival. This one, held at the Altamont Speedway just outside San Francisco, was a free concert that supposedly marked the coming-together of the two countercultural stalwarts of the time: the Stones and the ballroom scene. Originally scheduled as a shared bill with the Grateful Dead, the event grew to include Santana, the Airplane, and Crosby, Stills, Nash & Young. Creedence was wary and exhausted, but that didn't matter, since they weren't asked to perform anyway.

The Altamont Free Concert was conceived as a "Woodstock West" and a celebration of the Stones' US tour, which had just ended. The planning process alone made the summer festivals seem like Swiss watches in comparison. The venue changed multiple times. Altamont Speedway was ultimately only chosen on December 4. The Hells Angels were on hand for crowd control despite their reputation for violence and even rape. And of course the usual festival problems arose: an overexcited, overdrugged crowd, a lack of toilet facilities and food, and enormous numbers of attendees—supposedly three hundred thousand — that made proper event management all but impossible.

The result was an immediate, crushing metaphor for the era's dangers. The Angels fought with concertgoers, then with the Airplane's Marty Balin, who jumped offstage to stop them from beating a concertgoer. Balin ended up beaten himself, and things only escalated. A young Black man, Meredith Hunter, was ultimately stabbed and killed during the Stones' performance. Mick Jagger, who had spent the previous month cavorting and purring in a sparkly Uncle Sam hat on stages throughout the United States, impotently pleaded with the audience and the Angels to stay calm and cool out. After a year of hard-fought mass action and would-be utopian gatherings, Altamont was the easy proof that the doe-eyed optimism of the time had come to an end. Music, anger, drugs, and idealism had been uneasily mixed among young people for years now, with San Francisco as the acknowledged melting pot for all of them. The free concert seemingly proved that these elements would never be balanced again.

Creedence didn't play the concert. They weren't in the habit of playing local festivals alongside the Dead and the Airplane. On a bill with the Stones, they wouldn't have matched the range of hedonistic indulgence on display. But the most scene-friendly of the four, Stu Cook, was on hand as a spectator and amateur photographer. He was close to the stage to gets shots of the bands and ended up caught in the crush during the Stones, and nearly trampled.

For the members of Creedence Clearwater Revival, 1969 was the biggest year of their lives — the biggest year of any American band's life ever, and the release of *Willy and the Poor Boys* only solidified that. The album went to no. 3, which meant they purportedly achieved something that no other group had done in America since 1964: they outsold the Beatles for the year. In 1969, Creedence released three multiplatinum LPs and four double-A singles that sold more than two million copies each. Five songs from those singles ("Proud Mary," "Bad Moon Rising," "Green River," "Fortunate Son," and "Down on the Corner") went to the Top 10 and two others ("Lodi" and "Commotion") charted in the Top 100. They responded the only way they could, by continuing work. Creedence returned to Heider Studios with two new songs, "Travelin' Band" and "Who'll Stop the Rain," which they prepared to release as yet another double-A single early in 1970.

Outside their bubble, it had been a year of belonging, of claiming territory and camaraderie. Whether as part of a festival crowd, an Army unit, or an offshoot movement for equality like Redstockings, Red Power, or the Weathermen, young people sought fellow feeling everywhere. Creedence's music was a bear hug no matter your allegiances. They seemed relevant no matter what battle a person was fighting at the time. And so many of their 1969 hits, from their first, "Proud Mary," to their most recent, "Fortunate Son," concerned the difficult necessity of turning away from middle-class values, whether leaving a good job or decrying the military. A writer for the independent *Liberation News Service*, for example, listed the band among a handful of rock acts who embodied "soulful socialism," along with Janis Joplin, the Beatles, and the Stones, acts with "a life line to black music." "We're for drugs, rock, Janis, Creedence, Communes," he wrote of his young cohort, "but we're also for armed struggle, for the international revolution."

That wasn't the usual thought about the band. More often they were considered a little bubblegum, "one of those good bands that you somehow take for granted," according to Black Shadow, a writer for *San Francisco Good Times*. "Maybe because they don't put out a very heavy hype—just music. And if the music is always good, it's seldom great." He was reviewing *Willy and the Poor Boys*, which he claimed was their greatest work to date even though its pleasures were humble as always. "Sitting around yesterday, stoned, I looked over at Gary and yelled (we were playing it pretty loud) 'Hey, man, this is fine!' I never flashed before on how good a drummer Doug Clifford is; he steadfastly refuses to show off, just sits there and kicks the train down the track. Wheee!"

Finally Black Shadow described the experience of walking down Telegraph Avenue and hearing "Feelin' Blue" on a record store's speaker: "Sad/beautiful and funky as hell. People were standing around on the sidewalk, bopping and grinning at each other, so we went over and bopped some too." The review appeared in the December 11 issue, which otherwise had a near-exclusive focus on social violence, Altamont foremost of all. Creedence had become the house band for the end of the world.

And who better? They had played for sock hoppers during the Cuban Missile Crisis. They entertained Berkeley's drunkest during the Free Speech Movement. They played for older teenagers who were flying off to war. They stayed up all night at Woodstock with a half-million people who believed they could build a better world than the one they had inherited, if only for a weekend. Creedence were not strangers to the task of making people dance while the walls burned around them.

And that's exactly what they did themselves. Things among the four of them—and John's relationships to everyone around him—were as fragile and acrimonious as they'd ever been. They made the

TWENTY-SIX

WE SHOULDN'T BE TAKEN LIGHTLY

In late January 1970, Tom Donahue produced a veritable Super Bowl parade for the band: a single night at the Oakland Arena, with openers Booker T. & the MGs. Creedence played both songs from the latest single, released that month. "Travelin' Band," a plain Little Richard rip-off about life on the road, and "Who'll Stop the Rain," which found John in his messianic, lyrical mode. It was a subtle, melodic ballad about shared fate. It was also a forthrightly political song, with references to the USSR's five-year plans and the New Deal. And it was unbelievably catchy, enough that you didn't have to pay attention to the lyrics at all. It beggared belief that these things kept pouring out of him.

The night before the show, all the MGs except an ailing Al Jackson paid a long visit to the Factory to play music with Doug, John, Stu, and Tom. Tapes rolled as they covered "In the Midnight Hour" and a few other tunes, including "Born on the Bayou." No great artistic spark caught between the bands, but Creedence rarely had the chance to simply have fun. John rarely kept a recording that fell short of perfect. They kept these, though.

By this point, the admiration was mutual. Jones's eyes were so deeply set and his face was often so stoic, John perhaps didn't grasp how impressed the organist was. He might have been the only late-1960s band leader who could match John Fogerty for sheer demanding fussiness. Jones expected perfection from his trio as well, and he knew every aspect of music creation. The MGs were touring more now than they did earlier in their career, and Jones, in his quiet judgment, recognized when his band was in top form. That night in the Oakland Arena, with all four members of Creedence excitedly watching from the wings, Jones marveled at his guys. They'd never been better.

Doug found a similar brotherly rapport with Al Jackson. His hero was ten years older, a gentleman and generous. Having now played so many shows with the group, Doug saw how Jackson got his perfect snare sound, an airtight, cutting *thwack*. Every time he sat down at the kit, he pulled his bulging leather wallet from his back pocket and laid it on the edge of the drum's head. But as they spoke, Jackson shared his truer secret: adaptability. The MGs were a house band, and as a drummer he couldn't just play one volume or style. He had to change with the session's vocalist. Jackson instinctively changed his stick grip from song to song, or put more emphasis on his right foot, the bass drum, as in Sam and Dave's famous "Hold On, I'm Comin'," where he sprinkled sixteenth notes to match the horns' sprightliness. Jackson and Doug talked about drumming purely theoretically, without sticks. For

Doug it was heaven. He had found total acceptance from someone he revered.

After the show, in the arena's deepest hallways near the dressing rooms, Doug saw an older man approaching alone. He had to gather himself before calling out, "Dad?"

It was his old man, now gray. It had been years. They shook hands and stood talking awkwardly, long enough to establish that Mr. Clifford had been at the show. He'd enjoyed it. "I always knew you'd make it," he told Doug, and then he was gone as quickly as he came.

If only such validation came so easy everywhere. An interview with Tom, Stu, and Doug ran in the January *Hit Parader*, in which Doug griped, "It pisses me off good. We're worth more than just a 'ho-hum, another hit from Creedence.'"

The rest of his complaints bordered on whining. "We have something to say and we want to say it," Doug continued. "Everyone has the most fucking respect for the Beatles. Well, we're the biggest American group. We put out quality records. We go over and over our songs. We rehearse hours, every day. Nothing bad gets out under our name. We have artistic control. We even carry our own sound system. We shouldn't be taken lightly, barked at. You can't sell that many records and be taken lightly."

Another interview, the longest yet ever recorded with John, appeared the following month in *Rolling Stone*, conducted by Ralph J. Gleason. This was John's baptism, his debutante ball. The interview ranged over pages and pages of small print, accompanied by large pictures of John speaking with his hands, mid-pontification, fully framed to show his uniform of dark plaid shirt, blue jeans, and cowboy boots. Songwriters of that stature were required to be public

intellectuals of a kind. The audience needed to know their philosophy. "Who's your audience?" Gleason asked.

"Everyone," said John. "Literally everyone. That's why it's hard,
because I'm not trying to polarize hippies against their parents . . .
Because I think music, my concept of what music is supposed to be,
shouldn't do that. It should unite, as corny as that is."

He spoke about the band's entire long journey to supposedly
overnight success. He compared their early recordings, namely
"Brown-Eyed Girl," to the Monkees—a studio band, in his words.
Only as Creedence, with that specific combination of influences and
approaches, could he find a sound that breathed and felt his own.

John was unusually candid about the inner workings of the band
and their roles. He told Gleason that he managed the group because
"I wouldn't trust anyone else." He booked the tours at this point,
though he listed all the band's employees, including Bruce Young
and two other staffers, who he claimed to have "groomed" for the
previous eighteen months. "They'll know which way to move because they learned it from me," John told Gleason.

In 1970, Ellen Willis was at the complete opposite ebb. Depression came hard and when it did, the Stones, her onetime favorite
band, didn't deliver as before. Mick Jagger's power trip alienated
her. Instead, she took Creedence as her new sad-day music. It was
therapy to just be up and dancing. She played their records one
after another. Every time, it was like she took them for granted the
last time. John's gifts were not flashy ones, but to hear a song that is
genuinely perfect, a jewel-box combination of expert writing, performance, and presentation, is always a deep honor, and John honored
his listeners constantly. He was, in a sense, ego-less, if you saw his
single-minded ambition as an eagerness to satisfy his audience.

Their songs, Willis noted, were embraced by an unbelievable swath of society. She didn't have the hang-ups to think that this popularity somehow counted against their seriousness as artists. Instead, she considered it proof of Creedence's humanism. Their relative anonymity, the fact that most fans probably couldn't ID John on the street, was proof of it too, as was their head-down, nonstop work ethic. They were a band fully for the people, "the only 'serious' post-Beatle band to deliver one hit single after another, playing classic rock and roll without ever sounding archival," as she put it.

Laurie Zoloth, a twenty-year-old writer for the Berkeley feminist newspaper *It Ain't Me Babe*, attended a Creedence concert around the same time, "the first one I've been to since I started reading/talking/trying to live women's liberation—about a year . . . More important, it was my first concert since I used to go to them on dates." She was relieved that Creedence didn't feature "blatantly sick, male supremacist lyrics" as was typical among rock groups. She and her friends "didn't have to wince at being called chicks or being put down or verbally fucked over." Whereas most concerts were "an emotional ripoff," she felt that Fogerty's lyrics were "outasight."

Partly inspired by groups like Redstockings, feminist activism was taking new and more proactive forms, as in the case of Karen Nussbaum, a leftist antiwar activist working as a typist at Harvard who began to notice the gender-rights revolution burbling in the working class. She helped found 9to5, a Boston-area workers' rights group that advocated for maternity leave and opposed gender discrimination. They didn't expect to be taken seriously by their bosses, and they weren't. But to the group's dismay, the local unions weren't more engaging. She felt scorned by the institutional working class as much as she was by the business class. Left-wing sympathies didn't mean that a man wouldn't subject a woman to the absolute worst of human behavior.

In his unguarded moments with interviewers, John said he was aware of such female struggle. Thanks to enlightening conversations with Martha, he agreed that the "male superior attitude" had no place in the music industry. But even though he admitted that he'd written few songs about women, John didn't want an end to love songs, or "an end to pursuing." He worried about a "neuter society" without gender differences.

He made these comments to the *Liberation News Service*, during a sprawling conversation that occupied the entire back half of an issue whose only other interviewee was Jean Genet. The conversation was pegged as a follow-up to the one in *Rolling Stone* the previous month. He admitted to the *LNS* that "it started bugging me after a while that [reviewers] kept saying the same thing—dance music, good time, ad nauseum . . . there was nothing there but beat, etc." His interviewer pushed back, saying that their music reflected the "turmoil and unrest" of the time, including the persecution of the Black Panthers. But John demurred from that too.

"I'm trying to talk about at least what I'm personally frustrated about or what I see from the middle." He agreed that he leaned left, that it was the only moral place to be, and he dismissed Hubert Humphrey as too right-wing and expressed solidarity with rioters. But "academically you'd think the middle is the best place to be, right?"

Asked forthrightly if he were trying to compel young people to action and understanding, John said that he was a musician. He never sought to alienate. That was the impulse that he couldn't abide or understand among his cohort. Specifically, he dismissed Up Against the Wall Motherfucker, who had famously cut the fences at Woodstock and organized a series of free concerts at the Fillmore East, in addition to punching John's friend Bill Graham. "What the hell is Up Against the Wall Motherfucker? What is that? Screw it." AM radio play, he said, was still "part of the plan" as he saw it for Creedence.

The interviewer expected John to admit to some frustration or hassle as a result of his fame, and John could not accept it.

"That was really the whole point, for me . . . What we want to do is reach lots of people, lots of people that we haven't even begun to reach." He decried greed, on Wall Street and in the Rolling Stones' camp for their exorbitant ticket prices, but he acknowledged, "I have to admit that I'm a capitalist too. I mean I'm not doing all of this to end up with nothing."

These were big claims, but John was not lying. He certainly did keep the castle walls high, and no low-quality Creedence material emerged from it, regardless of context. Their Woodstock set, for example, he deemed insufficiently energetic or crowd-pleasing, and he didn't like the way that business deals were made with the festival organizers. So Creedence was nowhere to be found in the documentary about the concert, which was released in March 1970. As a film, *Woodstock* was an event to match its namesake: three hours of vérité footage and superstar musical performances. Even if the rumored half-million people made it to Woodstock, that left many, many millions who still wanted their first look at the proceedings. And for myth-building, no stage can compete with a movie screen. Creedence was not at all the only act to be left out of the final cut. The Band, the Dead, and Ravi Shankar, for starters, weren't included in the movie either. But for some of the lesser-known acts, first among them Creedence's close hometown peers Santana, it became their catapult to instant fame. For bigger stars like Hendrix

and Sly Stone, their *Woodstock* performances were the most intimate, instantly iconic images of them ever recorded.

Maybe it would have helped change perceptions of Creedence
to have their footage included. Certainly the band had no visual element to match Roger Daltrey's torso and microphone lasso or Pete
Townshend's aerial displays. They weren't capable of sudden musical shifts or improvisational outreach to the audience like Richie
Havens or Janis. Creedence didn't convey heroism or fellowship,
just rock and roll. Onstage, the most exciting presence was their
big-bearded, flailing drummer with the enormous hi-hats, and he
was sitting down. Maybe it would have earned them a new level of
respect to be included in the hippest movie since *Easy Rider*, and to
be remembered for all time as the headliners they were. They would
never know.

TWENTY-SEVEN

FORWARD TO
THE PAST

The band's next single, "Up Around the Bend" / "Run Through the Jungle," came out in April, to coincide with their first tour of England and Europe. Once again, the 45 offered the two sides of Creedence: unabashedly celebratory and vividly nightmarish. Yet both contained subtle expansions on their old ideas.

"Run Through the Jungle" began with an eerie sound effect like a helicopter (actually a backward piano and guitar reverb) before the drums entered playing a semi-Latin beat that reminded Tom of the Champs, the band who recorded "Tequila." The song was essentially "Born on the Bayou" with the imagery of "Bad Moon Rising," a perfect Creedence apocalyptic dance song. John claimed that his words about hundreds of millions of loaded guns were a reference to America's lax firearm laws. But the song had "jungle" in the title. The troops in Asia took it to heart.

Meanwhile, "Up Around the Bend" was an optimistic reimagining of "Fortunate Son." It had a chest-hitting riff like that song,
and the same insistent eighth-note bass. "Fortunate Son" was a call
to break free from chains, and "Up Around the Bend" was the welcome sign to the promised land. "There's a place up ahead and I'm
going," John sang. Everything else followed from that.

The verses of "Up Around the Bend" contained two chords. The
chorus added a third. The vocal melodies in both were just simple
repeating phrases of a few notes. John's musical and lyrical economy
was simply stunning at this point. No idea went to waste, no syllable
was extraneous. He led his listeners up a hill with this song, away
from destructive society and "to the end of the highway / Where
the neon's turned to wood." Ever since their debut record cover,
which abounded in trees both drawn and photographed, this was effectively the Creedence motto. Running forward into the past. "Up
Around the Bend" was John's catchiest, most powerful expression
of that idea so far, and his closest approximation of high-decibel
Seeger-style populist folk music.

John supposedly wrote both songs in one weekend and recorded the vocals to the existing instrumental in one day. Listen to
them back-to-back, and you can hear that his voice didn't change.
He sang the terrifying song with the same bracing, humorless
conviction that he brought to the secular gospel pop tune. The
trick was that he and the band were so musically chameleonic it
didn't matter. As songs, "Up Around the Bend" and "Run Through
the Jungle" had little to do with each other. As performances and
recordings, though, they were expertly balanced complements.
John's rasp and the band's skillful, pared-down interplay were both
instantly recognizable. Many successful bands of Creedence's stature might play together only at sound checks and gigs, or maybe at

specific practices before studio dates. Creedence practiced every day. They were in the Factory, making music like other men make airplane parts. When it was time to summon the very particular sound that made them famous ("swamp rock," as critics were now inevitably calling it), they could do it in an instant. That moniker made it sound like their music floated by on a slow river until they plucked it out with a net. In fact, they were the most diligently practiced and prepared group this side of the Duke Ellington Orchestra.

The European tour included sports stadiums in Germany, Sweden, and Denmark, places that didn't get too many American rock concerts. But the crowning achievements would be their stops at Paris's Olympia Hall and London's Royal Albert Hall, the kind of Old World palaces that Ellington and other older jazz icons played when invited to Europe like statesmen. Creedence would be there as an ambassadorial caravan for the new strain of boundary-breaking American pop.

They left from San Francisco in a private jet. Saul was along for these shows since they presented a rare opportunity to glad-hand the UK and European distributors that handled his essential clients' overseas sales. It was also a chance for him to show that he was the real wrangler here, the business mind behind this blues-indebted band that was set to entertain the country of Led Zeppelin and the Who. If the band was going to make their debuts on the continent's biggest stages, he deserved to spend the trip among his colleagues in the global record industry, toasting their shared luck.

They were used to young rock critics. Some *Rolling Stone* reporters were even younger than they were, and others from the underground press were occasionally teenagers. They'd spoken to the odd writer from *Life* and had been on TV quite a bit for a rock group.

Yet the British press was a new beast, perpetually girded for war. Creedence had never been set upon by cameras like they were on the Heathrow tarmac, where all four of them looked glazed from the trip. They stood tightly four abreast in their dark tousled hair and rumpled, unprepossessing jackets while the cameras clicked and bulbs popped. The journalists demanded sound bites and controversy if possible, and in the melee began asking why the band's ticket prices were so high. Stu blamed the promoters, a quick dashed-off comment that he didn't think much about. Then they were shuffled away to be greeted by label brass, driven to their hotel, and tasked with attempting some sleep before the night's welcome party.

That evening, aboard Liberty Records' chartered H.M.S. *Proud Mary*, they drank champagne with cute girls dressed in sailor suits. They spoke with the Englishmen who were making money from their records. They talked with British reporters who asked fusty questions that had little to do with their music. *New Musical Express* asked John the awkward question of why the tour was so short. He responded ramblingly, with an odd answer. "We're playing only the safe places, I suppose you'd say. The accepted ones. Other than that, I don't want to give you that old press release hooey about it's so wonderful to be playing for our fans! Of course, that's true, but people always make that an end in itself. Obviously we want to see the people who have been buying our records and that kind of thing. Also, we've never been there and we want to see what it's like."

Such tumult for such an innocuous question. John oozed anxiety about authenticity and a need to stay in the middle of the road. How easy it would have been to say, "We came for as long as the calendar permits and we can't wait to be back. Buy the new single." But nothing could ever be so simple.

The red-carpet treatment, with the boat and the girls, for example. It was fun, but John couldn't help but notice there had never been a boat in San Francisco. Fantasy hadn't done anything to celebrate them since Saul bought John's guitar amp two years earlier, and even that came out of their earnings. Then there were the other guys. In this moment of triumph, he heard constant griping from his bandmates, especially Stu. Whining about the stewardess, the size of their limo, about the disproportionate attention heaped on John. Tom seemed to be enjoying himself least of all, which was getting to be the usual case as John saw it. How could they grow more resentful as he made them more successful?

The tour didn't start in England. From London they went to Rotterdam for a show on April 11, then another in Essen the following night. They returned to Britain for two nights at the Albert Hall, April 14 and 15. As they left their hotel for the first show, their elevator opened and a barrister from the promoters tried to serve Stu with papers for a libel suit by a promoter, stemming from the statement about the high tickets. It took Stu's father's law firm to clear the matter up, and no harm came to the band. But they learned not to speak so freely among the British press.

Melody Maker reported that "straights, freaks, skinheads and greasers stood shoulder to shoulder" at the Albert Hall. The whole range of British youth were entranced by the new mythopoetic vein in American rock music, the groups that reinvigorated old traditions with contemporary energy. Only a few months earlier, in December, Delaney & Bonnie & Friends, the exemplary southern soul-rock band, had toured through the UK to astounded, disbelieving crowds, including at the Albert Hall, thanks to the invitation of Eric Clapton, who joined them on lead guitar. For the youth of Britain, American music radiated danger and meaning at the turn of the

decade. It was imbued with the struggle for racial justice and the
antiwar movement. Musically and philosophically, it was invested
with an adventurous spirit and a sense of purpose. Creedence embodied this, especially the guttural wail in John's voice and the
high stakes in his lyrics. In the UK, Creedence's hits didn't count
against their credibility, and neither did their coming from California rather than Louisiana.

They played their set and left the stage. Encores, often multiple
ones, were a part of the Hall's lore. The audience expected to be
able to call their favorite artists back, and Creedence's lack of appearance caused more confusion than anything. It was impossible
that they were somehow *refusing*. Saul waved away the appalled promoters and Creedence Clearwater Revival sat in the most historic
dressing rooms of their lives as their desperate, adoring fans stomped
away disappointed. Clapton was in the building with Harrison and
McCartney, but they couldn't make it backstage because of the angry throngs.

It was maddening. What a berserk relationship they all now had
with John, who had given them such incredible opportunities and
deprived them of crucial other ones. His talent had made the stakes
of their relationship so high, and his own need for control was making it impossible.

On April 17, one week into their European tour, they played
their fifth show, this one at the Tennishalle in Stockholm. "The
concert was absolutely heated: the audience jumped on the chairs,
sang along and screamed," one witness shared. They left Sweden
for Denmark, where they played the KB-Hallen, a sports venue in
Copenhagen, three nights later. While in Copenhagen John met
a woman named Lucy, a deejay, and became uncharacteristically
smitten. To his bandmates' surprise he even danced on a bar table

at one point after the show. Then he got her contact information as they left once again for Germany.

Creedence played Berlin's Sportpalast on April 22, before performing their final tour stop in Paris two nights later at the world-famous Olympia Theatre. They were in Europe for two weeks and one day altogether, and appeared in front of more than fifty thousand people. They were feted and interviewed and became, almost by the hand of fate, the unquestioned biggest band in the world. They pissed off the crowd at England's grandest concert venue and blew off three rock stars in the same night. The Royal Albert Hall concert was filmed and recorded. John even felt something like infatuation for the first time in ages. It was a time for unchecked optimism.

"Right now I'm where I've wanted to be since I was seven years old. But we've still just scratched the surface," John told one reporter during the trip. "We've studied hard what went before. Only the future can tell us how well we learnt."

They'd already released two singles since *Willy and the Poor Boys* came out in December. A couple more and they were almost through with another album. They could do it by summer, which would make it their fifth record in twenty-four months. That was the only way to stay ahead of the jealousy, the lousy label, the poor contract, the single-handed responsibility for carrying the largest rock and roll band on the planet.

TWENTY-EIGHT

BLOODBATH

While Creedence Clearwater Revival played in Berlin on April 22, their home country was enjoying the largest national celebration since the end of World War II twenty-five years earlier. The idea for the first Earth Day arose late in 1969, the year of Santa Barbara and the flaming Cuyahoga. The idea was initially boosted by Wisconsin senator Gaylord Nelson, who proposed a nationwide teach-in on environmental issues. But Nelson was not the face of the effort. Covering the campaign in its origins, the *New York Times* reported that it was largely youth-led, like so many utopian efforts at the time: "Rising concern about the environmental crisis is sweeping the nation's campuses with an intensity that may be on its way to eclipsing student discontent over the war in Vietnam." They yearned to turn the neon back into wood.

By late April, the event had grown beyond anyone's expectations, encompassing teach-ins on more than a thousand college campuses and ten thousand schools. Millions of people took part in marches and demonstrations across public parks, federal and corporate offices, and places of worship. Tens of thousands of people spoke at these gatherings, many of which lasted for a week or more despite the catchy holiday title, and a great number of those speakers were young. Environmental conservation was a universal cause that cut across cohorts. Federal bureaucrats and college professors could agree that humanity should not bake the world in smog and petroleum flames. This was one issue where students and young people could find common interest with older, less revolution-minded types.

These invigorating late-April displays emboldened the blood. The dawn of a new decade felt like a true dawn—a rising wind. And naturally, it disappeared like the breeze too. On April 30, when some of the last remaining Earth Day events were still smoldering on, President Nixon announced that he was reversing the drawdown of troops in Vietnam that he'd promised only a week earlier. The enemy was moving in, it was no longer safe, and military tactics suddenly required an invasion of Cambodia, or so he explained. "We live in an age of anarchy," Nixon told his television audience. He called it an era of "mindless attacks on all the great institutions which have been created by free civilizations in the last five hundred years. Even here in the United States, great universities are being systematically destroyed."

It was no accident that campuses, of all places, where a distinct minority of young people spent their time, were at the top of Nixon's list of worries. That college minority's antiwar faction, like its environmentally conscious one, was increasingly loud, effective, and prominent, and the broken promise to bring 150,000 troops home was its greatest recruitment tool.

Nixon's Cambodia speech led to antiwar protests at hundreds of colleges across the country. Campus leaders called for a National Student Strike. And though the surge was unprecedented, it wasn't unexpected. Governor Ronald Reagan, for example, who in 1966 referred to the Berkeley campus as "a rallying point for communists and a center for sexual misconduct," now directed the California Highway Patrol to force protesters into a makeshift park on campus. The police shot an innocent bystander during the ensuing standoff and injured dozens more. That set the tone for college and university collisions through the spring and early summer of 1970, as Creedence's hold on the mind of that demographic remained at a remarkable, sustained peak. "Up Around the Bend" / "Run Through the Jungle" reached no. 4 on the *Billboard* chart as May turned to June, the same time when many students were marching on their college administrations, some with firebombs and Molotov cocktails. Reagan didn't lead the ensuing crackdown; his attitude just encapsulated the wider feeling among America's weary reactionaries who had watched a decade of gains for Blacks and deviants. Right-wing America yearned to punish them.

"If it takes a bloodbath," Reagan said in early May, "let's get it over with."

First came Ohio's Kent State, where a confrontation between campus protesters and the National Guard ended with four slain students bleeding out on the quad walking paths. The photo published the next day, of a young woman kneeling and wailing above one of those bodies, became an instant icon of youthful agony at the outset of the 1970s. Eleven days later, city police opened fire on students at Jackson State College, a historically Black institution in Mississippi, leaving two young people dead and twelve more wounded. In between those two incidents, six additional unarmed

Black men were killed by police during an uprising in Augusta, Georgia, following the death of a teenager in police custody. At a May 19 demonstration, protesters held a sign with the recent tally: "2 KILLED IN JACKSON, 4 KILLED IN KENT, 6 KILLED IN AUGUSTA."

It wasn't only that young people were now literally under fire. According to many of their compatriots, they deserved it. Gallup found that nearly 60 percent of Americans blamed students for the Kent State massacre, against barely 10 percent who blamed the National Guard. Nixon issued a pitiless statement that all but held the protesters responsible for their own murder; for good measure, he called them "bums" in private. In Kent itself, an ad ran in the local paper thanking the Guardsmen, paid for by community business owners. The mayor received a flood of mail decrying "outside agitators," especially "hippies" and "longhairs," for the violence, while some residents began making a silent four-finger salute to each other—meaning, "At least we got four of them."

John Lindsay, mayor of New York City, declared May 8 a "day of reflection," and closed the city's public schools. Instead, a thousand college students marched down Wall Street, shouting, "One-two-three-four. We don't want your fuckin' war! Two-four-six-eight. We don't want your fascist state!"

Before long, a group of hard-hatted construction workers set upon these no-good peaceniks, beating them to the ground and kicking them once they got there. A few Wall Street workers in suits and ties joined in, and police officers looked on, not daring (or desiring) to disrupt the violence, but the energy of that assault, deemed the Hard Hat Riot, came from those supposedly salt-of-the-earth union men. The workers chased students back to Pace University and attempted to storm a dormitory to remove an antiwar flag hanging from a student's window. They forced their way into City Hall and successfully demanded that the half-staff flag be returned to full flight. In case there was any confusion as to their political loyalties, 150,000 teamsters, workers, and longshoremen marched through Manhattan in what the media termed a "parade for Nixon." The president invited the event's organizers to the White House, where they presented him with a hard hat of his own.

Crosby, Stills, Nash & Young's "Ohio," which was written and recorded in the immediate aftermath of Kent State, positively throbbed with sadness and anger. The quartet indicted Nixon by name and mourned "four dead in Ohio" so nakedly and repetitively that the single was banned on AM stations. The Steve Miller Band's "Jackson-Kent Blues," released later in the year, was similarly, straightforwardly contemptuous: "Shot some more in Jackson just to show the world what they could do." Creedence was busy in the studio as all this tragic mayhem ensued, finishing their latest LP. By comparison to those more direct protests, the four songs they had already released as singles *felt* timely even if they weren't specifically about the era's travails. "Who'll Stop the Rain" and "Run Through the Jungle" had the shape of protest songs. John's melodies were so simple that his choruses felt like group chants. "Travelin' Band" was an antic and uncreative throwback, a half-desperate effort to conjure simpler times. But "Up Around the Bend" atoned for it. It was a charging rallying cry, a promise for uplift and transcendence, the hard times gospel.

To fill out an LP, they resurrected a few cover songs, including their old favorite, "Before You Accuse Me," this time taking it at an unhurried, swinging lope. John swaddled his vocals in reverb on their rendition of Roy Orbison's "Ooby Dooby," and Doug and Stu stomped the beat like cavemen, heroically crude like the Stooges or Crazy Horse, as Neil Young's backing band was now known. Uncharacteristically, Creedence also drew on something more recent, "I Heard It Through the Grapevine," which both Gladys Knight and Marvin Gaye had recorded for no. 1 hits over the last few years. All four band members loved both versions, but Marvin was in a special class for them. Beyond a Motown act or an R&B singer, he was a true artist, and the chord progression for that single was right in their most comfortable place musically. Unlike the other covers, Creedence let themselves stretch a bit on this arrangement, turning the song into a dark, instrumental blues with a long and hypnotic guitar solo by John. Other than some overdubbed cowbell by Doug, the ten-minute final take was recorded in one go like all the rest, with the band members playing live together in Wally Heider's Studio C.

In his own compositions, John was pushing his creative limits too. "Lookin' Out My Back Door" was one of his goofiest, catchiest sing-alongs. It was nearly a kid's rhyme, with a literal cartoon parade: "A giant doin' cartwheels, a statue wearin' high heels." Then again, it was also the closest this famously straight band ever got to psychedelia. It was a cousin to "Lucy in the Sky with Diamonds," at least lyrically. He also wrote "Long as I Can See the Light," a soul ballad that would have suited Otis Redding. His metaphors—in this case, a candle in a window—were as starkly, immediately captivating as a cave painting. The narrator yearns to be close to home, and as long as he can see the light, he's close enough. The simplicity of that idea, and John's equally simple musical accompaniment, was its artistry, and the rhythm section gave the song a gorgeous, balanced foundation. Doug added small flourishes on the bass drum, barely noticeable on the radio, that reflected the mentorship of Al Jackson Jr. John added keyboards and a saxophone track, and the song became the closest the band had ever come to the real Stax sound. They chose it for the album's closing spot.

To open the new record, however, Creedence chose something even stranger and more impressive. It was a great mutant composition called "Ramble Tamble," another of John's '50s-inspired nonsense titles, but unlike "Chooglin'," the phrase was a total non sequitur, and the arrangement was the least beholden to rock and roll tropes of any music they had made to this point.

The song began quietly enough, just a spare country-funk riff on the guitar before Doug's drums and Stu's bass enter hard on the downbeat, like James Brown. But before that full-band effect even gathered steam, the quartet swerved into a double-time electric country feel, like "Bad Moon Rising" on speed. They quieted, suspending the beat on a pulsing high note as John's vocals entered with a familiar howl. He brought them down to the one again— "Down the road I *go*"—before the verse began in earnest. John's delivery was the bleakest, scariest narration he'd yet summoned, and his lyrics were all about a domestic nightmare. He screamed about a mortgage, bugs in the food, a highway encroaching on the property, and of course, polluted water. The song wasn't in first-person, but it was personal.

Then they swerved again. This time, they brought the raging country to a slow close, then hit and held one final downbeat to crush it to rubble. And as the rhythm section played the final grinding notes of that transition, John's guitar reappeared with an odd, almost English-sounding arpeggio that suddenly made perfect sense once the band reappeared behind him again, crushing a thunderous mid-tempo beat. John played some chicken-scratch patterns on his guitar that played off Doug's drums. It sounded heavy and dark but was far more adventurous than any Creedence recording to date.

They kept building. John's solo took the form of overdubbed, harmonizing guitar lines, an effect he'd never used before. The band was a steam train, unstoppable, and yet the effect was eternal rising. Up, up, with more guitar on the same sci-fi harmonies, until they finally crashed the whole thing again, and John came out of the wreckage with the old country two-step, now a little bit faster.

In the final verse, with the band fully atilt, positively out of breath, John decried "actors in the White House," but also . . . acid indigestion. The mortgage was now a "mortgage on my life." The personal and political, even the physical, had completely collapsed for him. The structure of the song even mirrored that collapse, as it swung from one genre to another, from the blues club to the honky-tonk to outer space and back.

Creedence was at the height of their influence and fame as they recorded this song, and that repute rested on their unique ability to straddle musical generations at a time when age cohorts were almost literally at war. They brought the sounds and record-making priorities of pre-Beatles rock and roll into conversation with young people who could now risk death at a rock concert or antiwar rally. It was never a single, only the album opener for one of the first hard-rock masterpieces of the 1970s, but "Ramble Tamble" embodied the ethos of Creedence as well as any song they made at their world-conquering peak. Listening to it would tell anyone exactly what this band was capable of. It explained their entire reason for being. And it was written as the country itself quaked in violence over its own values and direction, fighting a battle between old ideas and new.

There were other musicians who spoke more eloquently and personally about human concerns than John Fogerty in 1970. That spring alone, new records by James Taylor, Cat Stevens, and Joni Mitchell led a trend toward restrained, introspective, largely acoustic music that wrung its power and emotion from the words, not boundary-pushing instrumentation or structural experimentation. *Sweet Baby James, Tea for the Tillerman,* and *Ladies of the Canyon* were barely rock at all. They were records of supposedly confessional lyrical honesty, presented cleanly and smoothly, with hardly any bluesy grease or "in-between." Creedence's music remained incredibly popular, but John couldn't write this way. He made records, not autobiography.

For example, their growing batch of album material appeared to be another simple collection of singles with some long jams and new covers attached—nothing new from a band who had turned this formula into a cottage industry in under two years. Because this was the greatest band in the world, those jams and covers sounded as good as any rock music you could find on vinyl or hear on the radio. Musically, it embodied the era's elemental struggles, and it stood to be a massive commercial success. But it wasn't a *statement*. Creedence didn't make those. And after a year and a half in total sync with mainstream appetites, this was the first indication that Creedence might be diverging even slightly with popular taste.

TWENTY-NINE

GOOD BUSINESS

Tom was restless again. Feeling the odd man out. Doug and Stu had already convinced him not to leave the band a half-dozen times going back to the *Green River* sessions. They told him that a loss like that could end the band for everyone. Every time, he agreed to keep working through it. But things were getting worse. He didn't have Doug's capacity for explosive rage, but of the three, Tom was the one who felt most like he was being drowned by John. He felt his brother was reneging on some deal they'd made back in the haze of adolescence. Why couldn't they have more fun? Why couldn't Tom contribute a song here and there? He marched his kid brother into their first recording studio, showed him how to be a front man and how to sing for an audience, then stepped aside, and now he couldn't even write or sing album tracks? For a band that put out three albums a year? Doug and Stu could exercise some control over the songs simply because they played the drums and bass. They could take a fill here or there, or walk up the neck, whereas Tom was stuck eternally strumming. His desires were so simple, he just wanted to play songs and sing. Instead, he was left repeating to Doug and Stu, "I can't take this anymore."

John had already acknowledged to himself that his bandmates seemed miserable in Europe, and to his credit he made gestures toward a reconciliation as their next LP approached. There was the title, for one, which put the focus on Doug of all people: *Cosmo's Factory*. And in contrast to the previous few records, he stuck himself in the way back of the band portrait on the front cover, which was posed in the Factory. The picture was taken by Bob Fogerty, John and Tom's youngest brother, who was now band photographer and John's personal assistant. The shot was comically unaffected, especially by the standards of major album covers in 1970. Miles Davis's *Bitches Brew*, released that spring, featured minimal text and a double-gatefold psychedelic panorama. Led Zeppelin, meanwhile, were meeting with a graphic artist to dream up experimental designs for their forthcoming third album. And here was Creedence, arranged apparently haphazardly around their practice space, which looked like a garish patchwork quilt. There was the meaningful blue-velvet curtain, the bright orange shag carpet, Doug's wood-grain drums. Tom and Stu were sitting on the ground, each grinning in black-and-white stripes. Doug, in orange pants and layered athletic shirts, was atop a white bike and John, forever in blue plaid, was seated on his motorcycle. Both wore inscrutable glares. A little handwritten card was stuck to a white post in the center of the room. It read "3RD GENERATION" in tribute to Ralph Gleason. By this point, Creedence was the biggest pop act to ever come from the Bay. They didn't need a jazz man's approval. They didn't even need to stand for their album cover.

No one could accuse John of stealing the spotlight here. But that meant little compared to the credits, which once again showed him as producer, writer, vocalist, and lead guitarist. Tom's sole contribution: rhythm guitar. In a band with John Fogerty, what could be more superfluous?

Tom talked with John and explained that the band's steadfast focus on music, not image, had left them with so much "mystique" that they were invisible. He thought they should be known as four individuals, like the Beatles, like the Stones, the Mamas and the Papas, or Crosby, Stills, Nash & Young. On television, Creedence looked like three gentle guys behind a camera-shy front man. In interviews, John was avuncular but awkward and over-intense, and no reporter had any reason to talk to the rest of them. Creedence was just songs. They weren't a group with four personalities and names. But if people got to know all four of them, there would be fans of each. From there, Tom imagined, the opportunities would arise. If John wouldn't let him sing a song, maybe he would if the fan club asked for it.

Tom was right in one important way. Creedence was an almost completely undocumented band. They had no archivist. Jim Marshall, an increasingly famous rock photographer based out of San Francisco, had accompanied them to Europe and to Memphis, but other bands of that stature constantly had cameras rolling. And the few attempts to capture Creedence visually hadn't gone well. John rejected the Woodstock footage. The Oakland Arena concert movie had yet to air on local TV. In a rare moment of marketing generosity, Saul Zaentz even splurged on a documentary filmmaker to accompany the band in Europe, but John quickly felt the guy had an agenda. No usable footage emerged from the trip.

So Tom had a different idea. No cameras, no flashbulbs popping or lenses peering at his brother. Instead: a book. A real author could come visit them in the Factory, interview them and see how they all worked together. Something literary could be more lasting and impressive than a concert film or a photo montage on an album cover. John was never one to open their little kingdom to visitors. Outside of their marriages, the band's daily interactions were typically limited to Bruce Young, Jake Rohrer, and little brother Bob. But John acquiesced again. He gave the okay to Tom's idea.

Cosmo's Factory was released in July, and Fantasy bought a full page in *Billboard* that was less of an advertisement than a boast: "'COSMO'S FACTORY' is the new CREEDENCE LP that will earn a gold record on the day of release and a platinum record within 90 to 120 days. SELAH." The bottom third of the page was "a recap on the gold and platinum doings of Creedence," listing their six gold singles, four gold LPs, and three platinum LPs. "Lookin' Out My Back Door" / "Long as I Can See the Light" was released in early August and began its inevitable rise up the charts, peaking, like so many previous Creedence singles, at no. 2.

Obviously they enjoyed fame, though it was growing unclear what that meant. Creedence now demanded up to $50,000 per set, but they had priced themselves out of their favorite venues. John told a journalist at this time that the band would be happy playing only Fillmore West or Winterland Ballroom, but at their level of renown "good business, or whatever you want to call it, kind of dictates that you don't do that." Instead, they played larger and larger venues on tour and used benefit concerts as an excuse to play their preferred hometown venues.

On August 11 Creedence made one such benefit for the Haight-Ashbury Medical Clinic at Fillmore West and showed just how much they'd outgrown the place in under two years. Bill Graham was ecstatic: the line stretched for blocks and some kids even slept on the street to get tickets. Yet Creedence arrived as usual with their own sound system and limited roadies. Robert Hilburn, observing the group at this show for the *Los Angeles Times*, noted that they also did their own own booking and recorded for an independent label. In an interview with Hilburn, John made these choices seem natural. He started handling the group's business because "we couldn't find anyone else who could give us the quality of service we wanted." John was now a "copromoter" along with Artists Consultants and Concerts West. They had grown used to controlling their own sound when they were a regional touring outfit that played everywhere but proper music venues. Their performance itself belied the modesty. They owned the overspilled crowd, enough so that John was moved to a rare exhibition of loose fun: he played saxophone for the first time onstage during their opening medley of "Born on the Bayou" and "Run Through the Jungle." It was possible that his grip was actually loosening. Maybe his self-consciousness and worry were finally subdued by the smothering acceptance he had found in Europe. Now he could cut loose, let Tom coordinate a book project, play a sax solo instead of the pre-planned guitar jams. Perhaps it was possible. With the Fillmore once again fully serviced, they all four returned to Berkeley in separate limos.

Success was one thing. They were used to that. Used to selling a half a million records on preorders alone and commuting like royalty. The stranger thing was that the Creedence aesthetic had begun to seep into other parts of the culture. The guys that spent so much time studying and paying tribute to their influences were now themselves influential. In July, the Velvet Underground were veritable working stiffs. They spent their days recording a new

album in Atlantic Records' New York studio and their nights playing two shows at Max's Kansas City for an unprecedented nine-
week residency. A *Village Voice* writer attended and marveled at
the streamlined, down-home sound that Lou Reed and his current
cohort were making, barely two years after the ear-bleeding mul-
tisensory cacophonies that frightened San Francisco. "The Velvets
have changed considerably since they left Warhol's gang. No more
assaults on the audience, no more ear-wrenching shrieks of arts. No
more esoterica . . . It seems the Velvets are now back to where they
once belonged, functioning as a genuine rock 'n' roll dance band,
dedicated to laying down strong rhythms and a steady beat that gets
the vital juices flowing." The band performed stripped-down, solo-
filled versions of their underground hits, greeted rapturously by a
fawning multiracial crowd. Reed had made his name as a chronicler
of the dispossessed and strung-out, but now he was marrying his literary urge to music that explicitly summoned the 1950s and built
on the solid thump of a bar band, maybe one that could handle
Sundays at Deno & Carlo.

At the same time, Bob Rafelson was finalizing his latest project,
the culmination of his media career to date. After the huge success of *Easy Rider*, Rafelson and BBS negotiated a six-picture deal
with Columbia. They secured their right to their films' final cut by
agreeing to cover all production costs over a million dollars, and to
split net profits equally with the studio. "We didn't have any burning
ambition or slogan to change Hollywood," Rafelson told the *Los Angeles Press*. "We just knew there was a way to do something that was
groovier than the way it had been done."

The first product of this new arrangement was Rafelson's feature
directorial debut, *Five Easy Pieces*, with a script based on his idea.
Not quite an autobiography, it concerned the well-heeled scion of

a classical musician who throws his training and prospects away to become an oil worker rather than face the expectations of his family. That character, Bobby Dupea, was played by Jack Nicholson, the actor who cowrote *Head* and caught wide national attention in a supporting role in *Easy Rider*. At the film's outset, the audience meets Dupea as a dust-covered rig worker, and Nicholson played him with a glaring fury at the world, ready for a snarling match with a waitress or a dog, and overtly contemptuous of his country-music-obsessed girlfriend. Rafelson's insight was to show the true circumstances of Dupea's birth after introducing him as an anonymous laboring grunt. It revealed the character's brittle self-worth, and turned his interior failures, his inability to self-examine, into the movie's most poignant drama.

Bobby Dupea was an emotionally immature, work-obsessed, guilt-ridden musician, and someone who sought personal reinvention to avoid personal pressure and discomfort. He even wore flannel and work clothes. For those reasons alone, he could have made a perfectly suited fifth member of Creedence. He also worked in the California oil fields. A few years earlier and he could have been the kind of empty soul who sat on a barstool and tried to ignore the Golliwogs or the protagonists of *Fat City*.

These tiny pieces of the world now resembled Creedence's music and members, while other peers were falling by the wayside. The band played Shea Stadium in Queens, New York, on August 6 as part of the Festival for Peace, a multigenre day of music featuring Johnny Winter, Miles Davis, the Staple Singers, Dionne Warwick, and many other groups including Big Brother & the Holding Company, who were reuniting with Janis Joplin for the first time since she left the group. Unlike at Woodstock and the 1969 festivals, which were largely for-profit and paid handsome fees to most groups, most performed for free at Shea, and all the profits went to antiwar causes.

Creedence moved on to the Miami Beach Convention Center on August 15, then returned to the Fontainebleau Hotel, where they were staying in their usual digs, the Frank Sinatra suite. It was a two-story accommodation with a living space on the bottom and a full lounge above, accessible by elevator and spiral staircase. The lounge featured a library, pool table, grand piano, and an open area for entertaining. Post-gig, the band was on the second floor when a loud knock came from below. When Doug answered the door he found a visibly drunk Jim Morrison, in town for a court hearing after exposing himself to a Miami crowd months earlier. Morrison entered with his bodyguard, "Babe," and a young female hanger-on. The band invited him to play pool, which lasted only briefly until the Lizard King passed out. When the band emerged from their room in the morning, they found him still sleeping on the pool table, and left him there when they checked out.

Shortly after their run-in with a spiraling former rock god, drugs claimed three high-profile musicians in just over a month. The tragedy began with Alan Wilson of Canned Heat on September 3. Impossibly, Jimi Hendrix followed on September 18. And Janis was gone on October 4. The Festival for Peace was one of her final shows. They were all only twenty-seven years old, which was still older than every member of Creedence except Tom.

THIRTY

THE OLDEST
YOUNG MAN

J ohn Hallowell was not likely starstruck by these boys. He'd interviewed and written about many more glamorous stars than four flannel-decked Berkeley dudes, including huge names in Hollywood and on Broadway. He was Tom's age, nearing thirty, but also a Harvard graduate and a *Life* staff writer, which is how he got those plum assignments, enough to fill a book of his celebrity encounters, *The Truth Game*, which was published in 1969.

The Creedence project came together quickly. By late summer, with the band preparing to return to the studio for the follow-up to *Cosmo's Factory*, Hallowell was chosen as author and commissioned to write it for Bantam Books. Ideally, Tom's marketing coup would establish the individual band members as complex characters. It would reveal the band's unique backstory and showcase the four essential parts of the Creedence sound. Bass, guitar, drums, vocals.

They were a guitar quartet, born in February 1964 while watching *Ed Sullivan*. It was their balance that made the Beatles so astonishing. Multiple songwriters, multipart harmonies, four complementary personalities. Creedence created a different kind of balance, one more focused on the low end, a guitar-group's re-creation of keyboard boogie sounds: Stax, Motown, Chess, Sun. They pulled democratically from the United States' different traditions, then rearranged those sounds democratically in their instrumentation. The long journey to achieve that balance was their story and the reason for their success. But you'd never know that from singles. Tom wanted the full story told.

Hallowell joined the band for a few days and worked like a man on a tight deadline. He shadowed and interviewed each member individually, at home or in the studio, then observed some long rehearsals, a few recording sessions, and a big concert at the Los Angeles Forum. He was clearly a different ilk than the band. He was from a different coast and a more mainstream world, the world of glossy magazines. They weren't even on a corporate record label. But the difference was deeper. Hallowell knew Hollywood, especially old Hollywood, and he knew Broadway. He didn't know rock and roll. He didn't understand what motivated people to express themselves in the format of a three-minute single. He was Tom's age but seemed overwhelmed and overstimulated by the smallest whiff of hippie danger that this straightest of bands exuded.

Hallowell was the only journalist to write about Creedence primarily in terms of libidinal energy, and he was not subtle, either. "Is Creedence Clearwater Revival S-E-X?" he asked in the opening pages. "Is the pope Catholic?" The book proceeded in that manner for all eighty-four paperback pages. Hallowell wrote purple circles around the four band members seriatim, building gaseous metaphors everywhere. Backstage at the Forum, he observed the band "getting ready for that crucial character who's been in the wings till now, the character who makes them gods, and makes them sex and love: the audience." He barely mentioned their music. And he misnamed their set closer as just "Chooglin'."

Inside Creedence was published as a mass-market paperback and labeled as a Bantam "Rock Special." Padded with band photos and voluminous lyrics—John was effectively a cowriter—the slim book sold for one dollar. If the idea was to improve Creedence's critical standing or to make them, in Doug's formulation, incapable of being taken lightly, the book did not make the case.

But Hallowell saw certain things clearly. "Each one of Creedence Clearwater Revival has direct access to his childhood," for example. He recognized that the group's dynamic was forged when they were kids, and that in many ways they remained lodged there. Hallowell compared Stu to Oscar Wilde for being debonair and witty, but he also said his acid humor could come off like smart-assedness. Doug was a Tasmanian devil, perpetually climbing, eating, and flexing. John spoke about his formative records and TV shows of his youth. Like his conspirators, he was caught in the past, telling Hallowell, who inserted the italics, "That was when I learned about *gut*, the fifties . . . *I liked where it was.*" Though in general, John remained hard to read. Hallowell positioned him as an unquestioned genius and confounding as such. And certainly Hallowell could sense the heaviness in him. "John Fogerty is the oldest young man I have ever met," he wrote.

That left Tom, whose idea this whole book was, and who got the most dramatic treatment of all. His little chapter was titled "The Apostate," and revealed him as a tortured ex-Catholic. His time at St. Mary's, the high school John couldn't stand for more than a year,

had apparently scarred Tom harshly after all. He told Hallowell that
he could only "get free" by rejecting his residual "church guilt."
That was his youthful hang-up. But his story line, as Hallowell saw,
was knottier than that. The author opened by calling Tom "Gary
Cooper with an electric guitar." In one of his trademark space-filling
metaphors, Hallowell compared the band to a car, saying that John
would be the wheel, Stu the clutch, Doug "*has* to be the accelera-
tor," and Tom, simply, "the brake." Finally, his chapter ended with
a rhetorical question: "It must have been the bummer of all time to
be Leader, as Tom Fogerty was, not make it big, let kid brother take
over, and then wham! make it big." Even in his own vanity project,
Tom's value was being called into question. This was supposed to
be the chance to reveal their deeper characters, and he was stuck
explaining that he wasn't bitter about John after all.

The new record took time, which was a first. John was clearly
looking to establish a different reputation. "Hitmaker" was one thing,
but plenty of his peers were called "artist." He still didn't feel respected. Two years and millions in sales later, he still put "3rd Generation" on an album cover. The man could hold a grudge. The
new record was more immediately ambitious. First of all, he wrote
all the songs, a first on his records. No covers or borrowed jams. John
played saxophone, too, sometimes as a layered section unto himself.
He overdubbed keyboards and vocals, the latter at one point like
a full choir. All these new sounds meant that the other guys were
occasionally quieted in the mix. "Sailor's Lament," a breezy song
with a complex and gentle vocal arrangement, didn't need the usual
Doug and Stu thump. The carefully composed elements in "Have
You Ever Seen the Rain," like the Booker T.–style B-3 organ and the
piano lines that doubled the bass fills between verses, were show-

cases for John's record-making acumen, not a snapshot of a powerful band together in a room.

Stu, Doug, and Tom acquitted themselves nobly in service of John's changing artistic goals. "(Wish I Could) Hideaway" ebbed and flowed between loud and quiet sections of equal drama, most of it created by the keyboards. "Born to Move" was a blatant Stax rip with a long B-3 solo by John. He pushed them away from the swamp and toward Chicago, especially its R&B and blues clubs. Doug's drums were tighter. His snare cut and snapped, his kick drum hit like a punch. The tempos were faster. A few songs, like the opener, "Pagan Baby," which had a riff worthy of Albert King, went much longer than AM radio allowed. Others, like the mellow funk ballad "It's Just a Thought," required the guys to attempt completely new textures, and they sounded marvelous. All three adjusted their instruments' tones to match this brighter, punchier version of Creedence, especially on the single "Hey Tonight," which was unique for Creedence in having no swing at all, just a metronomic pulse. Yet on "Have You Ever Seen the Rain," the group had never been more effectively restrained. John even moved into full sonic experimentation on his album closer, "Rude Awakening #2." The band played every role he asked, on an album where he played more roles than ever. The result was an unlikely Creedence hodgepodge, but easily their most ambitious recording. They named it *Pendulum*.

The cover image this time was no woodsy scene. Instead, it featured only the four members' faces in stark black-and-white close-ups, staring unsmilingly back at the listener. A bit theatrical, though more democratic. They looked like Mount Rushmore groomed for the antiwar rally.

Inside Creedence bore the same cover. They prepared both products for release in early 1971. It went without saying that the record would sell massively. But the worry, as always, was that Fantasy wouldn't rise to the challenge. Their long-standing "thriftiness" meant that the songs had to live or die on their own merit, forget real advertising. Creedence got no innovative record packaging. The book was the band's idea. They did their own booking and tour management. Saul had no incentive to do more than sit back and watch money roll in. So if the band was going to make the most of their new sound and their first record of entirely original material, they would have to do it themselves. If John was to be taken seriously, like Lennon or Hendrix, he would have to set that narrative in motion. *Inside Creedence* wouldn't finish the job. It was a pocket-size paperback built for grocery racks and rear pockets.

Tom had one more idea. Something for the rock writers who dictated so much of the intelligentsia's taste. It took begging, but they convinced Saul that Fantasy should hire the Los Angeles public relations firm Rogers & Cowan, who were old money in Hollywood but looking to establish a presence in the pop world. Their biggest musical client so far was Motown Records. Bobbi Cowan, the niece of founding partner Warren Cowan and an established PR professional in her own right, was put in charge of the Creedence account.

In Berkeley, at the Factory, Cowan encountered four guys who seemed caught between urges. All four were nice as could be, and seemingly egoless. And that was the funny thing. This group of visibly tight-knit, codependent old friends were a little corporation making tons of money by pleasing only themselves. And still, their label was paying her company $30,000 to concoct a lavish publicity stunt purely to help them feel they were respected.

Cowan grasped that the band's magic really came through in their live performances. She also recognized that they were an inwardly focused group: they kept a small, closed circle. They had their little citadel at the Factory and local journalists could come by if they gave notice. But no other press throughout the country really knew them at all. No one saw the unprepossessing, hardworking boys she saw. She devised a big junket and created an invite list of a few dozen New York journalists. It was time for them to see Creedence in their element.

As she started making calls, it became clear just how unnecessary the effort was. Every critic was happy to go and had great things to say about the band. The nightmare scenario for a PR manager in such a situation would be to fly a writer out, wine and dine them, then have them write a dismissive review. But that was clearly not an issue. She heard the word "love" a lot over the phone.

In meetings with her, the band insisted that this not be a "Hollywood" event. They didn't want movie stars, or to be treated like movie stars. They just wanted to roll out their new album. Again, mixed messages. But that was manageable. She designed a weekend-long set of activities. The writers would be put up, fully fed, and plied with alcohol. They'd get an early copy of the new record and witness a short live set by the band in their own practice space and get to mingle afterward. An intimate, classy song-and-dance.

The low-pressure aspect of the event was true to the band's character. But a low-pressure junket is an oxymoron. In the meet-and-greet component at the Factory, the speakers played classical, not *Pendulum*, as one might expect. "It was strictly a flannel-shirt affair," wrote Robert Christgau, the *Village Voice* rock critic and confidant to Ellen Willis. The journalists were bused to a movie theater to watch the concert movie that resulted from the January show at the

Oakland Arena. The weekend's main event—the private set at the Factory—was in fact a perfunctory two songs from *Pendulum* and "I Heard It Through the Grapevine." According to Christgau, this "left everyone shouting for an encore that did not materialize. The guests, feeling frustrated and misused, almost stripped the factory of posters and other movables before receiving their complimentary copies of *Pendulum* at the door."

Coverage was generally positive. Perhaps it would have been anyway, even without spending thirty grand to make a bunch of press annoyed that you don't even play encores for private parties. And perhaps that wouldn't have revealed the band's ambivalence about the whole thing. In a feature about the party in *Rolling Stone*, Doug and Stu were quoted extensively and disbelievingly as they spouted silliness like "We want the world and we want it a week from Tuesday." They insisted on positioning themselves as ambassadors for clear heads rather than a party or a revolution. "We are interested in social causes, but aren't willing to go far left to prove it," Stu said.

The album received good—not rapturous—reviews. It went platinum quickly. Their double-A single, "Have You Ever Seen the Rain" / "Hey Tonight," was released in January and went gold, as high as no. 8. Only *Inside Creedence* flopped, which stung the band members a little. But that was a blip in an otherwise satisfying press cycle. They had a major tour lined up in the spring. Again, what more could a rock band expect, exactly?

Tom wasn't satisfied. Another record came and went, another tour approached. His kids were getting older. And even after all that effort to realign the band and get back a little leverage, the same narrative was moving along mercilessly. *Pendulum* was all John's songs. His vision was evolving and of course required him to play even more instruments while the others played only their rhythm tracks. The media wanted to talk with him, and why wouldn't they? It seemed like no one else had anything to say.

Gail, Tom's wife, advised against leaving, saying he should take a few months to decompress. But Tom was insistent. He felt he was becoming a stranger to his kids. He was in the most famous band on earth and it left him feeling bored and angry. Around the Christmas holiday, he told the other three that he was leaving the band. They had heard this before and he'd come to his senses every time. In the new year, they'd go back to work like always.

This time was no drill, however. Doug, Stu, and John tried to contact him but he wouldn't respond. The calendar turned over, 1971, the thirteenth year that this group had now spent investing their lives in a collective musical pursuit. Tom had been in the band for about ten years, six of which he'd spent as the lead or co-lead singer-songwriter.

In February 1971, when they made the announcement to the public in the *Fifth Street Flash*, Stu was in London, Doug was in the Sierras, and Tom was in Acapulco. No one knew where John was. "Of course it's a change for all of us," John was quoted in the fan club newsletter, "but change is implicit in music." It turned out to be the last issue ever sent.

THIRTY-ONE

BLUE AGAIN

They were furious. Years of talking Tom down from the ledge, then a full album promotional cycle given over to his demands—the book (god almighty) and the junket, which they now jokingly referred to as "The Night of the Generals," after the recent mainstream thriller about intrigue and backstabbing among Nazi brass. That's how cautious everyone was. Doug and Stu had spent years seeking a delicate balance between one brother's soaring ego and the other's broken one. The rewards were obvious: to play those songs, to those crowds, for that money. If John could ease up, let someone handle the business side, it would almost surely be more money. But if Tom couldn't ease up, if this was truly the end of a two-Fogerty Creedence, then it could be the end of the crowds. They had done so much to placate him, then he bailed anyway. Infuriating.

When they returned from their various pilgrimages, the trio needed to take stock. None of them wanted to end the band. Theo-

266

retically, they had their pick of rhythm guitarists. The most popular band, living in the hip music capital of the Western world, would not have trouble finding someone who wanted to tour in airplanes, playing set after set of monster hits for adoring fans. Yet the idea of auditions never came up. The band was such an organic creation that adding a member was always going to be more difficult than losing one. They briefly considered asking Duck Dunn to join on bass and having Stu move over to Tom's spot, but that was only a passing notion. Of all the MGs, Duck was easiest to get along with, the one with the nonstop sense of humor and musical personality. But they realized how hard it would be to have a fourth member based in Memphis, and weren't even sure whether Duck would want to join. It was also true that Duck, with his big hair, pipe, and bulging eyes, would have been a tough fit for a group so defined by their lack of image. John wouldn't allow himself to be upstaged, and Duck certainly wouldn't be told what to play.

They had to cancel the upcoming tour. Same with the TV special, the one they screened for the journalists, which was now a relic of their four-member past. Theoretically this was just the most significant in a line of fights stretching back years. Tom could come walking back in the door any day. But that seemed less likely as time passed, and soon all four members went about their own activities, the most prolonged such break in any of their lives since the summer of 1964. They had even gigged during the Army Reserve days.

Cast asunder in the spring of 1971, they faced very different obstacles. There was the obstacle of boredom, which Doug faced even when busy. Now he was positively cabin feverish. He practiced his drums, spent time with his young son, worked his garden, and walked in the nearby woods indulging his interest in insects and other natural wonders.

Finally some work came in. Fantasy signed the former Greenwich Village folk guitarist Mark Spoelstra and Doug got the chance to produce the record. Oddly, the sessions became a tryout for that alternate-universe Creedence that only existed in their imaginations. Doug played drums and Duck came in on bass, and for one song they had Stu on rhythm guitar. In that mellow, modest format, they were akin to the tight acoustic band that Booker T. had arranged that year for the West Virginia–born singer-songwriter Bill Withers.

Spoelstra was older than Doug by about five years. He had done his own time in some important but unglamorous places, including as an early folk-club collaborator with a young Bob Dylan. He was a conscientious objector too, a man with real feeling and principles working in a real musical tradition. And yet Doug felt no disrespect or commanding energy from the guy. Spoelstra had his way of making music, Doug had his, and neither had any problem accommodating the other. The record was titled *This House* and featured a back cover montage of Stu's black-and-white photographs of the participants.

For Doug this was no mere lark. He was finally able to view music- and record-making from a completely new perspective. He'd always had John looming to his left or listening to his playback with those remorseless ears. Working on *This House*, he was a full creative partner and the default music supervisor. Doug was Duck Dunn's goddamn boss for a few days, and as always with Duck, the ball-breaking and joking never stopped unless the tape was rolling. Russ Gary engineered, so the record sounded incredible. In Creedence, Doug was ostensibly the confident one, with the biggest smile and most outgoing personality. But in the studio with Mark Spoelstra, Doug found a different, deeper kind of confidence. He was thrown into a challenging situation, learning on the job every day. But he didn't feel pressure. There was a lot of laughter in the studio. Doug was on his own, making decisions that affected the entire project, selecting the players, helping choose takes. For this project, he didn't have John around to say no. It was joyous.

Stu threw himself into other people's work as well. His brother-in-law was shooting an independent film called *The Museum* and Stu shot, edited, and provided the soundtrack for it. He also recorded ten tracks by the country-rock band Clover, a recently signed Fantasy act who were regulars of the Deno Carlo Naval Base parties back in 1967. John unsurprisingly stayed close to home, nesting. He was now living apart from Martha and the kids and working toward his pilot's license. And, if the image of an imminently divorced man, aloft and alone, defiant even of gravity, was insufficient to show that John was seeking calm, he began to build a recording studio in his new place. An at-home recording rig where he could make something entirely independent, "sort of like what Paul McCartney has done, but without my wife on it," he joked to a journalist.

While they busied themselves, wondering about a future without Tom, they experienced a new achievement as a band. Ike and Tina Turner released a version of "Proud Mary" that was a cover song in the same way that Jimi Hendrix covered the "Star-Spangled Banner." Ike Turner's legendary early hit was "Rocket 88," and he brought exactly that kind of excess velocity to John's song. The slow riverboat strum-along became a steam-train showcase for his stunning, captivating wife. Tina Turner had already scandalized audiences on the Rolling Stones' 1969 tour. No one else could evoke such anatomically specific erotic longing with a microphone and stand. She had a huge soul-shouter voice too, and this jet-powered "Proud Mary," with its vaguely feminist title and familiar, easily remembered chorus, was the perfect family-friendly introduction to her talents. It peaked in March at no. 4, better than any song of her career so far. In May it went platinum. Turner was raised on Black church music and early electric blues, and "Proud Mary," which came out early in the year that she toured with the Stones, was a formative introduction to modern rock. She barely knew the Beatles at the time. But she intuited that Fogerty and his bandmates, like Jagger and Richards, were paying tribute to the music she knew as a girl. To play those songs was like giving something back. And like magic, the kind that only exists in pop music, the Tennessee girl's version of the California boy's song about the Mississippi River made her an indelible star.

That recording made money for Fantasy too, and Saul's priorities clearly lay outside small records by San Francisco rockers. Fantasy was about to open a new complex featuring three recording studios, a record mastering lathe, and three rehearsal halls. He bought the back catalog for Prestige Records, a thirty-year-old jazz label whose list included records by Monk, Coltrane, Miles Davis, and Sonny Rollins. He had his eye on Riverside Records and Milestone as well, acquisitions he would secure before long, which gave Fantasy a roster of contemporary jazz's greatest—and greatest-selling—luminaries. Between those steady sales and a young group of workaholic rock stars with a Midas touch, Fantasy Records could basically print money. When Arco Industries, holders of Little Richard's copyrights, sued Creedence for blatantly aping "Good Golly, Miss Molly" on "Travelin' Band," Zaentz simply bought the rights to the Little Richard song.

With things operating at that level, there was no reason not to let the Creedence boys take on a stray low-key project or two. Doug and Stu had their production duties, and in April, Tom Fogerty made his solo debut as a Fantasy artist with a 45, "Goodbye Media Man Parts

I & II." It was a rowdy song that showcased Tom's voice above all, especially in a big leaping vocal melody in the chorus. The second side contained a group jam with Bay Area keyboardist Merl Saunders improvising on a Hammond and drummer Bill Vitt skittering along behind him.

Tom met Saunders because he spent his post-Creedence life trying to scale down and regain a firmer connection to his music. He began hanging around the city's smaller venues: the Martin, Keystone Korner, New Orleans House. He called it his "freak out summer" but it was, like Doug's and Stu's own walkabouts, a splendid time. Saunders was a heavyset Black man with a jazz background and soul touch. He was a king of this small scene, and Tom made his acquaintance eagerly. Tom played on Saunders's recording sessions and gigs, where he ran across another of the Fillmore scene's genre-hopping folkway guides, Jerry Garcia, who kept a busy musical schedule outside of the Dead. The Garcia-Saunders band, which specialized in extended improvisational covers of familiar tunes, played at Keystone Korner on May 20, 1971, and Tom was in the crowd at Saunders's invitation. Within a week, Tom was playing in the group.

John, Stu, and Doug, meanwhile, made the decision to continue as a trio. Which was to say, they returned to the trio format. And with this change came sudden, noticeable shifts in the band dynamic. The three-man Creedence released their own debut material in May, a double-A single of John's new "Sweet Hitch-Hiker" and "Door to Door," which was written and sung by Stu. It was an unchallenging tune about the life of a traveling salesman, but if Stu was no match for 1969 John Fogerty as a writer, neither, apparently, was 1971 John Fogerty. "Sweet Hitch-Hiker" was pure energy with no melody and indistinguishable bayou yelping about a pretty

young one. Neither song sounded like it took more than a few minutes to write or record, and if that same formula had given earlier
Creedence songs their urgency, these new ones felt merely content.
Except for the cutting distortion tone, either could have been released fifteen years earlier.

Robert Hilburn interviewed them for a victorious feature in the
Los Angeles Times that announced they were lean and fit for fighting once again. In the article, the band admitted that they nearly
broke up in the wake of Tom's exit. Instead, talking leisurely with
Hilburn at the Factory, they were preparing for a two-month tour in
July followed by recording time and another tour in the fall. Stu's
songwriting contribution was a necessary change of procedure. According to the interview with all three members, there were times
when John overrode the other three members in the past, but he
was now more aware of the "power hungry" reputation he'd gotten.

"I wrote the songs and I knew how I wanted them to sound," he
explained. He said that he kept waiting for a leader to swoop in and
tell them what to do business-wise, but in the absence of a "second
Brian Epstein," he took control because it was assumed he would,
since he had long since taken the lead in music matters. But recently, John "was able to accept it finally in my head that each artist
has a valid contribution to make and that he is entitled to express it."

"What we have now is what I always dreamed we'd have," Doug
told Hilburn. "I couldn't be happier."

Commercial momentum and pure record-making talent en-
sured that "Sweet Hitch-Hiker" went Top 10. But it was a noticeable
step away from the conscientious and opaquely social-minded records
that made John's reputation. The song appeared as Marvin Gaye released his newest album, less than a year after Creedence's homage
and reinvention of his signature, "I Heard It Through the Grape-

vine." *What's Going On* revealed how fully Gaye's mind had evolved even since that transcendent 1968 single. Musically, nothing in Motown history compared to the sheer spaciousness of this LP, and few things in American pop compared to it, in 1971 or any other year. The singer had concocted a panoramic blend of orchestral strings, choral vocalizations, and Latin percussion to enhance the loosest Funk Brothers arrangements ever recorded. And lyrically, Gaye built his words around the endless contours of his voice. He wrote moral pleas to match his depth of feeling and sketched urban characters and scenes that were inseparable from his empathic shouts and conversational melodies.

It was not only Black people who bought *What's Going On*, which quickly became the best-selling LP ever released by Gaye or Motown. Black people recognized it as a revelation in their political and cultural expression, however. Not yet six months home from Vietnam, a Memphis-born soldier named Arthur Flowers heard *What's Going On* when it came out and suddenly felt less adrift in a fog of trauma and anger. He was smoking grass in a girlfriend's apartment at the University of Tennessee in Knoxville when the album's opening strains echoed from down the hall and Flowers immediately felt a commitment and a connection to the fight for Black freedom. He felt he was being lifted. Brother Marvin, as he was now known, gave Flowers and many others a sense of belonging to an important, ongoing history, a sense of duty to the generations.

It would be unfair to compare the scope of Creedence Clearwater Revival's musical vision to Marvin Gaye's in 1971, since almost no one of any genre or race matched him on those terms at the time. But Gaye had been Creedence's more successful fellow traveler across musical guises throughout the 1960s, and a thriving hitmaker and songwriter in the Factory- and factory-like confines of Hitsville, USA. Creedence had become a force to match him commercially, and John Fogerty had forged his own unique expression of youthful anxiety, but Gaye was now playing a different game entirely. He wasn't obliquely evoking wartime dread in metaphors and myths, he was speaking plainly about Vietnam and his brother Frankie, addressing poverty and environmental destruction without symbolism at all. He was using the LP format to make a statement as guilelessly personal as Joni Mitchell's *Blue*, released earlier that summer. Like *Five Easy Pieces*, these records found new ways to smuggle contemporary anxieties into mainstream art. A year before, Creedence were the kings of that approach. But in their amputated condition, the best they could hope for were good-time records, and those only work if listeners believe you're having fun.

THIRTY-TWO

THE SHIT KICKER THREE

On May 29, about sixteen months after it was recorded, the Creedence TV special aired in syndication. The delay resulted from corporate red tape and legal sign-offs over some Coke bottles and other things shown on-screen. Since the footage from Oakland in January 1970 showed a lineup that no longer existed, the band wanted to downplay the whole thing. So they arranged for a clause in their contract that allowed for limited televised exhibition followed by the destruction of the masters and all extant copies of the film.

Like *Inside Creedence, Creedence Clearwater Revival in Concert* was a middling attempt at multimedia crossover that still offered some rare unmediated glimpses into the band's offstage life. The director spliced interviews with the performance footage, and the up-close view did the band no favors. One clip showed John berating Stu to ease off the bass and play "Born on the Bayou" more like the record. At the end of the special, when the 14,000-seat Oakland Arena was empty except for janitors, John spoke some great rock star bromides to the camera: "Tomorrow night there will be a basketball game in here. But the kids who were in here tonight . . . are our people . . . and they won't be back until people like us come back."

"What makes John Fogerty think that he's all that hip anyway?" asked the *Los Angeles Free Press*. "His (film) manner suggested a superiority that is not evident in his imitative music. He is on an AM trip and judging from this film, he's a hypocrite if he denies not enjoying his role as a pop star. In explaining his music to the revered Ralph J. Gleason . . . Fogerty reinforced the lack of political clarity in the group's position and its lyrical outlook . . . As good as the group's music is (overlooking their blatant theft of the black culture), the boring monotony of their one-dimensional blues 'n boogie beat was graphically driven home." Few outlets paid the television movie this much attention. Like so many previous attempted documents of the band, it was buried quickly.

Tower of Power had formed on the San Leandro–focused youth scene that also produced Sly Stone. Emilio Castillo, a sax player formerly of a group called the Spyders, combined blaring Latin horns and San Francisco street-rock and created something akin to Santana but funkier and more earthbound. They had a standing Monday night gig in Oakland that soon became a popular destination for the city's musicians who wanted to see this blazing new stage show.

Doug was among those faithful. He and Santana drummer Michael Shrieve, who became a veritable celebrity when still a teenager after his heroic solo was featured prominently in the *Woodstock* film, came to watch Tower drummer David Garibaldi. This band was a horn outfit, not a Latin group like Santana. Garibaldi was the only percussionist and had no conga players backing him up. Instead, he was a master of four-limbed polyrhythms. Garibaldi had spent three years in the Air Force band, one of the country's most impressive proving grounds for musicians. He was a technical virtuoso on the drums, and Doug was still bruisingly aware that he could never impress his own band leader. He received crucial insights into the ineffable aspects of drumming from Al Jackson Jr., but Garibaldi could give him something more concrete: how to drive a band, how to play like a demon. Doug lived in Kensington and began having Garibaldi up to his house to give him lessons. Doug paid him, and asked Garibaldi not to tell John.

For his part, the Tower of Power drummer thought he'd ascended. His Air Force service ended in late 1969, and he'd come to San Francisco to play music just as Altamont transpired. By 1970 he joined Castillo's group, who were in the studio within a few months to record their debut LP, *East Bay Grease*. After a couple months of weekly lessons with Doug, the Creedence drummer asked if the new band would want to open for an upcoming tour with Bo Diddley. Tower of Power didn't even have a hit single or much of an audience outside the Bay. It took no discussion at all for the young band to agree, and they prepared for a trek through the country with these legends in the summer.

The warm-up for that tour occurred on July 4, the final show ever held at Fillmore West, which featured Santana on the bill as well. Creedence almost weren't hired; Graham assumed that they were in a delicate place after Tom's departure and the group had to volunteer their services. They headlined and donated their four-figure performance fee to Dr. Joel Fort's nonprofit, progressive addiction counseling center Fort Help.

That was a thoughtful gesture and one that showed the band's natural empathy. There were no drug problems in their group or their orbit, and that was a rarer blessing every year. Just the day before their Fillmore gig, Jim Morrison was found dead. Addiction and overdoses were a known problem in the Haight, and they were growing among Vietnam veterans too: in 1971, 15 percent of returning vets were addicted to heroin. Fort Help was a new attempt at humane rehab, though it had no trace of hippie. Dr. Fort was a physician in his forties who believed drug abuse was an illness, not a crime, and that its sufferers should be treated, not criminalized. This met the Creedence standard for social action: fairness, same as the Alcatraz fighters. As it happened, the last remaining American Indian occupiers were removed from the island by the federal government in June. The nineteen-month occupation ended ignominiously, with only a bedraggled few left from the height of their numbers. A child died during the occupation. Yet the effort had affected something outside itself. Indian self-determination had become a topic of discussion in the news and in the White House.

With his genuine support for these nationally recognized causes, John had claim to being more of a Bay Area guy than just about anyone. Yet he was now, in his secure fame and fragile smugness, more dismissive of the city's youth audience than ever. He showed up to the Fillmore swan song wearing a turquoise Elvis outfit. Doug felt he was mocking the band, telling the audience they were a Vegas act. Or maybe John still felt like an outsider in the last remnants of the ballroom that he'd transcended. He was still a self-conscious inheritor of traditions: old rock and roll, Memphis blues, Chess. Not the music he dismissed collectively as "'ride-Trans-Love-Airlines' stuff." He kept to himself, and was known for his withering, wordless rejections when offered hard drugs.

The tour began in Chicago. On one hand, Tower of Power's experience was brutal. Their band didn't share Creedence's drug-free policy, and they didn't travel by plane or comfortable bus. Things weren't glamorous, and they played every night to crowds who threw bottles and screamed for the band with a dozen-odd hits over the last few years. They played with the lights on.

But after those hard, strung-out drives and those thankless concerts, they pulled their equipment offstage and on came the godfather himself. Bo Diddley was an occasional Fillmore performer. The new breed of rock fan was not unfamiliar to him. For the untested newcomers on their first tour, he could not have been nicer. He played with a backing group that looked like children and kept the audience positively rapt. Every night, regardless of where the tour was stopped, he came onstage and said, "I'm so grateful to be here, where I got my start on this very day seventeen years ago." He got his first standing ovation before he even played a note. Then he got more.

Creedence were all that the Tower guys had hoped. Night after night, even without a second guitar, the trio went out and laid waste. They sounded exactly like their records, with just a bit more bite. Audiences loved it, even if the band barely interacted with them. It was all music. Even when they stepped offstage, Garibaldi could see they didn't get along well. But they all treated Tower of Power fine. Then it was off to the vans and the plane, respectively.

Not everyone was so impressed by the diminished lineup. A writer for the *New York Times* said that Tom's "loss was noticeable. The group's dynamic, hard rock and blues sounded flat on Saturday, rather a shell of the music it presented during last year's New York appearances. John Fogerty, the lead singer, lead guitarist and songwriter, remains a brilliant man but was at a loss to carry it all."

For their second trip to Europe, Creedence brought along Tony Joe White, a new down-home white southern soul singer whose signature 1969 hit, "Polk Salad Annie," was one of John's favorite songs — and Elvis's. White was a contemporary of theirs, born right between Tom and the others, and even though he was nowhere near as famous as Creedence, he drew from the same musical well. Except Tony Joe was a son of rural Louisiana. His drawl wasn't learned from radio, he had a breathy baritone that he probably got from the dinner table. "I gotta song I wanna lay on y'all," he'd tell his audience, and his voice sounded like a thick blanket. His swampy guitar picking looked as effortlessly cool as his face-framing sideburns. The real deal, in other words, and leading-man handsome. Tall, too.

John had clearly found another older brother figure whose approval he could set out to win. He marveled at Tony Joe's presence onstage, where he led a band with Duck Dunn on bass and an additional organist and drummer. Offstage, Tony Joe was just as mesmerizing. His songwriting, his face, everything. Something about "Polk Salad Annie," a tight, contained remembrance of a girl Tony Joe knew as a kid, spoke directly to John in a way he could not explain. He considered it one of the greatest records ever made. "If only I had your looks and my brain," John would tell Tony Joe, "we could be a big star," an odd thing to say to a man who was less famous than he was.

Creedence's private Learjet was a tiny thing, what their pilot called a "baby rocket," and they dubbed it "Mondo Bizarro." It had a range of fewer than two thousand miles, so Cap'n John, as they called the retired Air Force major who flew them, had to skip to Europe through Canada and Iceland for refueling. There was no onboard bathroom either, just a bedpan for true emergencies. Cap'n John had performed night raids in Vietnam, and like all airmen who came back from that, he was fearless. Whenever they had guests aboard, he'd throw the plane upside down and do barrel rolls just to hear people scream. Once he let John pilot a takeoff. Tony Joe wouldn't dare ride on the plane, but Duck braved it once and ended up vomiting in a moment of zero-gravity

This European excursion was much more relaxed than the first. They arrived in Manchester on the first day of September, having flown through the northern lights and filled the Mondo Bizarro with pot smoke. They brought along Russ Gary and a phalanx of tape recorders to capture the shows for a live album. They rode bicycles into hotel lobbies for press conferences singing "There's No Business Like Show Business." According to a writer in *Melody Maker*, they "blew an outrageously precise set of loud bitchy rock 'n' roll" at the Free Trade Hall. No surprise about the precision, but bitchiness was not a typical dynamic in a Creedence show. They still opened with "Born on the Bayou," played only an hour, and climaxed with "Keep On Chooglin'," two years after recording it. What once looked like strict professionalism now looked a bit like three men trying not to challenge themselves.

They had a full nine days until their next shows, held over two nights at the Concertgebouw in Amsterdam, and thank goodness: Doug got scarlet fever. Then three days off until another two shows at the Kongresshalle in Frankfurt. They played Hamburg as well as Berlin, where they were a sensation. The Mondo Bizarro was the first private jet to land at the Templehof airport in its fifty-year history. Two hundred police were on hand to monitor the rowdy fans in Deutschland Hall. Apparently the road had improved their per-formance. *Melody Maker* caught the Berlin concert and reported it was "ten times better than Manchester."

Their Creedence work was not what made them a tighter band. They played those songs for their contractual hour, then returned to the hotel where a new kind of ritual had begun. For this tour, John brought along some acoustic instruments and was play-acting a country singer onstage. Alongside Tony Joe, Duck, and their group, the trio dug into old-time and hard-core country tunes, playing for hours and passing bottles. They dubbed this hotel-suite-honky-tonk version of their band the Shit Kicker Three from Room 73, named for their first room in Manchester. And by far this endeavor occu-pied more of their time than the band they were paid to be in.

When they were previously a trio as the Blue Velvets, they were instrumental, and building a sound together. Now the dynamic was entirely different. They were performing an existing job in a hob-bled state. One simple piece removed and everything had changed. But as the Shit Kicker Three, they once again had no expectations. They were used to having a new name and working out a sound to match it. And while they still technically had a policy to play Cree-dence shows sober and drum-tight, they could work through George Jones, Merle, Buck, and Hank tunes until the dead of night and beer would only make it more fun. It was a way to have fun playing music as a trio while the core of their whole life together crumbled.

They took a long time in Copenhagen so that John could recon-nect with Lucy. Doug and Stu liked this woman, who was strong enough to stand up to John's grouchiness and dismissiveness of oth-ers. They could tell she was supportive of him, too, and this meant something even if he wouldn't admit it. In addition to his marriage problems and Tom's exit, John had fallen behind in his contractually required masters for Fantasy. If he was drinking more now, wearing rhinestone outfits, and playing the Opry songbook for hours at a time, it was likely because he needed a break from being John Fogerty, Boy Scout.

At their penultimate stop in Antwerp, they played the first rock concert ever held at the Sports Palace Arena, which was larger than anything in the more typical US band stopover, Brussels. Then they returned to the UK for back-to-back nights at the Albert Hall, ending on September 28. A full month in Europe this time, though with fewer festivities than the year before. It was simply a fact that there was less to celebrate. Thanks to low ticket prices, they actually lost money on the tour.

Back in the States, the schedule (and contract) demanded that they return to the studio. The reduced-size band had found a way to enjoy themselves on the road, something the quartet had never quite managed. The question remained whether they could produce music worth hearing at the pace they maintained for personal and financial reasons. John announced a plan in a limo, returning to the hotel after a gig at the San Diego Convention Center. Doug and especially Stu quickly realized it was an ultimatum. For their next record, John said, they would get what they'd been asking for, and what Tom wanted so badly that it drove him out of the band. The two of them, Stu and Doug, were each responsible for writing and singing a third of the material on the follow-up to *Pendulum*. And what's more, John wouldn't do his usual audio overachieving on their sides, either.

Doug felt like he was sitting back at the Italian restaurant in L.A., learning that he wouldn't be doing the background vocals on "Proud Mary." Or in the midwestern gymnasium, hearing that the encores were through. This was not what they had asked for. They only wanted greater input, greater say, not to pretend that they could do what John did. Perhaps with his help and effort they could record some lasting tracks, but they were not under the impression that they could step into his spotlight and deliver Top 10 miracles one after another. But this was John's way. He could pull a rug out when it suited him. He could throw up new regulations that didn't make the band better, didn't make him better, just changed the rules of the game.

By the end of 1971, Creedence had sold a total of $100 million in records and tapes. The year began with John Lennon telling *Rolling Stone*, "I like Creedence Clearwater. They make beautiful Clearwater music—they make good rock and roll music." It ended with Waylon Jennings, a honky-tonk singer who once played in Buddy Holly's band, singing their praises to the San Diego *Door*. Like millions of other existing Creedence fans, they had no way of knowing that a new policy was in place as the group reassembled to record their next album. As far as John thought, any disappointment from here on was out of his hands. Stu and Doug asked for this.

THIRTY-THREE

SAVAGED

They toured more as a trio than they had as a quartet. John's obligations to his family had shifted, for one. When Creedence went to New Zealand, Australia, and Japan in January 1972, his Danish girlfriend Lucy was along for most of the trip. She was a partier, a little rough around the edges as Doug would say, not without appreciation. He and Stu liked her company. The chemical rules for the band had relaxed as well. Theoretically, the sober-showtime restriction still applied, but it was hard to see how that could be when John was now drinking much more than he ever had before. He was into whiskey, which matched the cowboy affect. And he was certainly not alone. The trip began with an overlarge taste of pot brownies that San Francisco friends had given to Jake Rohrer before takeoff. That set the mood. The Shit Kicker Three were back.

Despite John's recent power move regarding the upcoming album, there was a juvenile kind of camaraderie at work as they made

their first visit to the Southern Hemisphere. The trio setup recon-
nected them to those plucky early days before the division of labor
became so stark. The drunken postshow carousing and the country songs gave them collective focus. And frankly, they were all still
pissed off at Tom. John felt betrayed, and Stu and Doug no longer
had to stick up for him. They didn't have to be the barrier between
brothers, and John didn't have to worry about simmering mutiny.

There was one show in New Zealand, then they moved to Bris-
bane, where they encountered a crowd so raucous it recalled the
Monkey Inn. Outside the venue, a cyclone caused flooding and
street closures. Inside, at least one beer bottle flew up to the stage
and crashed between band members. A day later they played a race-
track in Sydney in front of twenty-five thousand people, then went
on to Melbourne, where their concert was broadcast on the radio.
Before that concert, John visited a dying young fan in the hospital.
Word had reached the group that this was a sort of last request. John
sat at her bedside, unsure of what to say. She was too ill to attend
the concert, so John dedicated "Up Around the Bend" to her on the
broadcast that night.

The good feeling between the trio didn't mean their concerts
were better. Lacking rhythm guitar, John had to clip his melodies in
order to play chords. Stu had to hammer his bass to keep the bottom
end heavy enough. Doug, always excitable, kept the tempos hot.
They had lost their subtlety and substituted power. John even broke
a string in Melbourne.

The relative sloppiness was a particular shame in Adelaide, their
third Australian stop. Here, the band ran into Led Zeppelin, who
were crossing the continent from the opposite direction. The two
bands played the same venue on consecutive nights, Creedence going first, which meant the English group saw the trio perform in

their heedless new version. Doug felt embarrassed. These were the guys to beat now. They were also similar in many ways. Jimmy Page was a former session man turned record-making impresario like John. The two groups were reverent students of the blues and deep Tolkien aficionados. Yet from there they diverged, Creedence toward their unromantic, working-class-pop vision, and Led Zeppelin into full-scale mythmaking. Like John, Page was becoming an abler, more nuanced producer with every album, but he did it with a sense of grandeur that required trust and creativity from his bandmates. He made Robert Plant's voice sound like a screaming rocket and gave John Bonham's drums enough space that you could hear how much the air moved when he hit them. John Paul Jones contributed everything from riffs to orchestrations. Creedence was a great band, even in their shadow version on display in Adelaide. But Zeppelin were gods. Each of them summoned an elemental force.

After Creedence's hour-long show, the bands returned to the same hotel, where they each had private floors. Zeppelin was already infamous for debauchery and destruction while on tour, and the El Cerrito gang, even in their recent hard-drinking incarnation, was no match. The Creedence guys threw a TV out a window, nearly out of obligation. By night's end, John Bonham was tearing off the hotel wallpaper.

It was all good fun, but Doug could feel an undertow. This was the best kind of night that they were capable of having as a trio, and it wasn't consistent with the driving force that made them play together back in 1958. That wild night in Australia, none of them discussed music. They rarely did anymore. John was wearing his nouveau country suits and bell-bottoms with a bandana on his neck. He was clearly more interested in the songs they were working up in the hotel suites. He brought a banjo and pedal steel along for the tour though he'd never use them onstage. Doug could understand: John's industriousness and success had bought him only a debt and a contractual obligation to a man he now hated. He probably despised his own songs by now, Doug thought.

After a few dates in Japan, they returned home and John got a chance to model his annoyance plainly. They were calling the seventh Creedence album *Mardi Gras*, which could have been a wry joke given the mood in Wally Heider. They recorded eight songs to append to "Sweet Hitch-Hiker" and "Door to Door," one of which was a cover of Gene Pitney's "Hello Mary Lou" sung by John. Of the remaining seven, five were written or cowritten by Doug and Stu, including the latter's "Take It Like a Friend," which almost directly indicted John's selfishness within the band: "Thought you had the honor / Took special pride in all your well-laid plans / Forgot about the others / We moved out toward the light showing empty hands." John played the occasional guitar solo but gave nothing like his signature unstoppable effort. He explained the change in approach to journalist Joel Selvin by saying, all of a sudden, that he actually had no power in the band. "I'm not even in the realm of 'is the stuff any good or not.' That's not the criterion. If someone wants to do something bad enough, you're foolish to try and stop them after a point." He felt particularly bitter about Stu and Doug asking him to improve their songs; that wasn't the agreement. The idea was to finish their songs on their own, as John had routinely done for years after the others recorded their basic tracks.

Lucy was living with him now and accompanying him to the studio. His own two remaining contributions reflected the depth of his emotional struggles at the time. "Lookin' for a Reason," which was chosen to open the album, all but openly addressed John's desire to leave the band. "Every night I ask myself again / Just what it was that made our dream begin," he wrote in the first verse; "It seemed like a good idea way back then / But I'm wondering now what daydream took me in." He also wrote "Someday Never Comes," one of the most pensive and defeated songs he'd ever created, but one with greater emotional depth than any previous Creedence recording. Using the motif of a father asking his son to wait—for answers, for time together, for an understanding of why the father had to leave—John created a dramatic, heavy ballad about disappointment. He pointed the blame at his own father but reserved plenty for himself, since he was now in the habit of saying goodbye to his own kids, however briefly. Fathers always say it will all make sense someday, John wrote, but "You better learn it fast / You better learn it young / 'Cause someday never comes." He had become his own father, making inscrutable choices that affected his children, holding on to hope that they would come to understand and appreciate him. But he was also wise enough to know that understanding is illusory.

"Someday Never Comes" was as mature a statement as Creedence ever made, musically and emotionally. The band moved through odd minor keys, John added some lush piano, and the arrangement swerved from loud to hesitant as the lyrics changed. It was powerful and striking enough that it almost had to be the first single, and they prepared to release it simultaneous with the *Mardi Gras* album in April. The B-side was Doug's pseudo-Bakersfield touring anthem, "Tearin' Up the Country," a tuneful little song and the emotional opposite of John's compositions.

The record came out the month after Ike and Tina Turner won a Grammy for Best R&B Performance for their cover of "Proud Mary," and though only three years separated Creedence from their own initial triumph with that song, it had been nearly a year since their last LP. This was their first trio album and their first "democratic" one. Their plan was to release the record and the single, then head out for another tour. Creedence was already a wobbling enterprise, propped up by momentum and success, but the critical and commercial excitement for the group finally slowed to a near halt as the new record emerged.

For the first time, there was no picture of the band on the cover, just an image of a young girl and the band name spelled in hard-to-read font. Creedence was never known for their extended statements, but at ten tracks and twenty-eight minutes, including a cover and two previously released songs, *Mardi Gras* was a noticeably minor offering. Complaints of the group's stinginess had followed them since their first Fillmore shows. No encores, no improvisation, a tight fifty to fifty-five minutes. It worked when most of those songs were in the Top 10, less so when John was ceding album time to his bandmates who weren't practiced writers or singers, and not adding his own musical flourishes.

Reviews were not universally horrible. In *The Rag*, Austin's underground paper, reviewer Rockin' Raoul said he was relieved after hearing the album. The group had reoriented following Tom's loss and made "a very sensible change in direction." He praised Doug's and Stu's songs, John's solos, and called it "a very successful album." Greil Marcus, writing for *Creem*, said *Mardi Gras* wasn't a great album but "there was greatness in it." He considered it a "much more likable album than *Pendulum*, which is the coolest and most consistent Creedence has ever made. This one had more personality and more life." Marcus spent more than half of his long review praising "Someday Never Comes" and John's newfound lyrical depth. But Marcus grasped that the move toward democratization signaled the end of *something*, whether the band or just a previous idea of it. "I don't think Fogerty could survive as an artist outside of this little band. I think that working with musicians who have known him for more than ten years, who represent, in some way, his roots and his history, keeps Fogerty in touch with himself and keeps him honest, the way your roots, when you are in touch with them, act as a sort of conscience."

In the *New Yorker*, Ellen Willis's review was a chance for her to itemize what she loved about Creedence's music. She opened by recalling those halcyon days of 1970, when the band's audience stretched across "hardcore rock-and-roll fans and hard-core freaks, high-school kids and college students, AM and FM." This was the moment when her allegiance switched from the Stones to Creedence, and it happened to be the moment when the band's output slowed and they began their campaign to be taken seriously. Now she bemoaned their adoption of country-rock, "the number-one cheapo commodity in pop music." She noted that country music was once a way for rock musicians to explore different and exotic roots, but it had become an easy means of playing dress-up and escaping responsibility, an insightful reading of an album where multiple tracks explicitly mention leaving, running away, and finding safety elsewhere.

Willis believed in rock and roll, not country. It was the group's knowledge and celebration of history, and their unpretentiousness, that spoke to her initially. Their earlier music kept her sane as her other interests—politics, gender equality, civil rights, the antiwar cause—tested her patience and then sputtered out in partial victory at best. Creedence helped her dance through that tumult. They helped millions of others do the same. Even if the band stayed together, the loss of John Fogerty's overriding vision from the charts meant one less thoughtful, politically engaged, non-chauvinistic voice in a musical landscape that was desperate for them.

Rolling Stone was still the rock-world tastemaker, however, and the review by Jon Landau in that magazine was enough to mark the record for mockery. He held John responsible, calling the three-writer idea "Fogerty's Revenge," then ended his assessment by saying, "*Pendulum* was a disappointment but it was honest and it was useful—just because it showed Fogerty reaching for new directions. On this album he seems to have just given up. The result is, relative to a group's established level of performance, the worst album I have ever heard from a major rock band."

Mardi Gras went gold, achieving no. 12 on the album chart, while "Someday Never Comes" / "Tearin' Up the Country" went only to no. 25 and wasn't certified. The band went back on the road, mostly in the Midwest, playing their new songs about hating each other and their garage-band versions of the hits from 1969 and 1970. John felt foul onstage playing new songs he didn't care about. At one point in Denver, an audience member threw a quarter at the band. John picked it up and put it in his pocket. It was Creedence Clearwater Revival's final public show.

Not long after, Stu was at home when he heard a knock at the door. It was John, paying an uncommon house call, unprompted. They stood on the porch and John got to the point.

"I don't want to do this anymore," he told Stu.

"I don't think either one of us wants to do it anymore either," Stu responded, speaking for Doug as well. There was no fight, no tears, no punches. The band didn't explode, it dissolved.

THIRTY-FOUR

THE MUSIC IN
OUR HEADS

The band's breakup didn't change the requirements of their contract, so all four had to keep making music. Tom's self-titled debut solo album came out in May, featuring ten songs that he wrote and sang himself. The album, like its first single, "Cast the First Stone" / "Lady of Fatima," didn't chart. But he was thrilled with it. In an interview he said he wasn't thinking of money or recording plans. "I just enjoy the fact that people are coming along to see me and that I've got an opportunity of meeting and playing with some very down-to-earth people who aren't on any kind of personal trip."

John told a journalist that he tried to find new musicians when Creedence ended in the spring, but "couldn't find anyone on the same wavelength as me. So I learned one instrument after the other. Suddenly I thought my musical horizon had become endless. I could make my music the same as I heard it in my head." He learned the instruments he needed for a hot country group and started recording on his own. Those old covers he worked up with the Shit Kicker Three now had a place to go, and he didn't even have to worry about the other Two.

"Blue Ridge Mountain Blues" / "Have Thine Own Way, Lord" was released as a Fantasy 7-inch single in August and credited to the Blue Ridge Rangers. Both songs were traditional, with arrangements by "J.C. Fogerty." The same month, Doug released his own debut solo single, "Latin Music" / "Take a Train," which prefigured a solo LP, *Cosmo*, that arrived in September. Filled with guests including the Tower of Power horns, Steve Miller, Duck Dunn, Clover's John McFee, and Stu, the record also featured plenty of original Doug songs. It was released just as his second son was born.

An October 1972 press release announced the band's split but said everything was amicable. An article by Robert Hilburn confirmed it. Jake Rohrer told Hilburn, "Each of them felt it was necessary to explore their own musical interests and directions. The split wasn't bitter or vicious." He said the band continued to see each other every day at the Factory. That same month, Tom released another solo LP, *Excalibur*, and John put out another Blue Ridge Rangers single of two more old country tunes, "Jambalaya" and "Workin' on a Building." "Jambalaya," written originally by Hank Williams, went to no. 16.

In the aftermath of the breakup announcement, Saul found new product the only way he could: with a compilation. *Creedence Gold* was released in December 1972. An eight-song package, it included "The Midnight Special," "I Heard It Through the Grapevine," and six of the band's peak-era hits. There were no songs from *Mardi*

Gras and only "Have You Ever Seen the Rain" from *Pendulum*. The record went double platinum.

The Blue Ridge Rangers' self-titled debut LP came out on Fantasy in March. John wasn't exactly a recluse at this point, but his name didn't appear anywhere on the cover and the "band photo" was a lineup of five John silhouettes. He had written no songs for the record but played all the instruments. After the album's release, he took a trip to Troy, Idaho, with Jake Rohrer, where a family friend of Jake's lived. This man was heading into the deep backcountry to visit some back-to-the-landers and see how their camp was faring. John and Jake flew out to accompany him and commune with nature. They spent months among the rolling fields and in the rivers, fishing. They lived a life not far from what John's people in Montana had experienced. From then on, Troy, which had a population of only a few dozen, became John's frequent vacation spot.

In that moment, spring of 1973, he was optimistic. Truly. Since he was a child, every challenge had only strengthened John's resolve. Every loss of family, friends, mentors, confidants, and now bandmates was an opportunity to lose dead weight, just as he'd done with his music. Simplifying had never done him wrong. John was never afraid to shed things, but he was always very cautious about adding them. Now he'd finally done it. He could make music by himself, and he had a standing invitation to explore the outermost northern US wilderness. It couldn't get much simpler.

In the summer, a new youth-focused movie came out that bypassed the cynicism of *Easy Rider* or *Five Easy Pieces*. Instead, *American Graffiti* inaugurated a craze for nostalgia. The new movie was set in Modesto, California, in 1962, and concerned teenaged rock and roll addicts driving around at night in real time. Radio was nearly a character of its own in *American Graffiti*, and a reason why people loved it. In his review, Roger Ebert recalled his own early adolescence at this exact time and praised the literally endless pop soundtrack as "crucial and absolutely right. The radio was on every waking moment." Legendary deejay Wolfman Jack even played records on-screen. The movie was an enormous success, as was the accompanying two-LP set, *41 Original Hits from the Soundtrack to American Graffiti*, which functioned as an unofficial summary of Creedence's early influences, from "Do You Wanna Dance" to "Green Onions."

American Graffiti made so much money that it rekindled interest in a television pilot, *Happy Days*, that also starred young Ron Howard in the sock hop era. The show premiered in 1974, the same year as Linda Ronstadt's *Heart Like a Wheel*, which continued her previous solo records' mix of classic rock and roll and country with a few ace songwriters' original compositions. Her version of the Everly Brothers' "When Will I Be Loved" became the hit, but the inclusion of Hank Williams's "I Can't Help It If I'm Still in Love with You" was just as important for showcasing her taste and influences. A few years later she would show her debt, like Creedence, to Roy Orbison, and score a hit with "Blue Bayou."

Then there was Bruce. He announced himself with two records in 1973 alone, featuring dense, unspooling lyrics and arrangements that tumbled out of the speakers. He played an entrenched and enlightened member of the Jersey Shore underclass on those albums, but by his third, *Born to Run*, released in 1975, Springsteen moved beyond his beach-rat romanticism and found a style of music that echoed the *American Graffiti* soundtrack—a Bo Diddley beat in "She's the One," doo-wop affectations in "Tenth Avenue Freeze-Out," and monumental, Spector-esque production throughout. Then, between that album and his fourth, Springsteen underwent an artistic transition to match the change from the Golliwogs to Creedence. For *Darkness on the Edge of Town*, romance was all but gone, replaced by working-class worries and familial conflict. His songs were more grimly produced, too, with less reverb and air in the mix. On "Racing in the Street" and the title track, he wrung biblical emotions from drag racing, which featured prominently in *American Graffiti*, not to mention *Rebel Without a Cause*. Few of these artists proclaimed the influence of Creedence Clearwater Revival in the 1970s, but the band's interest in the music of the recent past, so untrendy during their brief reign, now looked prescient.

By this point no one needed to say they were influenced by Creedence anyway. The songs never really left. In 1976, Fantasy's double-LP compilation *Chronicle* collected twenty songs from *Creedence Clearwater Revival* through *Mardi Gras*, every one of their singles except "Born on the Bayou," plus "I Heard It Through the Grapevine." The result went instantly platinum and became the go-to introduction to Creedence for most people. The collection highlighted the band's awe-inspiring run of popular songs in such a short period, but it made their career seem smaller than it was. Twenty songs is an impressive number of well-known singles, but it wasn't enough to encompass all their great recordings or the range they were capable of. *Chronicle* lacked "Bootleg," with its perfect mix of acoustic and electric instrumentation. It lacked "Feelin' Blue," the one-chord marvel that showed off Doug's midtempo command like "Long as I Can See the Light." And it had no "Porterville" or "Walk on the Water," songs that connected them to an earlier stage of their career, one where Tom played a bigger role. Some of these were included on 1986's *Chronicle II*, which mostly proved that Saul and Fantasy were willing to oversaturate even the one-stop Greatest Hits market. *Chronicle* was ultimately

like a Creedence concert: astounding, entertaining, and after a bit
of consideration, maybe overcautious.

Saul Zaentz had been eyeing Hollywood for years, and his first
attempt at film production came when he backed an adaptation of
the counterculture-defining 1962 novel *One Flew Over the Cuckoo's
Nest* by Ken Kesey, the Grateful Dead confrere and acid test impresario whose events gave Bill Graham his first promotional opportunities in San Francisco. Saul used the money from Fantasy—which
is to say, money that Creedence made—to fund an independent
production that won multiple Academy Awards including Best Picture and Best Actor, won by *Easy Rider* and *Five Easy Pieces* star
Jack Nicholson. The numbers on the calendar may have changed,
but it seemed that the 1960s were not over, and not finished with
those who remembered them.

The '70s wore on and novelists and filmmakers kept trying to
make sense of the previous decade's existential challenges, particularly Vietnam. Creedence's entire public existence played out in a
brief window during those conflicts' darkest years. Now they became
a metonym for that time. *Dog Soldiers,* Robert Stone's 1974 novel
about a drug-running war correspondent, took place in Oakland and
Berkeley, and at one point a character even listened to their music
(though the band's name was misidentified as "Credence Clearwater"). When the book was turned into a movie in 1978, it was given
a new title, *Who'll Stop the Rain.*

From that point on, Creedence Clearwater Revival was nearly
synonymous with Vietnam. In 1981, when Bruce Springsteen dedicated a Los Angeles date of his ongoing tour to the plight of Vietnam vets, he opened his set with a cover of "Who'll Stop the Rain."
The movies kept telling the story of the war, too, and music super-
visors kept asking Fantasy for the rights to Creedence's songs. Saul

rarely said no, so the group's trademarks, "Run Through the Jungle" and "Fortunate Son" in particular, became soundtrack mainstays, enough that Fantasy released a cheap cash-in compilation under Creedence's name, *The Movie Album*, in 1985. Creedence's music was heard in *Born on the Fourth of July*, *Air America*, *1969*, *Distant Thunder*, *Powwow Highway*, *The Indian Runner*, and *Forrest Gump*, as well as in other period-set narratives like *My Girl* and *The Wonder Years*.

In a tragically familiar pattern, this success—cultural saturation, really—didn't stop the band members from seething at each other. At first, none of the others had much good to say about John in the press, and the leader was always quick to downplay their contributions or even dwell on how they held him back. John's general attitude toward the Creedence period of his life was not helped by Saul's flippant treatment of the music. Beyond *Creedence Gold*, *Chronicle*, and *The Movie Album*, Fantasy released 1973's *Live in Europe*, taken from their underwhelming trio tour of 1971, and 1980's *Live at Royal Albert Hall*, which had to be reprinted with a new title, *The Concert*, when it was belatedly discovered that the set was actually recorded at their triumphant Oakland Arena show in January 1970.

In the middle of all this, John discovered in 1975 that the money was gone. The lawyers had bungled everything, and the cash from millions of records sold and a hundred-plus worldwide sellout gigs was lost, completely unaccounted for. The Bahamian tax shelters were empty. The band spent years in court wresting $8.6 million from their financial advisors, years when John produced no music at all. All the while, the label repackaged and licensed his songs for every possible occasion, against his publicly stated wishes. Once again, Creedence Clearwater Revival's music remained the beloved soundtrack for innumerable shared moments of bliss, rage, sadness, and catharsis while the men who made it remained continually at odds with each other and their business partners.

They played together twice more. In 1980, Tom remarried and the four bandmates found themselves under the same roof with a willing audience for the first time in nearly a decade. The photos from that day are gorgeously garish. John, in amber-tinted glasses and sideburns to the hinge of his jaw, played a Gibson Explorer, Tom his own black Les Paul while wearing a white tux. They look sweaty, older, but neither looks bad. Behind them, Stu is singing background vocals for his life, still in glasses, a little heavier in the middle but obviously still in control of the bass. This reunited Creedence played a few songs on a tiered, Oriental-carpeted stage against a thickly striped wallpaper background. They posed for another picture together in the sun earlier that day. Tom beamed with his arms draped around Stu and John. Doug stood close by in a gray three-piece suit and a beard like a Wookiee. Like old album covers, they stood on the grass with the trees visible in the background. With the sun ablaze behind them, their legs cast long shadows that went far out of frame. Not long after the brief beauty of Tom's wedding, Ronald Reagan, old "Ronnie the Popular" as John had introduced him to record listeners on "It Came Out of the Sky," the same man who promised to fight college students to a bloodbath, was elected president.

A few years later, the twentieth reunion for the El Cerrito High School class of 1963 rolled around. How often were John, Doug, and Stu in the same room again, with people who remembered the Blue Velvets? Once again they played in their smaller form, the one they started in and could seemingly never avoid falling back to. But the night was celebratory. Could it have possibly been only twenty years? In his 1973 review of *American Graffiti*, Roger Ebert praised the film for conjuring "a world that now seems incomparably distant and innocent . . . Remembering my high school generation," he continued, "I can only wonder at how unprepared we were for the loss of innocence that took place in America with the series of hammer blows beginning with the assassination of President Kennedy." Now it was even ten years later than that. To be alive and among friends was enough justification to play those old songs again.

Tom was a regular gigging musician at this point, but only within a hundred-mile radius of his home in the Bay Area. He had his friends in the Keystone Korner scene and made a handful of solo albums in the '70s with studio musicians, including John, Stu, and Doug, who all played on his 1974 record *Zephyr National*, though John recorded his parts separately from the others. It was Stu on lead guitar for a song called "Joyful Resurrection," which celebrated Creedence's career. When it came out, Tom thought that it might be a good moment for the band to reassemble, but the moment passed. He told an interviewer in 1983 that things had changed for him. His crowds weren't as big as before and he didn't travel as much, which suited him fine. He was a family man now. "It really has to be something special to drag me out," he explained. "I'd like to visit some other countries but only if I could take my wife, make it a paid vacation." He didn't mention the others by name but noted, "I prefer the friendship of a gang, hanging out making music together. And I think the music's better that way."

By this point it had been long enough that plenty of people were alive who brought no twenty-year baggage like that to Creedence's music. "Proud Mary" felt like a standard in 1969. By the '80s, it and every other *Chronicle* track were part of the firmament of multiple subgenres of US popular music. Creedence songs had been covered, for starters, by Bob Seger, U2, Herbie Mann, Miriam Makeba, and the Minutemen. In 1986, the Beastie Boys' *Licensed to Ill*, the first hip-hop record to go platinum, closed with a track driven by a sample of "Down on the Corner." After Los Lobos recorded their first album in the late '80s, Jerry Garcia began sitting in with the Chicano group and was endlessly fond of calling out Creedence songs. Even self-consciously anti-mainstream bands loved Creedence. Kurt Cobain and Krist Novoselic played briefly in a CCR cover band years before starting Nirvana. Sonic Youth released their second LP, *Bad Moon Rising*, around the same time. Their guitarist Thurston Moore, who shared a peerless downtown-Manhattan résumé with his bandmates, affirmed to *Spin* that the title was a specific tribute. "John Fogerty is my life's blood," he said.

Tom contracted AIDS in the late '80s, purportedly from a blood transfusion during surgery. As he died in a hospital in 1990, only Doug visited. The drummer traded hours-long bedside shifts with Tom's family. John never came. He still felt something deeper than hurt. In 1985, after John willed himself out of retirement and recorded a hit album, *Centerfield*, he was sued unsuccessfully by Saul for plagiarizing "Run Through the Jungle," his own song. As John managed that latest surreal career struggle, Tom never came to his aid or said anything on his behalf. And as his older brother died an early, agonizing death, John could not bring himself to say goodbye in person. Tom supposedly wanted to play music together again. And that was too much to ask, too late.

Tom's son Jeff stood in for him when the band was inducted into the Rock and Roll Hall of Fame in 1993, their first year of eligibility. They were inducted by Springsteen, who gave a speech that honored all four members' contributions and told a story of his own early bar-band days in the late 1960s, a time he associated with *Easy Rider*. He said that his regular crowd was "eclectic": high school graduates of draft age, truckers, women in bouffants, and "a small but steady hippie contingent. A tough crowd to please all at once." But covering "Proud Mary" did it, and Springsteen marveled at how all these factions could stop and enjoy this out-of-time song during a moment of perpetual violent crisis and worry. Speaking at the height of grunge, Springsteen even credited John for his influential flannel-first fashion.

Stu and Doug arrived to the ceremony believing they would be playing the customary few songs onstage, but when the time came to rehearse, they learned that John would be performing the set himself with an all-star backing band including Springsteen and Robbie Robertson. The night left Doug and Stu feeling that a door had permanently closed. They resolved to start their own group to play the songs they knew were rightfully theirs to play. Calling themselves Creedence Clearwater Revisited, they began touring and even re-recorded classic Creedence tracks for their own albums. John sued. They had to change their name to Cosmo's Factory, then won back the right to Revisited.

In the late 1990s, the three remaining members of Creedence Clearwater Revival should have been taking victory laps. Fifty years since they started playing together and forty since they shifted the global consciousness in their small but entirely self-made way, they were an acknowledged influence on younger bands, they were Hall of Famers, and their records, *Chronicle* especially, continued to sell in the millions annually. But from their individual perspectives, their relationship to that music and era was in tatters. They were still fighting and struggling with outside forces and among themselves. John's songs were owned by his mortal enemy. His brother was dead.

His solo career was on hold again. One reliable source of income, Fantasy's liberal licensing practices, left him furious. After "Who'll Stop the Rain" was used in a paint commercial and "Fortunate Son" played for Wrangler jeans, he told the *Los Angeles Times* flatly, "I'm angry." And it wasn't just his own integrity, he was angry on behalf of the combat vets who associated his songs with those pivotal stolen years. He was angry that his memories were soiled. When he heard the Beatles in a commercial, he felt "they're stealing something from me . . . All my emotions welled up then at another nail in the coffin of the ideals of the '60s." In his mind and his heart, even in his legal battles, he was stuck in those years and in the swirl of youthful feelings that grew and overtook him then. Now his old bandmates were touring on the group's name and his songs.

For Doug and Stu, the situation was possibly more desperate. They had fought for a professional musician's most basic right: the ability to play the songs they made famous for an audience that wanted to hear them. And the man whose name they'd made, whose ideas they'd given everything for, had tried to prevent that.

Death and lawsuits and thirty years of publicized infighting didn't stop young kids like me, born in the '80s, from discovering those songs in movies, on the radio, at sports games, in documentaries, and for many of us, on *Chronicle*. In the CD era, a record like *Green River*, which isn't even thirty minutes long, wasn't exactly a deal. *Chronicle* offered more than twice as much music, all of it familiar or famous, for the same price. I must have known a few songs by the time I got that disc, but it was my first prolonged exposure to the group, and as designed, it killed. The opening duo of "Suzie Q" and "I Put a Spell on You" worked like a feint. It made them sound like a good, if indulgent, garage band. And then "Proud Mary" began, and *Chronicle* proceeded like a one-stop jukebox.

I was a suburban teenage drummer then, stuck on classic rock and grunge, and these songs made perfect sense. I was more in awe of the heavier British stuff, the Who and Zeppelin, because they had drummers who could have been comic book heroes. At least on record, Creedence couldn't match their sheer bashing power. But they had their own unique four-man movement, a feel that started in Doug's right foot and went up to John's top register. I could hear how John's arrangements, heavy on the low end and filled with scuzzy guitar tones and twisted blues lines, were a touchstone for Pearl Jam or Soundgarden, but the influence wasn't immediate or obvious. The newer groups were flashier. They were influenced by the Who and Zeppelin too. Creedence was still their own island. They could be felt everywhere, but nothing felt like them.

Few things could challenge my obsession with drumming during those years, but *The Big Lebowski*, released in 1998 when I was thirteen, came close. My friends and I were among the many millions who watched the DVD and received its dialogue like scripture. We understood little of the story's context, few of the western, war movie, and film noir tropes that it employed, or the Gulf War–era setting. But then I'd never heard Dale Hawkins sing "Susie Q" before Creedence introduced me to it either. We only loved the movie's madcap stupidity. We loved the profanity, the dick humor, the absolute refusal to give the story a higher meaning or gravitas.

But beneath its transcendent vulgarity, *The Big Lebowski* is ultimately about its characters' relationships to the 1960s. It is *The Big Sleep* rewritten for '90s California, where the private eye is a burned-out hippie whose clients stretch across a decadently liberated Los Angeles: the luxury art world, real estate development, and the pornography industry. Jeff Bridges, whose star was made in BBS Productions' 1971 release *The Last Picture Show*, plays the Dude,

a walking ghost of Woodstock Nation thrown into the plotting me-
chanics of the 1940s and contending with the commercial reality
of the present day. He has a permanent pot high but was also apparently close with the Seattle Seven and helped write a draft of
the Port Huron Statement. His best friend Walter is still haunted
by traumas from Vietnam. And so naturally, almost inevitably, the
Dude's favorite band is Creedence Clearwater Revival.

The Big Lebowski needed a way to identify the Dude with the
'60s as economically as possible. The Beatles were too obvious,
the Stones too dark for his personality. The Byrds were closest, especially for an L.A. denizen, but they were too gentle. The Dude
was gruff but tender, idealistic if self-defeating. Creedence's songs
were the soundtrack to his youthful triumphs, such as they were.
Their tuneful, bluesy sound, spiked with an underlying sense of
rage, matched his spiritual temperature. He sounded perpetually
frustrated that his party was being interrupted by real life.

The movie reset the band's reputation after the implosion of the
Hall of Fame. It put the emphasis on the greatness of their music,
how perfectly suited to this indelible, endearing character. As the
movie's cult status grew, an entire cottage industry sprung up just to
parse its every line, and Creedence was the unofficial house band
of this odd little community of die-hard in-jokers.

The twenty-first century has been quiet, relatively speaking.
There is Creedence merchandise now, and a line of luxury vinyl
reissues commemorating the classic years. This is better audiophile
treatment and marketing than they received at their peak, even
though everything is still owned by Fantasy. The label is part of the
Concord Music Group now, bearing no corporate resemblance to
its former self.

In 2019, after a quarter century as Creedence Clearwater Revisited, Doug and Stu decided they wanted off the train. I saw them perform in Annapolis, Maryland, one year earlier and they spoke from the stage in gratitude for their sixty years of friendship and music-making. They played the Creedence catalog with deep love and authority, knowing that these songs were born from ten years of hard luck and ugly nights without money or outside enthusiasm. Those songs came together at the Shire, in Doug's shed, at the Factory, at Woodstock and the Albert Hall and so many lesser arenas. They were John's songs first but they were not John's alone, not the way people knew and loved them. It was a Tuesday night in a small city in a small state, but the thousand-capacity venue was filled. People danced in the aisles, especially during "Down on the Corner." The guest-pass stickers looked like little *Lebowski* carpets.

In the years leading up to his ex-bandmates' retirement, John was in the middle of a well-deserved artistic stride as well. He was touring regularly with his son on guitar and a crack band behind him, one that never made mistakes or pushed the beat. He published his memoir, *Fortunate Son: My Life, My Music*, in 2015. And he was many years remarried to a woman, Julie, who he credits with all his clarity and positivity. He has reclaimed his songs for himself and, by all accounts, found the joy in them again. He plays and presents them now as John Fogerty songs, not Creedence songs, as on his 2013 album *Wrote a Song for Everyone*, where he dueted with a raft of contemporary stars from Brad Paisley to the Foo Fighters. When he plays with his band, they make a relaxed and warm sound, and John is visibly happy onstage. Knowing where he has been, I find this happiness almost unbearably poignant. He credits Julie.

In early 2021, on the day that antidemocratic insurgents attacked the Capitol, John released a gospel-hued ballad, "Weeping in the Promised Land," that addressed the previous years' civil unrest and police violence. The music video featured him on a hill above Los Angeles, seated alone at a grand piano. Close-ups of his face were intercut with images of contemporary street protests and uprisings. By this point it had already become a cliché to ask if the post-Obama years were crazier or scarier than the 1960s. John's reappearance as a sagely commentator, what Ellen Willis called an interpreter, was one more reason to think that history was repeating.

That song did not enter the vernacular. But Creedence, as routinely happens, emerged again. First, President Trump used "Fortunate Son" at his 2020 rallies. It blared as he disembarked from Air Force One. John issued a cease and desist and recorded a video for social media denouncing Trump's use of the song. He explained, with grandfatherly patience and clean language, what the Vietnam draft was and why the famously bone-spurred president with a millionaire father was exactly who the song was aimed at.

More surprising was the news in July 2021 that "Have You Ever Seen the Rain" had taken the no. 1 spot on the *Billboard* Rock Digital Sales chart, fifty years after its release. Catalog songs are routinely on that list; Creedence's two-week reign coincided with "Sweet Home Alabama" at no. 2. But the fact remained. With one member fallen, two retired, and the last still going under his own name, a brotherhood built and broken, it was the band's first no. 1 single.

Acknowledgments

Thank you first and foremost to Doug Clifford and Stu Cook for their participation in this project. This book could not exist without their input and willingness to talk about these years for many hours and with great candor.

I am indebted to Geoffrey Cannon, Robert Hilburn, Jesse Jarnow, Michael Kramer, Ken Levy, Joel Selvin, and Craig Werner for sharing their work on Creedence and the era. Special thanks to Michael Byrne, who, when asked about his time with John Fogerty in Portland in summer 1964, wrote a long, incisive, and entertaining memoir in response. Few researchers are treated so well. Additional, sincere thanks to Jane and George Lukes, and to Nona Willis Abramowitz, Daphne Brooks, and Van Truong.

Cherished friends and readers from all walks: Elon Green, Bradley Greenburg, Ted Scheinman, Rumaan Alam, Kaleb Horton, Dave

Stack, Andrew Stack, Pete Backof, Alex Cameron, Daniel Polansky, and Will Crain.

Deepest thanks to Ben Schafer, Carrie Napolitano, Fred Francis, and everyone at Hachette. RIP Da Capo Press.

To David Patterson, who is full of good ideas. A great agent and a wonderful person.

Love to my siblings, Ishai, Anna, and Jake, who grow more important to me every year, especially these last few. A lifetime of thanks and love to Mom and Dad, whose own memories of the era were my introduction to "the '60s"—and Creedence. Thanks to Denise and my extended family, whose support and love mean everything and never fail. To my uncle, Bob Lingan, who deserves to have his name in a book about CCR.

To Nina, Albert, and Roch. Always play your music loud. God how I love you all. And to Justyna, after years of challenge and exuberant joy. Thank you for keeping the music in my life.

Bibliography

INTERVIEWS AND EMAILS

Over the course of 2020, I interviewed Stu Cook and Doug Clifford for more than ten hours each. The many uncited, intimate band details in *A Song for Everyone* stem from those conversations, as do my insights into Stu's and Doug's points of view or thoughts over the course of the book — to cite them all would be cumbersome, and in any case it should be clear when these details inform the story.

Every effort was made to speak with John Fogerty, including emails and calls through multiple representatives. In lieu of his participation I have relied on his own memoir and on the many interviews he has granted since 1969.

I conducted additional phone interviews with Bobby Cowan, Emilio Castillo, Steve Cropper, Booker T. Jones, David Garibaldi, Joel Selvin, and Stu Steinberg, whose specific memories are cited in the text.

Email memories came in from alumni of St. Mary's in El Cerrito, where Tom and John Fogerty attended high school: Dan Reiley '59, John Young '63, Ernst Becker '63, and Baynard Cheshire '63.

BOOKS

Abbey, Edward. *Desert Solitaire: A Season in the Wilderness*. New York: Touchstone, 1968.

Anderson, Terry H. *The Movement and the Sixties: Protest in America from Greensboro to Wounded Knee*. New York: Oxford UP, 1995.

Appy, Christian G. *Working-Class War: American Combat Soldiers and Vietnam*. Chapel Hill: University of North Carolina Press, 1993.

Austerlitz, Saul. *Just a Shot Away: Peace, Love, and Tragedy with the Rolling Stones at Altamont*. New York: Thomas Dunne Books, 2018.

Azzerad, Michael. *Come As You Are: The Story of Nirvana*. New York: Broadway Books, 1993.

Barlow, John Perry. *Mother American Night: My Life in Crazy Times*. New York: Crown Archetype, 2018.

Bang, Derrick. *Vince Guaraldi at the Piano*. Jefferson, NC: McFarland & Co., 2012.

Bingham, Clara. *Witness to the Revolution: Radicals, Resisters, Vets, Hippies, and the Year America Lost Its Mind and Found Its Soul*. New York: Random House, 2016.

Blecha, Peter. *Sonic Boom: The History of Northwest Rock, from "Louie Louie" to "Smells Like Teen Spirit."* Milwaukee: Backbeat Books, 2009.

Block, Alan A. *Masters of Paradise: Organised Crime and the Internal Revenue Service in the Bahamas*. New Brunswick: Transaction Publishers, 1998.

Booth, Stanley. *The True Adventures of the Rolling Stones*. Chicago: Chicago Review Press, 2014.

Bordowitz, Hank. *Bad Moon Rising: The Unauthorized History of Creedence Clearwater Revival*. Updated Edition. Chicago: Chicago Review Press, 2007.

Boyle, Kay. *The Long Walk at San Francisco State and Other Essays*. New York: Grove Press, 1970.

Bradley, Doug, and Craig Hansen Werner. *We Gotta Get Out of This Place: The Soundtrack of the Vietnam War*. Amherst: University of Massachusetts Press, 2015.

Branch, Taylor. *At Canaan's Edge: America in the King Years, 1965–68*. New York: Simon & Schuster, 2006.

———. *Parting the Waters: America in the King Years, 1954–63*. New York: Touchstone, 1988.

———. *Pillar of Fire: America in the King Years, 1963–65*. New York: Touchstone, 1998.

Carroll, James. *An American Requiem: God, My Father, and the War That Came Between Us*. New York: Mariner, 1996.

Clear, Rebecca D. *Jazz on Film and Video in the Library of Congress*. Washington, DC: Library of Congress, Motion Picture, Broadcasting and Recorded Sound Division, 1993.

Cottrell, Robert C., and Blaine T. Brown. *1968: The Rise and Fall of the New American Revolution*. Lanham, MD: Rowman & Littlefield, 2018.

Cowie, Jefferson. *Stayin' Alive: The 1970s and the Last Days of the Working Class*. New York: The New Press, 2010.

DeCurtis, Anthony. *Lou Reed: A Life*. New York: Little, Brown, 2017.

Diski, Jenny. *The Sixties*. New York: Picador, 2009.

Ferlinghetti, Lawrence. *A Coney Island of the Mind*. New York: New Directions, 1958.

Fogerty, John. *Fortunate Son: My Life, My Music*. New York: Little, Brown, 2013.

Fornatale, Pete. *Back to the Garden: The Story of Woodstock*. New York: Touchstone, 2009.

Gaillard, Frye. *A Hard Rain: America in the 1960s, Our Decade of Hope, Possibility, and Innocence Lost*. Montgomery: New South Books, 2018.

George-Warren, Holly. *Janis: Her Life and Music*. New York: Simon & Schuster, 2019.

Gioia, Ted. *West Coast Jazz: Modern Jazz in California, 1945–1960*. New York: Oxford University Press, 1992.

Gleason, Ralph J. *Music in the Air: The Selected Writings of Ralph J. Gleason*. New Haven, CT: Yale University Press, 2016.

Gordon, Robert. *Respect Yourself: Stax Records and the Soul Explosion*. New York: Bloomsbury, 2013.

Grogan, Emmett. *Ringolevio: A Life Played for Keeps*. New York: New York Review Books Classics, 1972.

Hallowell, John. *Inside Creedence*. New York: Bantam Books, 1971.

Hoskyns, Barney. *Across the Great Divide: The Band and America*. Milwaukee: Hal Leonard, 2006.

Kaliss, Jeff. *I Want to Take You Higher: The Life and Times of Sly & the Family Stone*. New York: Backbeat Books, 2008.

Kitts, Thomas M., ed. *Finding Fogerty: Interdisciplinary Readings of John Fogerty and Creedence Clearwater Revival*. Lanham, MD: Lexington Books, 2013.

———. *John Fogerty: An American Son*. New York: Routledge, 2016.

Kramer, Michael J. *Republic of Rock: Music and Citizenship in Sixties Counterculture*. New York: Oxford University Press, 2013.

Krieger, Susan. *Hip Capitalism*. Beverly Hills: SAGE Publications, 1979.

Lauterbach, Preston. *Bluff City: The Secret Life of Photographer Ernest Withers*. New York: W. W. Norton, 2019.

MacDonald, Ian. *Revolution in the Head: The Beatles' Music and the Sixties*. New York: Henry Holt, 1994.

Mathhiessen, Peter. *Sal Si Puedes (Escape If You Can): Cesar Chavez and the New American Revolution*. Berkeley: University of California Press, 1969.

McNally, Dennis. *A Long Strange Trip: The Inside History of the Grateful Dead*. New York: Broadway Books, 2002.

McNeill, Don. *Moving Through Here*. New York: Alfred A. Knopf, 1970.

Morrow, "Cousin Brucie." *Doo Wop: The Music, the Times, the Era*. New York: Sterling Publishing, 2007.

Reich, Steve. *Writings on Music, 1965–2000*. New York: Oxford University Press, 2002.

Ritz, David. *Divided Soul: The Life of Marvin Gaye*. New York: Da Capo Press, 1991.

Rorabaugh, W. J. *Berkeley at War: The 1960s*. New York: Oxford University Press, 1989.

Rudd, Mark. *Underground: My Life with SDS and the Weathermen*. New York: William Morrow, 2009.

Sandoval, Andrew. *The Monkees: The Day-by-Day Story of the '60s TV Pop Sensation*. San Diego: Thunder Bay Books, 2005.

Savage, Jon. *1966: The Year the Decade Exploded*. London: Faber & Faber, 2015.

Slick, Grace. *Somebody to Love? A Rock-and-Roll Memoir*. New York: Warner Books, 1998.

Smith, Sherry L. *Hippies, Indians, and the Fight for Red Power*. Oxford: Oxford University Press, 2012.

Steinberg, Stuart Allan. *This Is What Hell Looks Like: Life as a Bomb Disposal Specialist During the Vietnam War*. Stroud, UK: Fonthill Publishing, 2018.

Stone, Robert. *Dog Soldiers*. New York: Mariner Books, 1974.

Talbot, David. *Season of the Witch: Enchantment, Terror, and Deliverance in the City of Love*. New York: Free Press, 2012.

Turner, Tina, with Kurt Loder. *I, Tina: My Life Story*. New York: It Books, 1986.

Watson, Bruce. *Freedom Summer: The Savage Season of 1964 That Made Mississippi Burn and Made America a Democracy*. New York: Viking, 2010.

Werner, Craig. *Up Around the Bend: The Oral History of Creedence Clearwater Revival*. New York, Spike Books, 1999.

Willis, Ellen. *Beginning to See the Light: Sex, Hope, and Rock-and-Roll*. New York: Random House, 1981.

——. *The Essential Ellen Willis*. Minneapolis: University of Minnesota Press, 2014.

——. *Out of the Vinyl Deeps*. Minneapolis: University of Minnesota Press, 2011.

Wolfe, Tom. *The Electric Kool-Aid Acid Test*. New York: Picador, 1968.

Wollenberg, Charles M. *Berkeley: A City in History*. Berkeley: University of California Press, 2008.

ARTICLES, ARCHIVAL INTERVIEWS, ETC.

"About . . . Teens 'n Twenties Promotions." Promotional handout, undated (likely 1966 or 1967).

Abramovich, Alex. "The Velvet Underground in California." *New Yorker*, published online December 8, 2015.

Baker, Bob. "Their 'Son' Was Fogerty's Baby." LATimes.com, October 23, 2002.

Berkeley Tribe. "Gay Fest." March 27–April 3, 1970, 10.

Billboard. "Heider Opens New Studios on W. Coast." April 26, 1969, 18.

Billboard. "Personal Appearance Dates Rack Up B.O. $ for Creedence." May 24, 1969, 24.

Black Shadow. "Record Wrap." *San Francisco Good Times*, December 11, 1969, 12.

Bordowitz, Hank. "The 1969 Creedence Clearwater Revival Recording Contract." *Journal of the Music and Entertainment Industry Educators Association* 12, no. 1 (2012): 69–89.

Bosso, Joe. "John Fogerty Talks About the Creedence Musical Process." MusicRadar.com, July 1, 2013.

Boston Globe. "John McKey Hallowell, 1942–2014." December 29, 2014. Reprinted at www.legacy.com/us/obituaries/bostonglobe/name /john-hallowell-obituary?id=17977074.

Brown, G. "Jimi Hendrix's Colorado Connection—Denver Pop Festival." Blog post, Colorado Music Experience, https://colomusic.org/blog /jimi-hendrixs-colorado-connection-denver-pop-festival/.

Bruce, George Henley. "Creedence in It for the Money." *Rebirth*, September 1969, 4.

Buday, Don. "Fogerty's 1-Man Quartet on the Tube." *Los Angeles Free Press*, May 28, 1971, 12.

Byrne, Michael. "My Life with John Fogerty." Private memoir shared with author, 2020.

Cannon, Geoffrey. "Creedence Clearwater Revival: Royal Albert Hall, London." *The Guardian*, April 17, 1970.

———. "Family, the Rolling Stones: The Rolling Stones in Hyde Park: Out of the Way." *New Society*, July 10, 1969.

Cashbox. "Embarrassed on the Bayou." January 31, 1981, 14.

Christgau, Robert. "Creedence: Where Do You Go from the Top?" *Village Voice*, February 1971; reprinted at robertchristgau.com.

Clash, Jim. "CCR Drummer Doug Clifford Releases 'Doug Cosmo Clifford' LP." Forbes.com, June 20, 2018.

Coley, Byron. "Sonic Youth." *Spin*, August 1985, 52–54.

"Color Them Creedence Art Contest." Advertisement in the *Los Angeles Free Press*, September 19, 1969, 12.

"'COSMO'S FACTORY' is the new CREEDENCE LP." Fantasy Records advertisement, *Billboard*, July 26, 1970, 49.

Crisafulli, Chuck. "Russ's Factory: The Man Behind Creedence's Sound." Gibson.com, November 11, 2010.

Daloz, Kate. "The Hippies Who Hated the Summer of Love." Longreads .com, August 2017.

Dare, Michael. "Five Easy Pieces." Liner notes to Criterion laser disc. Available at www.criterion.com/current/posts/884-five-easy-pieces.

de Benedetti, Chris. "Local Garage Bands of 60s Chronicled." *East Bay Times*, August 12, 2006.

di Perna, Alan. "Inside Creedence Clearwater Revival's Breakthrough Year." *Guitar Aficionado*, September/October 2016.

Door to Liberation. "The State of Our Music Message." September 24, 1970, 10.

Dubro, Alec. "Willy and the Poor Boys." *Rolling Stone*, January 21, 1970.

Durham, Michael. "A Short Talk with a Debut Novelist." *Life*, August 29, 1969, 10.

Ebert, Roger. "Review: *American Graffiti*." *Chicago Sun-Times*, August 11, 1973.

Ehler, Jay. "Waylon Jennings." *Door*, December 9–23, 1971, 17–18.

"Enter Tom Fogerty." Jerry Garcia's Middle Finger, May 28, 2018. Available at http://jgmf.blogspot.com/2018/05/enter-tom-fogerty.html.

Fenton, David. "An Interview with John Fogerty of Creedence Clearwater Revival." *Liberation News Service*, March 28, 1970, 24–32.

Gibson, Caitlin. "What Happened in Chicago in 1968, and Why Is Everyone Talking About It Now?" *Washington Post*, July 18, 2016.

Gilbert, George. "Rock Radio in the Streets." *San Francisco Chronicle*, March 19, 1968, p 3.

Gilliland, John, and Harry Shearer. "Pop Chronicles Interviews #41— John Fogerty and Creedence Clearwater Revival." Audio recording, 1969, University of North Texas Libraries, UNT Digital Library.

Gladstone, Howard. "The Robbie Robertson Interview." *Rolling Stone*, December 27, 1969.

Glazer, Nathan. "Negroes and Jews: The New Challenge to Pluralism." *Commentary*, December 1964.

Gleason, Ralph J. "John Fogerty: The Rolling Stone Interview." *Rolling Stone*, February 21, 1970, 17–24.

Goldberg, Michael. "John Fogerty Looks Back at the Glory Days of Creedence Clearwater Revival." *Rolling Stone*, February 4, 1993.

Goldman, Albert. "Purity, Not Parody, in a Real Rock Revival." *Life*, May 9, 1969, 8.

Goldstein, Richard. "Pop Eye: San Francisco Bray," *Village Voice*, March 3, 1967.

Great Speckled Bird. "Patton." March 16, 1970, 15.

Greene, Andy. "Q&A: John Fogerty on All-Star Duets LP, Unlikely Cree-
    dence Reunion." RollingStone.com, May 12, 2012.
Gross, Jane. "At Lunch With: Herb Caen; Romancing San Francisco in
    1,000 Words or Less." *New York Times*, May 26, 1993, sec. C, 1.
Hamill, Pete. "The Revolt of the White Lower Middle Class." *New York
    Magazine*, April 14, 1969.
Havers, Richard. "Creedence Clearwater Revival Take Europe."
    Udiscovermusic.com, September 1, 2012. www.udiscovermusic
    .com/stories/creedence-clearwater-revival-take-europe/.
Hilburn, Robert. "200 Police but No Hassling." *Los Angeles Times*, Sep-
    tember 22, 1971, F16.
———. "Antwerp Gets Rock 'n' Roll Message." *Los Angeles Times*, Septem-
    ber 28, 1971, F1.
———. "Creedence—A Rock Group That Means Business." *Los Angeles
    Times*, August 30, 1970, M1.
———. "Creedence in a Return to Recording Wars." *Los Angeles Times*,
    June 20, 1971, T1.
———. "Creedence Moves Ahead with Album." *Los Angeles Times*, De-
    cember 15, 1970, H19.
———. "Creedence Split as Working Band." *Los Angeles Times*, October
    18, 1972, E19.
———. "Delta Sound Dominates Rock Concert." *Los Angeles Times*, De-
    cember 1, 1969, D1.
———. "Fogerty Rocks Again as Lone Ranger." *Los Angeles Times*, April
    8, 1973, Q1.
———. "Fogerty's Nightmare Is Over." *Los Angeles Times*, January 6, 1985,
    U54.
———. "Popular Records: 7th Creedence Album Also a 1st." *Los Angeles
    Times*, April 9, 1972, S44.
———. "Tardy but Worthy Look at Creedence." *Los Angeles Times*, May
    28, 1971, F19.
Hoberman, J. "One Big Real Place: BBS from Head to Hearts." *America
    Lost and Found: The BBS Story*. Criterion Collection, 2010.
Hopkins, Jerry. "Crashers, Cops, Producers Spoil Newport '69." *Rolling
    Stone*, July 26, 1969.
Hurwitz, Matt. "Classic Tracks: Creedence Clearwater Revival 'Fortu-
    nate Son.'" *Mix*, March 1, 2009, www.mixonline.com/recording
    /classic-tracks-creedence-clearwater-revival-fortunate-son-366079.

Ingles, Paul. "The Beatles' Yearlong Journey to 'The Ed Sullivan Show.'" *All Things Considered*, February 7, 2014.

Jahn, Mike. "Bo Diddley Returns on Guitar at Forest Hills Rock Concert." *New York Times*, July 19, 1971, 31.

——. "Californians Play Refreshing Rock at Fillmore East." *New York Times*, March 24, 1969, 52.

James, Gary. "Gary James' Interview with Doug 'Cosmo' Clifford of Creedence Clearwater Revival." ClassicBands.com, www.classicbands .com/CCRInterview.html.

——. "Gary James' Interview with Executive Assistant to CCR and John Fogerty Jake Roher [*sic*]." ClassicBands.com, www.classicbands .com/JakeRohrerInterview.html.

——. "Gary James' Interview with Stu Cook of Creedence Clearwater Revival." ClassicBands.com, www.classicbands.com/Creedence StuCookInterview.html.

"John Lennon: Hear Jann Wenner's Legendary 1970 Interview." *Rolling Stone Music Now* (podcast). Original print interview appeared in *Rolling Stone*, January 21, 1971.

Johnson, Dr. Troy. "We Hold the Rock: The Alcatraz Indian Occupation." National Park Service, Alcatraz Island website, November 19, 2019, www.nps.gov/alca/learn/historyculture/we-hold-the-rock.htm.

Karp, Josh. "Bob Rafelson Emerges to Reflect on His Feud-and-Brawl-Filled Career." Esquire.com, April 2, 2019, www.esquire.com /entertainment/movies/a26454547/bob-rafelson-interview/.

Kleinhans, Charles. "The Great Atlanta (White) Pop Festival." *The Spectator* (University of Indiana–Bloomington), July 15, 1969, 16–17.

"KMPX Radio Protest Strike." Bay Area Television Archive. KTVU-2 News, March 15, 1968.

Lepore, Jill. "Kent State and the War That Never Ended." *New Yorker*, May 4, 2020.

Levy, Ken. Unreleased audio interview with Tom Fogerty, February 25, 1983.

Lombardi, John. "Creedence Clearwater Throws Serious Party." *Rolling Stone*, January 7, 1971, 3–6.

Long, Everett. "Creedence Clearwater Revival." *Kudzu*, November 12, 1968.

Lynskey, Dorian. "John Fogerty: 'I Had Rules. I Wasn't Embarrassed That I Was Ambitious.'" *The Guardian*, May 29, 2013.

Marcus, Greil. "Creedence Clearwater Revival: Mardi Gras." *Creem*, June 1972, 62.

Margolis, Lynne. "John Fogerty: The Extended Interview." *American Songwriter*, May 28, 2013.

Maron, Marc. "Episode 392: John Fogerty." *WTF with Marc Maron* (podcast), May 27, 2013.

McCormick, Patricia. "The Girl in the Photo." *Washington Post Magazine*, April 24, 2021, 8–15.

McFadden, Robert D. "Saul Zaentz, 92, Producer of Oscar-Winning Movies." *New York Times*, January 5, 2014, A21.

Meister, Dick. "1968: San Francisco's Year of the Strike." LaborFest.net, 2008.

Moon, Tom. "Creedence Clearwater Revival's *Green River* at 50: Our Essential Guide to Early CCR." NPR.com, August 2, 2019, www .npr.org/2019/08/02/744929605/creedence-clearwater-revivals -green-river-at-50-our-essential-guide-to-early-ccr.

Myers, Marc. "'Proud Mary,' from John Fogerty to Tina Turner: Anatomy of a Song." WSJ.com, May 13, 2013.

Ng, David, and David Colker. "Saul Zaentz Dies at 92; Oscar-Winning Producer of 'Amadeus,' 'Cuckoo's Nest.'" *Los Angeles Times*, January 4, 2014.

Nixon, Richard. "Address to the Nation on the Situation in Southeast Asia." April 30, 1970. Archived at www.nixonfoundation.org/2017 /09/address-nation-situation-southeast-asia-april-30-1970/.

Nusser, Richard. "No Pale Imitation." *Village Voice*, July 2, 1970.

Orloff, Kathy. "Creedence Clearwater Revival Is Unique." (Toledo) *Blade*, May 23, 1969, 30.

Palao, Alec. "Pre-Creedence: The First Decade." Liner notes to *Creedence Clearwater Revival: Box Set*, Fantasy Records, 2001.

———. "Rumble on E. 14th St. in San Leandro: The East Bay's Garage Heyday." Liner notes to *You Got Yours! East Bay Garage, 1965–1967*, Ace Records, 2007.

Pilgrim, Eric. "52 Years Later, Rock Legend John Fogerty Remembers Time in Army." Military.com, September 26, 2019, www.military .com/off-duty/2019/09/26/52-years-later-rock-legend-john-fogerty -remembers-time-army.html.

Prevert, L. "Far-Out News Shorts." *Fifth Estate* 5, no. 11 (October 1–14, 1970): 17.

Radin, Rick. "El Cerrito Centennial: Longtime Merchants Take Fond Look Back." *East-Bay Times*, March 2, 2017.

———. "El Cerrito Era of Gambling, Vice and Racketeers Recounted in Talk." *East-Bay Times*, March 16, 2017.

Raskin, Jomo. "Dear Abbie: A Review of Woodstock Nation by Abbie Hoffman." *Liberation News Service*, November 13, 1969, 16–17.

Record World. "Assoc. Inks Creedence." May 17, 1969, 22.

Record World. "Germany's Top Ten." June 14, 1969, 48.

Reed, Lou. "The View from the Bandstand." *Aspen*, December 1966.

Rezos, Ray. "*Bayou Country*." Review. *Rolling Stone*, March 1, 1969.

Rockin' Raoul. "Creedence Clearwater Revival: *Mardi Gras*." *The Rag* (Austin, TX), May 1, 1972.

Rohrer, Jake. A Banquet of Consequences: *True Life Adventures of Sex (not too much), Drugs (plenty), Rock & Roll (of course), and the Feds (who invited them?)*. Portland, OR: Inkwater Press, 2014.

Rome, Adam. "The Genius of Earth Day." *Environmental History* 15, no. 2 (2010): 194–205.

Rothman, Lily. "This Photo Shows the Vietnam Draft-Card Burning That Started a Movement." Time.com, October 15, 2015, https://time.com/4061835/david-miller-draft-card/.

Schlesinger, Arthur. "Joe College Is Dead." *Saturday Evening Post*, September 21, 1968, 24–30.

Schonfeld, Zach. "How Creedence Clearwater Revival Became the Soundtrack to Every Vietnam Movie." Pitchfork, February 20, 2018, https://pitchfork.com/thepitch/how-creedence-clearwater-revival-became-the-soundtrack-to-every-vietnam-movie/.

Silvers, Emma. "How One Tenderloin Recording Studio Shaped 'The San Francisco Sound.'" KQED.com, November 10, 2016, www.kqed.org/arts/12279498/hyde-street-rock-how-wally-heider-and-the-tenderloin-shaped-the-san-francisco-sound.

Simkins, J. D. "Creedence Clearwater Revival's John Fogerty Talks Military Service, Music's Role in War." MilitaryTimes.com, November 11, 2019, www.militarytimes.com/off-duty/military-culture/2019/11/11/creedance-clearwater-revivals-john-fogerty-talks-military-service-musics-role-in-war-2/.

Smith, Sharon. "The Workers' Rebellion of the 1960s." *Socialist Worker*, December 1990.

Tannenbaum, Rob. "Roger Daltrey Recalls the Mud, Music and Madness." *New York Times*, August 11, 2019, F18.

Taruskin, Richard. "A Sturdy Musical Bridge to the 21st Century." *New York Times*, August 24, 1997, sec. 2, 29.

Tiegel, Eliot, et al. "San Francisco: A Cauldron of Creative Activity." Special section of *Billboard*, May 6, 1967.

"Tom Fogerty Unreleased MTV Interview, 4/26/1986." Music Vault, uploaded September 25, 2014, www.youtube.com/watch?v=CTJ 6j5zPc_I&t=1s.

Trakin, Roy. Liner notes to *Creedence Clearwater Revival—The Studio Albums Collection*, Craft Recordings, 2019.

US News & World Report. "Race Troubles: 109 US Cities Faced Violence in 1967." August 14, 1967.

Vanjak, Gloria. "State of Florida vs. Jim Morrison." *Rolling Stone*, October 1, 1970.

Wasserman, John. "The Hottest in the World." *San Francisco Chronicle*, December 20, 1970. Republished on SFGate.com, October 10, 2013, www.sfgate.com/entertainment/article/The-hottest-in-the-world -1970-4886424.php.

"A Weekend of Folk Music on the Berkeley Campus of the University of California." Event program, 1958.

Wharton, David. "The Lost Love-In: It Was the Woodstock They Forgot: Newport '69, Los Angeles' Own Weekend of Music, Masses and Mayhem." *Los Angeles Times*, August 6, 1989.

Zoloth, Laurie. "Sisters at Rock Concert." *It Ain't Me Babe*, July 2–23, 1970, 7.

Notes

INTRODUCTION

xiv **an unusually terse answer:** MacDonald, 294; and "Paul McCartney Interview: Beatles Break-up 4/9/1970," Beatles Interviews Database, www.beatlesinterviews.org/db1970.0417.beatles.html.

ONE: CLASSMATES

2 **height of doo-wop airplay:** Morrow, 200.

3 **residents burned a cross:** Kaliss, 24.

4 **a hundred thousand people . . . half a million:** Rorabaugh, 49.

4 **Sears and Safeway:** Rorabaugh, 49.

4 **pushed into the sleepier suburbs:** Rorabaugh, 55.

4 **"second Gold Rush":** Wollenberg, 105.

4 **tripled:** Kitts, *American Son,* 2.

4 **haven of sin:** Radin, "El Cerrito Era of Gambling."

5 **Stu grew up hearing:** Werner, 19.

TWO: THE COMBO

11 **furniture store:** Werner, 27.

12 **escape:** Fogerty, 30, 36, and 38 has information about John's alcoholic parents and the shame, failure, and self-consciousness he felt as a young man. Only music brought him joy during the chaotic time. On page 39 he immediately connects this joy with the need to make money, to "get anywhere."

12 **Great Falls, Montana:** Kitts, *American Son*, 2.

12 **Stephen Foster:** Fogerty, 5.

13 **"air":** Fogerty, 42.

13 **"I Want You"** . . . **"Rock Around the Clock":** Fogerty, 41.

13 **"Bumble Boogie":** Gleason, "John Fogerty," 24.

14 **Johnny Corvette:** Werner, 15.

16 **his band:** Fogerty, 68.

16 **self-consciousness:** Lynskey, and throughout Fogerty's memoir.

17 **Jean Ritchie and Frank Warner:** "Weekend of Folk Music," 2.

18 **the bookstore:** Talbot, 26, 27.

18 *I thought I was Tom Sawyer:* Ferlinghetti, 60, 61.

THREE: A GROWN MAN

21 **the Five Satins, the Penguins, and the Medallions:** "Tom Fogerty Unreleased MTV Interview."

22 **Del-Fi Records:** Werner, 34.

26 **a thousand students:** Anderson, 59.

FOUR: BLUE AND GREEN

28 **drove a truck:** Werner, 54.

28 **served his ex-classmates:** Email correspondence with Dan Reiley, St. Mary's class of 1959.

28 **St. Mary's:** John's recollections of this period are in Fogerty, 80–84.

28 **He formed a group:** Email correspondence with Baynard Cheshire, St. Mary's class of 1963.

29 **sole "long-hair":** Email correspondence from Ernst Becker, St. Mary's class of 1963.

29 **bicycle pump:** Rohrer, 62.

29 **small tape deck:** Werner, 91.

31 **"Come On Baby":** Werner, 35.

33 **Sierra Sound Laboratories:** Fogerty, 84.

34 **"Green Onions":** Gordon, 67.

34 **Booker T. & the MGs:** Fogerty, 125. He calls them "my favorite band." Doug Clifford confirmed the Blue Velvets' group-wide adoration.

35 *The First Family*: Branch, *Parting*, 674.

35 **above all others:** Fogerty, 46.

37 **After finishing:** The details of the incident are purposefully vague. In Werner, 37, John contends that a Black man approached the group at the El Cerrito High School class of 1953 reunion and said that the band was missing an "in-between thing" in their sound. In his own memoir, he only says that it happened at *a* high school reunion, but he now somehow remembers the attendee's name, R. B. King, and that King said that there was "somethin' missing" in their Booker T. rhythm. In interviews for the current book, Stu Cook concurred that they received similar feedback from a slightly older Black listener, but he recalled it as a cab driver who arrived early to pick the band up from a gig. Doug did not recall the incident at all.

FIVE: FANTASIES

39 **Phase A-2:** Talbot, 61.

40 **Pat Boone:** Bradley and Werner, 20.

41 **genre were since toppled:** MacDonald, 8fn.

42 **initially aired:** Ingles.

42 **ten hours:** Branch, *Pillar*, 174.

43 **seventy-three million:** Booth, 136.

43 *Newsweek*: Gaillard, 191.

43 **no major youth crimes:** Booth, 136.

44 **March 18:** Clear, 8.

44 **Soul:** Bang, 22, clarifies the spelling of this name, which is atypical.

44 **Max:** Palao, "Pre-Creedence."

44 **made quick plans:** Bordowitz, *Bad Moon Rising*, 21. This contrasts with John's own telling of this event in his memoir, where he claims to have made the trip solo. Bordowitz draws on earlier quotes from both he and Tom where they state they went as a pair.

45 **"the city":** Fogerty, 91.

45 **Jack Sheedy . . . Dave Brubeck:** Gioia, 62.

45 unusual colors . . . Chinese opera: Bang, 22–23.
47 Bob Rafelson: Karp has the details of Rafelson's early life.
48 screaming match about recuts: Sandoval, 17–18.

SIX: FREEDOM SUMMER

49 Mustang . . . "buyingest age group": Branch, *Pillar*, 229.
49 thirty-mile stretch: de Benedetti.
50 Sly Stone: Author interview with Emilio Castillo.
50 Mike Byrne: The bulk of what follows about the Apostles and Portland is drawn from Byrne's short memoir, "My Life with John Fogerty," which was written and supplied to the author specially for this book. Byrne is misidentified as "Mike Burns" in John's memoir (96) and the entire Portland episode is only briefly noted in that book, as well as in Bordowitz and Werner. Tom Fanning died in 2010.
51 The Portland scene: Blecha, 163.
51 Supro: Fogerty, 73–74.
53 James Brown, Wilson Pickett, and Little Richard: These three are mentioned as John's specific vocal influences in Fogerty, 98, along with Don Ford, Billy Gordon of the Contours, and the Sevilles, a Twin Cities band with a 1961 hit, "Charlena," who are the only white singers he lists as inspiration.
53 manlier: Fogerty, 98. John specifically writes of his vocal influences: "That's where I was trying to go. That alpha thing."
53 "The white man": Branch, *Parting*, 709.
54 90 percent . . . "middle-class stamp": Watson, 16, 19.
56 John's voice: Bordowitz, *Bad Moon Rising*, 27 quotes Tom from a 1971 interview, where his exact phrasing is "I could sing, but John had a sound." Bordowitz notes this was "rather magnanimous."
56 largest-ever college enrollment: Bingham, 38. To be precise, Bingham notes that the 1964–1965 school year saw a 37 percent increase in student enrollment over the previous year.

SEVEN: HUMILIATION

59 Howard Zinn: Anderson, 86.

59 **Barry Goldwater:** Gaillard, 236, contains an excellent summary of this coalition and its unifying principles.
59 **Union Square:** Reich, 19–22.
60 **physical sensation:** Taruskin. Reich is quoted more than thirty years later as saying, "The sensation I had in my head . . . was that the sound moved over to my left ear, moved down to my left shoulder, down my left arm, down my leg, out across the floor to the left, and finally began to reverberate and shake . . . [finally coming] back together in the center of my head."
62 **'58 Volkswagen bus:** Bordowitz, *Bad Moon Rising*, 40.
64 **US war industry:** Rorabaugh, 169.
64 **deployments to Vietnam:** Cottrell and Brown, 20–21.
64 **Alice Herz:** Branch, *Canaan's Edge*, 120–121.
65 **"teach-ins":** Gaillard, 263. The first such event at UC Berkeley took place in May.
65 **25,000-person march:** Gaillard, 265.
65 **late July:** Branch, *Canaan's Edge*, 268–269.
65 **amendment to the Selective Service Act:** Cottrell and Brown, 25.

EIGHT: A MAN OF NATURE

69 **Mick Jagger:** Savage, 50.
70 **the first "John" record:** Palao, "Pre-Creedence."
70 **Pope Paul VI:** Carroll, 158.
71 **Hells Angels:** Austerlitz, 76.
71 **Raybert:** Sandoval, 25–26. The pilot for the show was written by Larry Tucker and Paul Mazursky.
72 **DC street-corner group-harmony scene:** Ritz, 28.

NINE: NITTY-GRITTY

73 **Charles Sullivan:** Talbot, 63.
73 **Wolfgang Grajonca:** Talbot, 69.
74 **"the big ballroom":** Wolfe, 252–253, which has the further details from this scene as well.
75 **New York Times:** Gaillard, 369.
75 **US soldiers died:** Branch, *Canaan's Edge*, 452.

76 **Them's first US show:** de Benedetti.
76 **grand press release:** "About . . . Teens 'n Twenties Promotions." Archival material about Teens 'n Twenties materials is available online, www.teensntwenties.com/.
77 **ten thousand copies:** Kitts, *Finding*, xiii.
77 **Monkees:** Werner, 47.
77 *Washington Post* . . . **Monkees recording sessions:** Sandoval, 34, 37.
78 **"draft card burning":** Savage, 84–85.
78 **Hoover:** Lauterbach, 154.
80 **collage of sensory experiences:** Slick, 97.
80 **microphones and speakers:** Kramer, 46–47.
80 **Hertzberg:** McNally, 175.
81 **"Perversion U.S.A. element":** Abramovich.
81 **short memoir:** Reed.

TEN: THE VALLEY OF THE BLACK PIG

83 **Reagan:** Gaillard, 315.
84 **Martha:** Fogerty, 112. The hypothesis that Martha pleaded is John's.
86 **Canby:** Sandoval, 56.
87 **major US fighting units:** Appy, 121.
87 **185,000 . . . 385,000:** Savage, 81.
87 **Project 100,000:** Appy, 32.
87 **President Johnson:** Gaillard, 372.
88 **Lady Bird:** Branch, *Canaan's Edge*, 552.
88 **one of the Grateful Dead's associates:** This and the naked Bob Weir story are in Barlow, 49–50.
88 **"Superspade" . . . "Free Frame of Reference":** Grogan, 245–249, though he spells the man's name as two words.
88 *Berkeley Barb*: Gaillard, 416.
88 **twenty thousand people:** Daloz.
89 **Larry Beggs:** Talbot, 43–44.
89 **Judge Raymond J. O'Connor:** Talbot, 48.
89 **their ass-kickings in January:** Gilliland and Shearer.
90 **Fort Bragg:** Pilgrim. This interview, conducted in 2019, years after John's memoir, presents a very different view of his experience in the military. The memoir does not mention hearing music, though

he does recall an incident where he stands up to a fascistic sergeant. But the Pilgrim interview isn't necessarily more reliable; in it, John claims to have seen Elvis Presley's signature on a wall at Fort Knox, though there is no record of Elvis ever having been there.

90 **barracks leader:** Fogerty, 113.

91 **After his initial charm offensive:** Fogerty, 114–118.

92 **shadows:** Fogerty, 112.

92 *The Doors:* Simkins. *Fresh Cream* is assumed because John only tells the interviewer "something with Eric Clapton" and that album would fit the timetable. Interestingly, he never mentions any of these records in his memoir except *Sgt. Pepper's*, which he only dismisses in passing: "After *Sgt. Pepper* [sic], rock and roll grew up and everybody got all brainy and highfalutin and introspective and impotent—I mean important" (137).

93 **moral grounds:** Fogerty, 114. His exact phrase is: "This was a very volatile time in America, with all kinds of confrontations and conflicts and philosophies floating across the cultural windscreen. People chaining themselves to government buildings."

93 **David Miller:** Cottrell and Brown, 22.

ELEVEN: FULL-TIME

95 **$1,250:** Bordowitz, *Bad Moon Rising*, 31.

95 **he understood why:** "Tom Fogerty Unreleased MTV Interview"; this observation seconded by Stu in Werner, 67.

96 **caught himself in the mirror:** Werner, 54.

97 **The profits from a car sale:** Bordowitz, *Bad Moon Rising*, 31.

97 **"See you on *Ed Sullivan!*":** Levy.

97 **marching endlessly:** Fogerty, 121–123.

99 **He wore Doug out:** Fogerty, 89. John spends three full paragraphs explaining his complaints with Doug's drumming, the dream he had about it decades later, and the effort it took to get Doug to play correctly.

99 **That was their salary:** Werner, 53.

100 **Saul was born:** Saul Zaentz biography from Bordowitz, *Bad Moon Rising*, 37; McFadden; Ng and Colker.

100 **bookkeeper at a music publishing company, then as head of sales:** Bang, 49.

100 **$1,500 for a new amp:** Gilliland and Shearer.

100 "not even the ghost of it": Bordowitz, *Bad Moon Rising*, 37.

100 The Golliwogs' new contract: Bordowitz, *Bad Moon Rising*, 38, 31; Fogerty, 126. "I will tear this contract up" verified by Doug Clifford in an interview with the author (and as John suspects it would be in his memoir).

TWELVE: REVIVAL

102 Herb Caen: Gross.

102 "the most turned-on city": Goldstein.

102 About a hundred thousand young people: Daloz.

103 "Rape is as common as bullshit": Anderson, 175.

103 Haight-Ashbury Medical Clinic: McNeill, 136.

103 "Death of the Hippie": Daloz.

103 Rolling Thunder: McNeill, 141.

103 "What you people are going through": McNeill, 143–144.

104 Walked around the makeshift bazaar: Author interview with Steve Cropper.

104 Weekday traffic jams: Boyle, 141.

104 Thomas Cahill: McNeill, 151.

105 General Lewis Hershey: Cottrell and Brown, 25.

105 Ramsey Clark: Cottrell and Brown, 27.

105 Superspade was murdered: Grogan, 444.

105 "Bloody Tuesday": Gaillard, 450.

105 March on the Pentagon: Cottrell and Brown, 24.

106 Coast Recorders: Palao, "Pre-Creedence."

106 living a double life: Kitts, *American Son*, 41.

106 new names: The following details of renaming come from Werner, 55–57.

107 no more needed to be heard: Werner, 56.

107 Now it was up to them: Werner, 57. John's exact phrase, spoken in 1970, is "*Finally* we were a working band, and we had a real name. It was up to us to make that all mean something."

THIRTEEN: STRIKE TIME

108 "We poison their water": Gaillard, 380.

109 "oozes rather than flows": Gaillard, 571.

109 **"If industrial man continues":** Abbey, 211.

110 **returned to Coast Recorders:** Palao, "Pre-Creedence."

110 **five-night residency:** Werner, 74.

111 **John added feedback:** Bordowitz, *Bad Moon Rising*, 46.

111 **ten- and twelve-minute durations:** Werner, 76.

112 **more imitative than expressive:** Maron.

112 **Deno & Carlo:** Bordowitz, *Bad Moon Rising*, 41. He refers to the venue as Deno-Carlo, perhaps because of John's pronunciation in Gilliland and Shearer, though variations abound, including "Deno and Carlo's" (Werner, 77) and "Dino and Carlo's" (Fogerty, 144). In advertisements from the late 1960s in the *Berkeley Barb* and the *San Francisco Express Times*, "Deno & Carlo" is the most frequently used name for the Vallejo Street address, though the separate venue in Muir Beach was advertised as Deno Carlo Naval Base.

112 **no cover and no minimum:** Kitts, *American Son*, 43.

112 **Sunday night residency:** Gilliland and Shearer, recorded in 1969, is where John refers to the residency as happening on Sundays. Other sources, collected years later, refer to Tuesday or Monday nights, but the band's participation in the KMPX strike, which started on a Sunday night, reinforces John's earlier claim.

113 **two-dollar parking and gas:** Gilliland and Shearer.

113 **bands that hadn't even been signed:** Fogerty, 136.

113 **Janis Joplin, Bob Dylan, Jefferson Airplane's Jorma Kaukonen:** Krieger, 71.

113 **validate the work or not:** Gilliland and Shearer.

114 **Autumn Records:** Kaliss, 21–22.

115 **young men under thirty-five:** Rorabaugh, 141.

115 **"The Chicks on Sunday":** Kramer, 79.

115 **pot dealers . . . marijuana delivery . . . "bird engineers":** Kramer, 80.

115 **read the news on air:** Rorabaugh, 141.

116 **KPPC:** Krieger, 70.

116 **Near 3 a.m.:** Gilbert. This source was also highlighted in an extremely helpful post on the *Lost Live Dead* blog, dated September 3, 2010: http://lostlivedead.blogspot.com/2010/09/march-18-1968-pier-10-san-francisco.html.

117 **Traffic:** McNally, 157.

117 **no one brought the amps:** Gilbert.

117 **"the Creedence Clearwater band":** Gilbert.

118 "total assault on the culture": Anderson, 329.
118 "the first hippie strike" . . . Aquarian imagery: Kramer, 87, 81–83.
118 the strike was on television: "KMPX Radio Protest Strike."

FOURTEEN: AN INCIPIENT FAD

121 antimacassar-strewn dream palaces: Savage, 520; Gleason, *Music in the Air*, 186.
121 "Pure sensuousness" . . . "seven different centuries": George-Warren, 137–138.
122 the English bands knew: Gleason, 185–187.
122 a little guitar figure that felt new: Goldberg.
122 He kept a notebook: Fogerty, 155.
123 his own irreplicable tone: Fogerty, 142–143.
124 a Grateful Dead show at Fillmore West: Stu and Doug agree they saw the Dead in spring 1968, which likely means they saw the band on March 30, which happens to have a low reputation among bootleg collectors, for what it's worth. John doesn't mention this incident in his memoir.
125 American Federation of Musicians union: Bordowitz, *Bad Moon Rising*, 47.
126 mourned King as one of their own: Meister.
127 The Everly Brothers and Muddy Waters: The Everlys moved toward country-rock and arrived there simultaneous with the Byrds, one of many bands that bore the Everlys' direct influence. Their album *Roots*, the Byrds' *Sweetheart of the Rodeo*, and Muddy Waters's *Electric Mud* were all released in 1968.
127 "incipient fad": Willis, *Vinyl Deeps*, 194.
127 "prophets are the translators": Willis, *Beginning*, 25.

FIFTEEN: GRIEF

128 Howlin' Wolf: Werner, 81; Gleason, "John Fogerty," 24.
128 May 22: Fenton, 32.
130 John even sent him a postcard: Werner, 81.
132 *Swamp Water*: Margolis. John misremembers the movie as *Swamp Fever*, and though the imagery on-screen matches his song, it is actually set in the Okefenokee Swamp in Georgia, not the Louisiana bayou.

134 "turn this country around": Cowie, 75.
134 His mind was full: For John's songwriting process and mental state in the wake of Kennedy's assassination, see Gilliland and Shearer; Lynskey; and Goldberg.

SIXTEEN: A CRIME TO BE YOUNG

137 "THE FACTORY": Werner, 126.
138 Chicago's WLS: Trakin.
138 Bill Drake: Gleason, "John Fogerty," 20; Werner, 78.
138 "a crime to be young": Mary McGory quoted in Gibson.
138 "an emotional marathon": Willis, *Beginning*, 127–129.
139 "oldies updated and dressed": Bordowitz, *Bad Moon Rising*, 49.
140 he just tried to outwork them: For John's work ethic and stress level at this time, see Bosso, where he says, "I looked at our situation. I said, 'Man, we have no manager. We have no publicist. We have no producer. We're on the tiniest record label in the world.' I felt almost death to my bones, to my toes. I thought, 'We're in the position of being the next one-hit wonder.' Our next thing had to be good. I said, 'OK, if I don't have all the things that The Beatles have or the Stones have, I guess I'm going to have to do it with music.'"
140 Stax Soul Explosion: Gordon, 224.

SEVENTEEN: DISHARMONY

143 "Rolling on a River" and "Riverboat": Gleason, "John Fogerty," 19.
145 back to the gas station: This exact worry is expressed in Goldberg.
148 *Kudzu*: Long.
148 Up Against the Wall Motherfucker: McNally, 283.

EIGHTEEN: ROLLING

150 1,800 B-52s a month: Carroll, 90.
150 When Gallup polled students: Bingham, xxvii.
150 pulled over a twenty-three-year-old: Talbot, 129.
155 *Stereo Review*: Bordowitz, *Bad Moon Rising*, 58.
155 "A few more fresh ideas": Rezos.
155 Albert Goldman: Bordowitz, *Bad Moon Rising*, 59.

156 took home a Peugeot: Rohrer, 65–66.
156 John also indulged himself: Werner, 126.

NINETEEN: RISING

157 violent, vile abuse: Willis, *Essential*, 14.
158 "Washington has destroyed that illusion": Willis, *Essential*, 15.
158 Florynce Kennedy: Gaillard, 561.
158 "friends dead or in agony" . . . "Lesbians!": Willis, *Essential*, 234.
158 "hair-pulling": Gaillard, 561.
158 a property in Berkeley's old warehouse district: Werner, 128.
160 new guitar strings before every gig: Rohrer, 114.
161 *Ed Sullivan Show*: Clash.
162 Wally Heider: Information about Heider and the studio in Silvers.
162 An item: *Billboard*, "Heider Opens New Studio on W. Coast."
162 Russ Gary: Hurwitz.
163 standing in a hallway: Crisafulli.
166 Mark Rudd: Rudd, 214.

TWENTY: SMOLDERING

167 "Revolt of the White Lower Middle Class": Hamill.
168 "countless lives lost": Gardner, 75.
169 "Negro slang": Durham.
170 Omega Seamaster watches: Fogerty, 167, corroborated in interviews
     with Stu and Doug.
170 "hard, firm rock": Jahn, "Californians."
172 "From the records": Orloff.
173 that critics respected: Tom's interview with Levy goes into detail
     about this, and Doug and Stu echoed that sentiment in interviews
     with the author.

TWENTY-ONE: AT THE FEET OF THE GODS

174 new milestones: *Billboard*, "Personal Appearance Dates."
174 $6 million: Bordowitz, *Bad Moon Rising*, 74.
176 Ryman Auditorium: Fogerty, 192; Maron.

176 **10.5 percent:** Bordowitz, "The 1969 Creedence Clearwater Revival Recording Contract," 73. This article provides the details for the entire business negotiation process for this contract as well as its aftermath.

177 **different arrangement:** Block, 268–271.

178 **Associated Booking Corporation:** *Record World*, "Assoc. Inks Creedence."

179 **$350,000:** Hoberman.

180 **Vietnam Moratorium Committee:** Bingham, 165–168.

183 **respect for regimen:** Gordon, 77. The final phrase is Jones's own.

183 **dismantle an M1 blindfolded:** Gordon, 109–111.

TWENTY-TWO: SONGS FOR EVERYONE

185 **"Newport '69":** Hopkins; Wharton.

188 **Denver Pop Festival:** Brown.

188 **Atlanta International Pop Festival:** Kleinhans.

190 **"It's years since any one number":** Cannon, "Family."

190 **Germany:** *Record World*, "Germany's Top 10."

191 **John gave the kid the Rickenbacker:** Maron.

191 **second quarter of 1969:** Bordowitz, *Bad Moon Rising*, 68.

191 **A phrase entered John's mind:** Fogerty, 174, which includes his sympathetic feelings about the "generation gap," older people who couldn't speak to their children.

192 *The Andy Williams Show:* Moon.

193 **red-eye to New York:** Fogerty, 182.

193 **Biblical, Tom thought:** Levy.

193 **first band to sign on:** Fornatale, 158–164 and elsewhere, though the claim has been disputed.

194 **the only one with that opinion:** Bootleg audio of Creedence's Woodstock footage circulated for years and was officially released for the fiftieth anniversary in 2019 by Concord Music Group. We can compare the group's performances from *The Concert*, recorded six months later, to hear the consistency in setlists, song lengths, and, in the case of "Keep On Chooglin'," ostensibly improvised solos. John has also claimed in interviews and in his memoir (184) that the crowd was so quiet and uninterested he could hear a single audience

member's voice, which the official *Creedence Clearwater Revival at Woodstock* album does not confirm.

194 **sounded like one thing:** Levy.

196 **Leslie West . . . John Sebastian:** Fornatale, 158–164.

196 **Roger Daltrey:** Tannenbaum.

TWENTY-THREE: THE ACCEPTANCE OF DEATH

198 **"E-O-fucking-D!":** Steinberg, 77. Creedence-specific details about Steinberg's Vietnam experience come from the author's interview with him.

199 **Music was a shared language:** For more on leisure and bonding time among US troops in Vietnam, see Bradley and Werner, 95.

199 **half a million radios:** Bradley and Werner, 95.

200 **tank crew:** Bradley and Werner, 70.

200 **Buffalo Soldiers:** Maron; Fogerty, 120.

200 **music worthy of those moments in the jungle:** Bradley and Werner, 146.

200 **"Lollin' on a liver":** Bradley and Werner, 16.

200 **GIs rarely performed:** Bradley and Werner, 177.

201 **"acceptance of death":** Appy, 279.

201 **a mistake to send troops:** Bingham, 114.

201 **"upstanding citizens" . . . prison sentence:** Anderson, 159.

202 **Harvard, Princeton . . . James Reston:** Anderson, 159.

202 **hammering the music down:** Margolis.

202 **Vietnam Moratorium Day:** Bingham, 185.

202 **"Fortunate Son":** Fogerty, 190–191.

203 **December 1969:** Steinberg, 231.

TWENTY-FOUR: TOGETHER AND APART

206 **based all the characters on the four Creedence members:** Fogerty, 187.

206 ***Fifth Street Flash:*** Rohrer, 80.

207 **"No encore tonight":** The change in encore policy is described in Werner, 113–115. In John's memoir (199–200) he seems nearly apologetic for this decision. He claims other bands had stopped playing

encores at the time, in part due to safety concerns around hysterical crowds, and ends by saying, "Of course, things have changed. I now play encores!"

208 **Doug grabbed the table:** In interviews with the author and through-out the decades, including Werner's book, Doug has insisted that John was seated on the table when he threw it, and that he lifted it above his head, sending the singer tumbling. John has dismissed this claim as macho bluster, including in his memoir, where he says, "I don't remember any violence, or a specific confrontation with Doug" (200). Stu remembers an upended table incident following the no-encores announcement, but not John's being seated on it. In 1998 he said, "Doug just exploded on John. It stopped just short of a head-bashing. It was a bad moment" (Werner, 114).

209 **Phoenix Memorial Coliseum:** Bruce.

211 **favorite song of the year:** Bordowitz, *Bad Moon Rising*, 58.

211 **third album in the calendar year:** An unbelievable-but-true ac-complishment, though it's important to note that Fairport Conven-tion met Creedence's LP productivity, if not their sales, in 1969. Fairport's records *What We Did on Our Holidays*, *Unhalfbricking*, and especially *Liege & Leaf* were also phenomenally influential in the UK.

212 **"a very few minutes":** Dubro.

212 **"Do you need $500":** "Color Them Creedence Art Contest."

213 **Alan Lomax . . . John's call:** Werner, 118.

213 **swimming alone:** Kitts, *American Son*, 4.

TWENTY-FIVE: AN ARMY GROWING IN YOUR GUTS

214 **"FROM HERE ON":** Bingham, 130.

214 **"Greetings and welcome Rolling Stones":** Booth, 142.

215 **March of Death:** Bingham, 200.

215 **Alcatraz Island:** Johnson.

216 **purchased a boat:** Werner, 121–123; Sherry L. Smith, 97.

216 **folk music:** Maron. John expresses his political beliefs as "anything Pete Seeger would say, that's where I'm at."

217 **"the Electronic Front Page":** Savage, 399.

217 **Inglewood Forum:** Hilburn, "Delta Sound."
218 **December 3:** Dubro.
219 **two nights starting on Thanksgiving eve:** Abramovich. These shows are captured in beautiful detail on *The Complete Matrix Tapes* (2015).
221 **spectator and amateur photographer:** Hallowell, 54.
222 **outsold the Beatles:** An impossible claim to accurately gauge, though it has been made many times, including in Havers.
222 **"soulful socialism":** Raskin, 17.
222 **one of those good bands:** Black Shadow.
224 **Robbie Robertson:** Gladstone.

TWENTY-SIX: WE SHOULDN'T BE TAKEN LIGHTLY

226 **They'd never been better:** Author interview with Jones. The phrase is his.
227 **"'ho-hum'":** Werner, 131. To be sure, Robert Christgau used almost this exact phrase ("Ho-hum, another Creedence album") within the year, in his review of *Pendulum* in the *Village Voice*. Tom recalls feeling disrespected in his interview with Levy, as well.
227 **conducted by Ralph J. Gleason:** Gleason, "John Fogerty."
228 **Ellen Willis:** Willis, *Vinyl Deeps*, 90, from an essay that was originally published in 1972, a review of *Mardi Gras*.
229 ***It Ain't Me Babe*:** Zoloth.
229 **Karen Nussbaum:** Cowie, 63.
230 **"male superior attitude":** Fenton, "An Interview."
231 **didn't like the way that business deals were made:** Levy.

TWENTY-SEVEN: FORWARD TO THE PAST

233 **the Champs:** "Tom Fogerty Unreleased MTV Interview."
233 **lax firearm laws:** Bordowitz, *Bad Moon Rising*, 88.
234 **in one weekend:** Hilburn, "Fogerty's Nightmare."
236 **glazed:** Moon contains a great picture of this arrival taken by Michael Puttland of Getty Images.
237 **constant griping:** Fogerty, 197, in which he explains his mystification at the band's lack of appreciation on this and other occasions.
237 **The tour:** Havers.

237 a barrister from the promoters: Bordowitz, *Bad Moon Rising*, 91, and author interview with Stu Cook.

237 "straights, freaks, skinheads and greasers": Bordowitz, *Bad Moon Rising*, 92.

237 Delaney & Bonnie & Friends: This band was of course recorded for *On Tour with Eric Clapton* (1970). A four-disc reissue released by Rhino Records in 2010 contains the Albert Hall set in full.

237 the youth of Britain: Diski, who writes that in the late 1960s, "America became a synonym for violence and structural racism" (28) but that West Coast US musicians in particular "all played our tune." By comparison, English music was "a little softer, lacking the desperate edge of the Americans" (43).

239 "Right now I'm where I've wanted to be": Havers.

TWENTY-EIGHT: BLOODBATH

240 "Rising concern about the environmental crisis": Gaillard, 574.

240 grown beyond anyone's expectations: Rome, 194–195.

241 "We live in an age of anarchy": Nixon.

242 "If it takes a bloodbath": Lepore, which also contains information on the Hard Hat Riot.

242 six additional unarmed Black men: Lepore.

243 they deserved it: The aftermath of Kent State is in McCormick, 12.

TWENTY-NINE: GOOD BUSINESS

250 "I can't take this anymore": In John's memoir (208), he references Tom's "mutiny," which supposedly took the form of angry rants about John at rhythm section rehearsals at the Factory. In interviews, Doug and Stu said that Tom expressed this sentiment on various occasions, and not strictly in anger.

251 Tom talked with John: This version of the origins of *Inside Creedence* is based on original interviews with Stu Cook and Doug Clifford in which they corroborated the same basic details of Tom's motivation. From the specificity of their recall, it seems clear they were in closer contact with Tom at the time than John was. In John's memoir, *Inside Creedence* is relegated to a single paragraph, one of the strangest in the entire book. In it, John claims that Hallowell

cried in the studio after hearing the band perform "Have You Ever Seen the Rain," recognizing it as a metaphor for the group's coming breakup. John then claims that the other band members have never understood his inspirations or song meanings, and that they still don't. At the very least, Stu's interview in Gilliland and Shearer would dispute this.

252 **full page in** *Billboard*: "'COSMO'S FACTORY' is the new CREEDENCE LP.'"

252 **"good business"**: Werner, 67.

252 **Haight-Ashbury Medical Clinic**: Hilburn, "Creedence—A Rock Group."

254 **"The Velvets have changed considerably"**: Nusser.

254 **six-picture deal with Columbia**: Hoberman, 75.

254 **"something that was groovier"**: Hoberman, 77.

256 **Miami Beach Convention Center**: The details of the band's encounter with Jim Morrison can be found in Vanjak, and in James, "Interview with Doug Clifford." Stu remembers the bodyguard's name as "Babe," not "Babes."

THIRTY: THE OLDEST YOUNG MAN

257 **John Hallowell**: *Boston Globe*, "John McKey Hallowell 1942–2014."

258 **overwhelmed and overstimulated**: This is the unwavering tone of *Inside Creedence*, as described in the following pages, but Hallowell's personal fascination with the band's gruff and unruly California machismo was brought up unprompted in interviews with Stu and Doug.

258 **"S-E-X?"**: Hallowell, 4.

259 **"that crucial character"**: Hallowell, 32.

259 **"oldest young man"**: Hallowell, 35.

260 **"church guilt"**: Hallowell, 22.

260 **"Gary Cooper with an electric guitar"**: Hallowell, 1.

260 **"the brake"**: Hallowell, 6.

260 **"It must have been the bummer of all time"**: Hallowell, 24.

262 **Rogers & Cowan**: Author interview with Bobbi Cowan. Details of the event from Christgau.

264 **a feature about the party in** *Rolling Stone*: Lombardi, 6.

265 **"change is implicit in music"**: Bordowitz, *Bad Moon Rising*, 118.

THIRTY-ONE: BLUE AGAIN

267 **their own activities:** Information on the band members' respective forced sabbaticals is in Hilburn, "Creedence in a Return," and Bordowitz, *Bad Moon Rising*, 122.

269 **"but without my wife on it":** Bordowitz, *Bad Moon Rising*, 122.

269 **Ike and Tina Turner:** Turner, 151, 160.

270 **Saul's priorities:** Bordowitz, *Bad Moon Rising*, 124, 133.

270 **a new complex:** Lombardi, 9.

271 **post-Creedence life:** "Enter Tom Fogerty."

272 **Robert Hilburn:** Hilburn, "Creedence in a Return."

273 **Arthur Flowers:** Bradley and Werner, 193. Flowers's exact quote is: "It just didn't let go it just kept taking me higher and deeper and further . . . I could feel my plan, my contribution to black folks' freedom taking shape."

THIRTY-TWO: THE SHIT KICKER THREE

275 **The delay:** Lombardi, 3.

276 **John berating Stu:** Buday.

276 **"Tomorrow night there will be a basketball game":** Hilburn, "Tardy."

276 *Los Angeles Free Press*: Buday.

276 **Tower of Power:** Information about the band's start and their experience touring with Creedence and Bo Diddley taken from author interviews with Emilio Castillo and David Garibaldi.

277 **almost weren't hired:** Bordowitz, *Bad Moon Rising*, 128.

278 **15 percent of returning vets:** Talbot, 124.

278 **turquoise Elvis outfit:** Werner, 65.

279 **"seventeen years ago":** Author interview with Emilio Castillo.

279 **"loss was noticeable":** Jahn, "Bo Diddley Returns."

280 **Tony Joe White:** This band is captured on this exact tour, including tracks from the Royal Albert Hall, on a 2010 compilation called *That On the Road Look (Live)*.

280 **another older brother figure:** Fogerty, 229–230, in which John recalls being closer to White than other opening acts, White's magnetism and musical personality, and his own relatable attempts to win

White's approval and compliments, especially for his singing. The quote is drawn directly from John's book.

280 **private Learjet:** Rohrer, 97–99.

281 **This European excursion:** Bordowitz, *Bad Moon Rising*, 128–131.

281 **"loud bitchy rock 'n' roll":** Havers, who has the 1971 European tour details as well.

281 **the first private jet:** Hilburn, "200 Police."

282 **while the core of their whole life together crumbled:** The emotional state described in this section was elaborated on by Stu Cook and Doug Clifford in interviews with the author. Stu said that he enjoyed the country work because it meant "playing with the other two guys while the core was crumbling."

283 **Antwerp:** Hilburn, "Antwerp."

283 **John announced a plan in a limo:** This is likely the most controversial episode in Creedence lore. Only three people were involved in the conversation. Two of them, Stu and Doug, agree that John presented the idea for democratically divided duties during this ride. Stu is particularly adamant on this point. John has rejected this story ever since, averring that he never made such an ultimatum. He instead claims that Stu and Doug made the demand for greater artistic control when they spoke to *Rolling Stone* about the new changes in the band's power structure (see Lombardi) and he was merely "relinquishing" power, as he writes in his memoir (223). Bordowitz all but closes the book on this case, especially with a lengthy block quote from Jake Rohrer on page 134, in which Rohrer astutely says that John "held Doug and Stu to Tom's idea of 'artistic democracy.'" There is also the fact that John had an acknowledged history of unilateral decision-making by that point already.

284 **$100 million:** Bordowitz, *Bad Moon Rising*, 133.

284 **John Lennon:** "John Lennon: Hear Jann Wenner's Legendary 1970 Interview."

284 **Waylon Jennings:** Ehler.

THIRTY-THREE: SAVAGED

285 **pot brownies:** Rohrer, 112.

286 **a crowd so raucous:** Rohrer, 113.

286 John visited a dying young fan: Rohrer, 114.

288 "I'm not even in the realm": Bordowitz, *Bad Moon Rising*, 135.

288 He felt particularly bitter: Fogerty, 225, explains this thought process.

290 "a very sensible change in direction": Rockin' Raoul.

290 "much more likable album than *Pendulum*": Marcus.

291 Ellen Willis's review: Willis, *Vinyl Deeps*, 89–93.

292 "Fogerty's Revenge": Bordowitz, *Bad Moon Rising*, 143.

292 an audience member threw a quarter: Bordowitz, *Bad Moon Rising*, 140.

THIRTY-FOUR: THE MUSIC IN OUR HEADS

293 "people who aren't on any kind of personal trip": Werner, 184.

293 "same wavelength": Werner, 176.

294 "Each of them felt it was necessary": Hilburn, "Creedence Split."

295 Troy, Idaho: Rohrer, 122–126.

296 "every waking moment": Ebert.

298 "Credence Clearwater": Stone, 154. Stone was an associate of Kesey's Merry Pranksters as well.

298 nearly synonymous with Vietnam: Schonfeld.

298 he opened his set with a cover of "Who'll Stop the Rain": Bradley and Werner, 186.

299 *Live at Royal Albert Hall*: *Cashbox*, "Embarrassed on the Bayou."

299 $8.6 million: Hilburn, "Fogerty's Nightmare."

301 Tom was a regular gigging musician: Levy.

302 Los Lobos: Author interview with Joel Selvin.

302 Kurt Cobain: Azzerad, 54. The band was called the Sellouts and they never played a show.

302 "John Fogerty is my life's blood": Coley, 52.

304 "I'm angry": Baker.

Index